ASPECTS OF INDIAN SOCIAL ANTHROPOLOGY

About the Author

In anthropological fraternity **Dr. R.S. Mann** needs no introduction. He is one among the seniormost Indian anthropologists. Dr. Mann specialised in social-cultural anthropology and obtained Master's and Doctoral degrees from Delhi University. Over three decades of his professional career kept him engaged in research and teaching. One finds in him a combination of theoretic concerns and substantivism. Dr. Mann's scholarly insight and contribution are reflected through his numerous books and papers. Some of his more popular books include: *Culture and Integration of Indian Tribes; Anthropological and Sociological Theory; Social Change and Social Research; Social Structure, Social Change and Future Trends; The Ladakhi; Nature-Man-Spirit Complex in Tribal India;* and *The Bay Islander*. Dr. Mann's contributions are well recognised in national and international seminars.

Careerwise Dr. Mann has been holding high positions. He remained the Director of Anthropological Survey of India. Dr. Mann is the President of Indian Anthropological Association. Now he is teaching in the Department of Anthropology, University of Delhi, as Professor of Social Anthropology.

ASPECTS OF INDIAN SOCIAL ANTHROPOLOGY

R.S. MANN
Professor of Social Anthropology
Department of Anthropology
University of Delhi
Delhi

CONCEPT PUBLISHING COMPANY, NEW DELHI-110059

ISBN 81-7022-586-8 (Hard Bound)
ISBN 81-7022-587-6 (Paper Back)

First Published 1996

Published and Printed by
Ashok Kumar Mittal
Concept Publishing Company
A/15-16, Commercial Block, Mohan Garden,
NEW DELHI - 110059 (India)
Phones : 5554042, 5504042

PREFACE

The tribal social structures all over the world largely maintain their exclusiveness and uniqueness when compared to non-tribal communities around. Alongwith the commonality of many socialogical, ideological and technological components of tribal ways of life and thought, there can be viewed divergent elements of social organisation, economic pursuits and ideology among the tribals themselves who are spread far and wide in various parts of the globe. By and large this holds true even in intra-continent as well as intra-subcontinent social and cultural situations. The argument is further authenticated when one views and reviews tribal cultures and social structures spatially and temporally. Further, a large number of contemporary trends, generated in the process of change, even speak of togetherness of thinking at the level of tribal mind. Though a very important part of human society the tribal fabric constitutes the 'other world' in terms of many of their life-designs encompassing even the attitude, belief system and the world view. And for that matter Indian tribes are no exception. This is well supported by their quality of life, value system etc., as reflected through many unique social and cultural institutions and practices. Existence and continuity of many distinctive customs and values, of which the tribals themselves have been proud of, seak impetus through emic explanations which sound so convincing when put to analysis in their overall context. Should we not search for such explanations in the existing tribal social-cultural orders and the mental rationality and philosophy holding them? Yes, the present book is in response to such a requirement.

In the atmosphere of ignorance or under the climate of partial and superficial understanding of tribal life and culture people simply underrate the tribal scenario. Wrong impressions aroused within this background do not help in putting forth the realities of tribal thought, living and standards as visualised and perceived by the insiders themselves. And when the logic and rationalities prevailing in tribal thought and culture remain beyond comprehension the ball of sufferings stays in the court of tribals alone. The tribals are unnecessarily charged on various counts. This is evident from many irrelevant initiatives and actions of non-tribals who intend to diffuse innovations among the tribals. Such a situation paves way to resistance and opposition from tribals in many instances. The argument seeks support from rising indifference in case of many tribal belts within and outside India. In general those who matter at political level seem to have, of late, shown mounting concern for the tribals and their plight. When seen in terms of evolutionary perspective, at no stage the words 'tribe' and 'tribal' could be used and flashed, at different echelons, with such high frequency and tone as is the case now.

But what has happened on the surface or at grassroot level, in terms of experience of tribals in general, poses more for unpleasantness than reward. Why have the tribes, their social structure and culture have not been channelised in right direction, under the umbrella of change, remains an imposing question. This can largely be attributed, among other factors, to the fact that the tribals have not been understood in correct perspective. For lack of knowledge and understanding the tribal affairs could not be directed the way they should have been. Even the policy and approach lacked direction and clarity especially at the level of their implications. The trends of the above nature led, in many instances, to disorganisation and even to the creation of new problems which the tribals did not confront at their earlier stages of existence. Such trends, more so in the absence of cognitive mapping in right perspective, not only adversely affected the mundane life but also impaired the tribal thinking in respect of their native philosophy. A climax of mounting threat to tribal cultures got generated even in those aspects of life which speak of commendable adaptation to specific environmental niches. Instances of enforced imbalances in man-nature rèlationship in tribal millieus are no less reported from tribal scenes in India and abroad. Popular and pampered slogans from outside tribals frontiers do not serve the purpose of usefulness as reality content in them is shallow. This comes all the more damaging in the background of not properly understanding and interpreting tribal life and culture. To overcome such difficulties this book was planned though with references to certain selected aspects and in the context of Indian tribes alone. The contents elaborate upon comprehensive understanding and interpretation. What is happening in the sway of change is equally emphasised as part of analytic framework. The account speaks of what is happening to tribal cultures, in certain specific sense, for a variety of reasons. However, the hallmark in this exercise is the consolidation of essence in respect of institutions and practices which are typical of many Indian tribes.

Though sporadic mentions on the aspects of tribal life and culture, dealt herein, were frequently reported even in past, one usually remained short of catching the essence thereof. The reason could be traced to weak ethnography and lack of indepth analysis at formal level. With a strong focus on substantivism, as it is suggested to be sought after in the recent times, the account in this book provides ample explanations of what is holding this reality from beneath in terms of cognition generated out of long experience and adaptations of tribal societies. In other words the institutions, customs and practices dealt in the pages that follow, not only comprehend the totality of their matter-of-fact world but also present the thought-of-order attached thereto. During the course of this exercise numerous dimensions poured in which helped in the consolidation of essence of each aspect presented herewith as part of Indian tribal scenario. More studies on similar lines among the tribes, including those beyond Indian frontiers, would help strengthen this new stream of understanding, analysis and interpreting tribal cultures and the image thereof. And consequently the strength of such dispositions would go in the interest of not only the academic fraternity but also to those whose structures of culture are analysed.

R.S. MANN

CONTENTS

1

POLYANDROUS MARRIAGE
A New Theoretic Construct

In the institution of marriage, polyandry assumes a special form and is of rare existence in the contemporary world. To most of the people such a form of marital institution, though widely but scantily distributed, appears very unusual kind of feature. Accounts from India and abroad, wherever this custom existed or still survives, reveal that such a way of marrying is not of any recent origin. Rather, it is an ancient custom and existed, more so in India, from time immemorial. Existence of polyandry is supported by *Rig Veda* and *Atharva Veda*. As reported by Parmar (1975:80), "the Maruts are pictured as united to a common bride and Rodasi, who was devotedly attached to her husbands, probably lived with them by turns. Again, we find that a wife is exhorted to perform her duties towards her husband's brothers and to love them. The marriage of five Pandava brothers with Draupadi is well known. A lady of the name of Jatila is narrated as having been married simultaneously to ten brothers".

The origin of the word polyandry is believed to be an outcome of the combination of two Greek words *i.e., poly* or "many" and *andria*, the "men". In other words, the polyandry refers to the marriage of many men to one woman. It therefore, becomes plain that there could be no polyandry without marriage. According to the Notes and Queries on Anthropology (1954:71), the polyandry is defined as an institution or custom "by which a woman is permitted to have more than one husband at the same time. Where the husbands are brothers the term adelphic is used. If one of the husbands has a superior position to the others, the polyandry is disparate". Some writers have even reported of fathers and sons polyandry among Tibetans. From the analysis of polyandry in time and space, it appears that this institution, more so in the earlier explanations of social scientists, has been crudely and inseparably mixed with cicisbeism and conjoint marriages. Many have labelled all as polyandry, though it does not suit to the essential requirements of the custom. Some like Marvin Opler, Piddington, H. Fischer pointed to the weaknesses involved in the treatment of polyandry. Certain groups, known to have polyandry, were termed by them as non-polyandrous but having cicisbeism, polykoity or plural mating. They put forward two major criteria *i.e.*, stability of marriage and its legitimacy as essential ingredients of polyandry. When analysed in these dimensions, many groups are eliminated from the polyandrous purview. Likewise some groups would be dropped out when polyandrous marriage and conjoint one are differentiated. While becoming more specific about such a distinction Peter (1963:29) stresses that "the conjoint marriage develops naturally out of polyandry by the combination of polygyny with it in the same union. It simply means that instead of a group of men sharing one woman, they share more than that number". Likewise the significant element in cicisbeism is that a man makes arrangement for sex with any woman not related through marriage. Under the conditions the man remains only a *cicisbeo* (lover) rather than a husband. As such, there is the need of differentiating the situations of sexual connection, as that of lover and mistress, free love and conjoint marriage from polyandry. But it is also true in some cases that two of these are found simultaneously existing in the same group. There is, then, need to highlight, in the interest of academic demand, such features categorically. Therefore, the polyandry, as being lately stressed, involves a few fundamentally important issues. Plurality of husbands whether brothers, real or socially ascribed, or beyond; public recognition of such husbands of particular women; assumption of status of spouses of husbands and wife and the holding of mutual rights and obligations by the partners are the major requirements to call a union as polyandrous one.

Before making mention of the polyandrous groups on the above criteria, another aspect of polyandry, based on the nature of descent and succession, may be given a mild treatment. Like the fraternal and non-fraternal kind, the nature of polyandry can also be matriarchal and patriarchal. In case of the former the succession is traced through the female and in the case of the latter through male. Patriarchal form is more connected to fraternal polyandry. But then there are groups who have both, the patrilineal as well as matrilineal practices, say the Lahulis. However, patriliny is the feature among most polyandrous people. The same people can even simultaneously be found observing fraternal as well as non-fraternal polyandry. Even a polyandrous union can and does in some cases, suddenly turn to conjoint; in other words it can be said that the latter form is an outcome from the former. Mention may be made of the process as to how it happens. Living with a common set of husbands, if a woman, say among Jaunsaris, keeps on bearing female children alone, her sister is brought as second wife. Bringing in of a second wife is also resorted to when the common wife fails to produce a child for quite some time. A third reason for arranging an additional wife is the disparity in age between the first common wife and the youngest brother. In latter case, the additional common wife is brought in the name of the youngest brother.

It would be necessary to give an account of the existence of polyandry in three perspectives. Firstly, when the cicisbeism, plural mating, free love, etc., were all amalgamated within polyandrous fold. Such a view, by and large, continued to persist till, say, the fifties of the present century; secondly, when this custom was largely studied in isolation of the above kind of sex relationship and was seen strictly within more rational and accepted qualifications meant for calling a group as polyandrous; and thirdly, in the light of declining trend of the custom because of diverse reasons. Going systematically along these lines would screen out many groups from the earlier recognised gamut of polyandrous unions. Only a few are now truly polyandrous groups and the declaration of Majumdar, made at one time about the existence of polyandry, would not be found very appropriate. Majumdar (quoted by Peter 1963:84), in his lecture delivered at the Indian Science Congress of January 1940 remarked that 'nearly forty million people all over the world are polyandrous'.

Without, at times, being categorically isolating the determinants of polyandry, and rather many times taking even non-marital relations between men and woman as case of polyandry, which is not something dependable, Westermarck in the book, *History of Human Marriage* and *Encyclopaedia Britannica* gives a long list of polyandrous people. The Institution has been reported as widely spread as America, Asia, Australia and Africa. Among the American polyandrous people the author includes Avanoes, Maypures, Warru, Zaparo, Canaris Indians, Seneca, Iroquois, Crow Indians, Eskimos, Aleuts. Among the Asians and others are included Chukchees, Ainus, Tibetans, Hill Miris, Daflas, Abhors, Khasis, Bhutanese, Santals, Bhuiyas, Korkus, Oraons, Todas, Kurumbas, Badagas, Coorgs, Kammalans, Tiyyans, Kaniyan, Nayar, Kallans, Reddies, Russian peasants, Ossetes, Kadyans, Punans, Dyaks, Maoris, Dieri, Gippsland blacks, Merina, Hottentots, Bantu, Basuta. Lowie mentioned of polyandry among the Wahuna of Africa and so did Linton for Marquesans of Pacific islands. Likewise Mary Tew explained polyandry in Belgian Congo.

More specifically about India, within the frame of pre-fifties views, mention has been made of a large number of polyandrous groups. McLenan (Census of India, Punjab 1892:224) reported polyandry in Kulu valley and Lahul and Spiti. Likewise E. A. Gait (Census of India,

1911 volume I, part I) expressed polyandry of Todas, Kurumbas, Talkolans, Kaniyans, Kammalans Ishavans, Muduvas, Bhotias, Kanets, Thakkars and Meghs, and Ghonds. J.H. Hutton gave an account of polyandry of United Provinces, more so of Jaunsar Bawar area of Dehra Dun in Census of India, 1931, vol. I, part I, 1933 edition. Then the excess of married men over married women, in the districts and states of Ambala, Bashar, Sirmor, Kalsia, Ludhiana, Maler Kotla, Ferozepur, Faridkot and Amritsar has been explained on the basis of polyandry in Census of India 1931 vol. XVII Punjab, part I, 1933 edition. Kanets, Kolis, Brahmins of Bashar state, Kanawar and Rohm were dealt as polyandrous in Simla State Gazetteer, 1910. The inhabitants of Sikkim were reported having polyandry in Census Report of Bengal, 1901. Izhuvans, Ishavanas, Tiyas or Thandans castes of Malabar were said, by Aiyappan, having the custom of polyandry.

Drastic revision, however, was made in the above list of polyandrous people by the writers of third quarter of twentieth century. The elements involved in such a scrutiny were more rational, scientific and acceptable. In the reclassified category, the cases resembling cicisbeism and free love were eliminated. Thus, the picture lately emerged, in Indian context, about the distribution of polyandry is as dealt below. It has systematically been recorded areawise.

In the north and north-west, the institution of polyandry is found in the cis-Himalayas as well as trans-Himalayas. More popular places, from this point of view, are Kinnaur hills, Ladakh of Jammu and Kashmir state, certain areas in Rawai and Jaunsar-Bawar region of Dehra Dun, Uttar Pradesh. Lahaul and Spiti are also prominently marked by this marital form. The custom of polyandry is also popular among some inhabitants of Sikkim.

The polyandrous groups in Himachal Pradesh include Kinnars or Kanowars or Kinnauras. Many of them are Buddhists and dedicate the surplus females to monasteries where they lead the life of celibacy as Jomos. Writing on the polyandry prevalent in Himalayas, especially of Sirmur, Parmar (1975:89) has mentioned that, "polyandry is practised by every caste and tribe in Sirmur region. It is common for three or four brothers to have only one wife but even seven brothers are known to have one wife". The fraternal polyandry is the feature among Rajputs, Brahmins or Bhats. Members of lower castes, including Dumras, Chanals, Kolis etc., practice non-fraternal polyandry. The hold of polyandry in certain areas of Himachal Pradesh continues. For Bashar region of Himachal Pradesh, Parmar (1975:81) has categorically mentioned that "the polyandry exists in both forms, higher and lower (fraternal and non-fraternal). In the higher form, the joint husbands are own brothers and in the lower they are not so. There are scattered instances of the latter. What happens in the latter type is that at times strangers of even different castes become *Dharam Bhais* (brothers not by blood but by performing a ceremony by which they become like brothers) and share a wife. Cousins and half-brothers sometimes have a joint wife. In the Bashar tract, a form of group marriage coupled with polyandry is found. Instances of a group of brothers marrying a group of sisters jointly are not unknown and at times when the joint wife is barren, her sister is brought in as the second wife.

Chakrata, an area adjoining to Himachal Pradesh has a tract popularly known as Jaunsar Bawar and is particularly polyandrous. The people who live in this area are known as Khasas. It is a combination of various ethnic groups, especially the Brahmins and the Rajputs. The other inhabitants of the area are the Doms and Koltas. It is mainly because of the intermarriage between the Brahmins and the Rajputs that the both have been labelled together as one group. Jaunsari polyandry has been described as more complete and tenacious. It is essentially of a fraternal type.

Polyandry is again, quite popular among the Ladakhis or Bhot or Bhautta of Ladakh, the most northwesterly district of India. Some writers have reported that a woman keeps upto four and five husbands in Ladakh. But then during the course of my fieldwork, I could not come across more than three brothers sharing a common wife. The Bhots are the fraternal polyandrous people. Instances of polyandry could also be reported from the Dards of Dah in Ladakh. Zanskaris of south Ladakh and the Chanspas of highlands are also found practising this custom. Rare instances of non-fraternal polyandry among the inhabitants of Ladakh are also reported. In case of the latter, a man, known as Phorsak, also shares a wife. This man is not one from amongst the brothers. Adjoining to Zanskar division of Ladakh are the Lahaul and Spiti areas of Himachal Pradesh. Like Ladakh, the Buddhist inhabitants of Lahaul and Spiti have the institution of polyandry. Pattern of polyandry among the Lahulians and the Spitians is almost the same as among the Zanskaris of Ladakh. Like the Kinnauras, the conjoint or polyandrous marriages are also, according to Peter, found among the Ladakhis and the Lahaulis. However, it may be mentioned here that among the Ladakhis of Leh division (I am not very sure of the Zanskaris), I, at least, could not come across any instance of conjoint polygynandrous marriage. In Ladakh and Lahaul, the rule of primogeniture has been prevalent. Like Ladakh, Lahaul, Kinnaur, Sirmur and Jaunsar-Bawar, the instances of real polyandry have also been reported from the Bhotias of Sikkim. Among rest of the tribes and castes of Himalayas, mentioned specifically by Westermarck and others as polyandrous, the system of true polyandry does not seem to be prevalent. Rather, the relationship could be of the type of cicisbeism and free sex. Even the Lepchas of Darjeeling are described to be having cicisbeism rather than polyandry.

At the same time, the regions between the Himalayas, including foothills, and the southern peninsula, including Indo-Gangetic plains and other areas, are described to be completely devoid of the custom of polyandry. Writers on polyandry almost have a unanimity on this view; exception being some stray case where the author lacked depth of data. Polyandry of Indian subcontinent again is highlighted in the works on various castes and tribes of south India, especially of Kerala and Tamil Nadu. Unlike the northern region of Himalayas, some elements of controversy does exist in case of certain groups of south India in their labelling as polyandrous or non-polyandrous. But still, an equation of tolerable compromise can be struck, and hence groups crystalized in and outside the garb of polyandry.

Frequency of polyandrous unions is stated to be quite high among the Todas of Nilgiri hills. The small group of Todas practises polyandry of fraternal as well as non-fraternal types. Another view, however, is that the latest trend is towards regression of the custom and its becoming scarce.

About the other groups, in sysmbiosis with Toda, including Badaga, Kurumba and Kota, there is little difference of opinion. However, the weighty side holds that they are more involved in the relationship of cicisbeism than one of real polyandry. The Kerala Tiyas, bearing different names of Thiyyas, Iruvans, Thandans, Irava-panikars, Iravas etc., are explained to be fraternal polyandrous people. Like the Kota controversy, in the matter under reference, say between Mandelbaum and Prince Peter, some diversity of views is noted in case of Nayars. K. Gough searched for the trait but came to a different conclusion. The kind of situation prevalent among the Nayars does not conform to genuine polyandry but to a different kind of non-marital sexual relationship. According to K. Gough, the real marriage ceremony of Nayars involves the tying of the Tali. But afterwards the woman develops her other sexual relations with Nambudri Brahmins or her own caste men, and the union of this kind is termed *Sambandam*. The latter hardly involves any religious rites and is rather a plain sexual cohabitation. At the same time, such a relationship does not involve any major element of obligation in the man-woman relationship. The case is more akin to cicisbeism than one of polyandry. Contrarily, Peter (1963:173) while reporting on Kerala State polyandry has stated that,

> "Various castes including Nayars, Tiyas, Kammalans, Karuvans, Asaris, Musaris, Tol Kolans, Mannans, Panans, Pulluvans are polyandrous. In spite of it being said that Nayars are no longer polyandrous in Kerala, I was able to find some families left who do still live matrimonially in this way. In the very closed Court circles of Cochin and Travancore, polyandry of the old type is still practised by Nayar ladies, who consort with wealthy Tamil Brahmins and Pillais from the east coast."

A word about the terrain and other physical ecological conditions, whereunder polyandry is prevalent, may be of relevance in the later stages of analysis, if not now.

More commonness and only a little divergence can be observed in the eco-systems of the areas marked by the prevalence of polyandrous marital form. A more or less uniform characteristic is of the existence of hard external ecological conditions. In Ladakh, the fertile tracts are only a very few. Most regions present a barren and desolated look. There are towering hills with snow-capped peaks. People, living at a height between 9,000 and 15,000 feet above sea level face freezing cold and frowning weather. The atmosphere is extremely dry and there is a severe problem of erosion of hills. The hills are nude and even the valleys are devoid of trees. The vegetation, in general, is scarce because of the high altitude and a very little rainfall of the average of about three inches an year. Nothing can be grown in winter which extends for about seven months. Acreage of cultivable land is small. More or less similar conditions exists in Lahaul. Altitude ranges from 9,000 to about 21,000 feet above sea level. With extreme cold, the average rainfall is about six inches in rainy season and more in winter. The land-holdings are small, roughly below two acres. The inhabitants grow crops during months from May to November. For rest of the year, the ground remains covered with snow. In polyandrous regions of Himachal Pradesh, it is quite a difficult job to plough the fields as the latter are in the form of sloping plots and very small in size. A common method is the hoeing. The small plots are having lot of stones. Certain area, say Bashar, are characterized by precipitous rocks and the mountains. Earning, under such conditions, is a difficult job. It is more of hand to mouth living. More or less similar conditions prevail in Jaunsar-Bawar, a region of succession of hills and mountains. Sexena pointed out that there is not a single spot of one hundred yards of level ground in the whole Purganah. One has to struggle hard to exist in the teeth of environmental difficulties. With this are the conditions of severe winter and heavy snowfall which most of the villages, situated between an altitude of five to seven thousand feet above sea level, face. A vivid description of nature in Jaunsar-Bawar is given in the *District Gazetteer* (1911:6) "Even in the hills, Jaunsar-Bawar has the character of being one of the wildest and most rugged tracts, affording naturally very little level ground, and that only in small patches. The mountains are peculiarly rough and precipitous, there is much cliff and rock and few villages, so that the cultivation is necessarily small and very laborious". The geographical conditions in Kerala and Nilgiris differ, to a considerable extent, from those prevalent in high Himalayas. Nilgiri, though is at quite a height, is free from snowfall and severe winter. There the Toda polyandrous tribe does not depend on the cultivation of land. They rear buffaloes and depend on their milk and its products. Kerala, of course, is an undulating terrain consisting of small valleys, having agriculture fields, and hillocks and mountains. There is a great deal of vegetation. Though the cultivation landholdings are small, people take more than one crop as the rainfall is sufficiently high. Many groups, including polyandrous Tiyas, however, remain economically hard pressed. This may not have been true for Nayars.

Views about Polyandry

There are quite a few views in respect of polyandry. Such views, in many cases, are marked by contradictions and incompatibilities. What one says is turned down by the other on the basis of study of a different group. Westermarck stressed that polyandry is confined to non-Aryan, Mongoloid and Dravidian tribes and castes. In general too, there has been a belief that polyandry did not prevail among the Aryans. On the contrary, mention has been made in Briffault's *Mother* that the custom prevailed among the Indo-Aryans and other Aryan races such as the Medes. According to him, the constitution of Vedic family was the same as of other polyandrous families. Tracing polyandrous belt from Jaunsar-Bawar to Hindu Kush and even beyond, Saxena quotes Briffault's (*The Mother*, Vol. I, p. 691) remark, "The practice of polyandrous marriage among the Indo-Aryans of the Punjab is associated with other survivals of a more archaic and tribal order of society, which are culturally identical with usages of the polyandrous people of Hindu-kush, whence the invaders came to India". Peter concludes that most primitive people rarely practise polyandry. He feels that it is so because the necessary environmental conditions for it do not exist everywhere. Majumdar, too, reported polyandry among the Rajputs and Brahmins of Jaunsar-Bawar who belong to Indo-Aryan Stock. The same is true in case of Indo-Aryan Mons of Ladakh. Linton has been of the opinion that the institution of polyandry remained a character of lower classes. But his looks just the other way round when the argument is seen in the context of Indian tradition linked with *Mahabharata*. The custom, explained in Indian mythology with special allusions to the *Pandavas,* princess Kanha, Varkshi and Jatila Gautami, reveals that it was limited to class of Kshatriyas and ruling castes. Referring to the Himalayan polyandry, Parmar opines that the custom is confirmed to any caste or tribe. Rather, it extends even to the highest castes.

In regard to Ladakhi polyandry, Parmar writes that it is a feature of poorer classes. Those who are rich can independently have wives, and at times even more than one. The same view gets supported by Rockhill who has expressed that the custom is found among the poor and scorned. But Turner's assertion is that the polyandry is found among the wealthiest. The same was observed by me in Ladakh where rich Kalhons were found sharing a common wife. Rockhill further asserted that the agriculturists alone are polyandrous and not the nomads. But Baker reported that polyandry is common among the shepherds (who ar nomads) of the uplands. Chatterjee, Jha and Moris mentioned of polyandry among the farming families of Jaunsaris. But then polyandry is also found among the herders and hunters. In Ladakh, as I studied, polyandry exists among the agriculturists as well as the herders. Then the custom is prevalent, almost in equal proportion, among the wealthy and the poverty-stricken or those who face economic hardship. It is also not supported that polyandry is categorically meant for nobles or for commoners. The sample covered by me included polyandrous families of Kalhons (socially and economically superior class of Ladakhis) and other important persons like Lharje (medicinemen), and the commoners. Peter puts forward the view that the practice of polyandry creates male jealously. But contrary to such a viewpoint is the finding of Saxena who firmly holds that there is absence of male jealously. That polyandry breeds cooperation has also been reported in many cases. Even I observed the same in Ladakh. About fraternal polyandry it has been pronounced that it helps set up an intense form of joint family. Even Parmar has given that the fraternal or communal tendencies are encouraged and individualism suppressed in polyandrous societies.

According to Parmar (1975:130), "Polyandry enables a family of brothers to get the full benefit of several sources of livelihood. One can cultivate the joint land, another breed cattle, a third engage in trade and so on". It has further been explained by Parmar that polyandry probably results in the procreation of more boys than girls. A related version of Cunningham, in respect of Ladakhi polyandry is worthy of mention. He feels that custom is a principal check to the population increase. Population growth remains small because of low birth rate. Cunningham further states that, "however, revolting it may be to our feelings, it was a most politic measure for a poor country which does not produce sufficient food for its inhabitants" (quoted by Parmar, 1975:130). Further, it has been reported, more so for Himalayan polyandry that the polyandrous custom is prestigious. Such a value judgment is applicable, at times, to the common wife and, at times, to the common husbands and the children. But at the same time some people feel that the custom of polyandry encourages the formation of corrupt society. The example, in support, are cited from the Jaunsaris and the Ladakhis—more so from Jaunsaris from amongst whom many surplus women, who specially do not get married, adopt prostitution as their profession. They even go to the big cities for such a business. Many Ladakhi girls, who do not find husbands, come to Leh, the district headquarters of Ladakh, in the name of *Chhang*-seller girls and many of them become mothers even without being married. When the Central Asian Trade route, through Ladakh, was opened, such girls indulged in sex with the traders who temporarily halted at Leh. But now, there has evolved a regular group, known as Argon, of the descendents from Ladakhi females and non-Ladakhi Muslim males. Polyandrous areas of Himachal have also been stated suffering from lack of sexual morality. Then the comparatively more sexual freedom among polyandrous societies is also held responsible for the origin and spread of venereal diseases. A bulk of Indian polyandrous population is not free of such disease. The induction of such a disease is further held responsible as a cause of sterility. In addition, there are many who attribute sterility, more so for Jaunsari women, to some kind of sexual atrophy which is resulted from excessive sex indulgence-otherwise a common feature among all the polyandrous communities.

Position of Woman

It may be of some relevance to discuss a few aspects connected to the position of woman, more so of the common wife, among the polyandrous castes and tribes. Of quite an interest is the thing to know of the personality assessment of women in accordance with the insider's point of view. To an outsider, the common wife, in a polyandrous wedlock, may appear very taxing. But this does not seem to be true in the eyes of those who practice the custom. In most of the cases the treatment with the woman is of liberal nature.

Elements of oppression and suppression do not seem that apparent. About the women of polyandrous Sirmor region, it has been stated that the common wife is dominant in sexual matters. She even controls the household in matters related to food, fodder, fuel, cattle, fields, kitchen, etc. In most of the polyandrous groups of Himalayas, she is, most of the time, consulted prior to bringing in a second wife. Among the polyandrous families of Ladakh, the wife enjoys a good status. Although she shares sex with the younger brothers of husband, she does have an upper hand over them. She prevails over them and her authority is exerted. Only after she grants permission, any of them can marry to a second female. Ladakhis are, by and large, submissive enough to honour the privileges of common wife. Writing about the women of Himachal Pradesh, Parmar (1975:33) stated that,

> "A woman appears to be subservient to man, is regarded as chattel and bought and sold to the highest bidder, and may be inherited by her husband's kin. If the husband wills it, he may repudiate his marital obligations and divorce her on the flimsiest pretext, and receive compensation for her in the shape of Reet. But her drudgery is, in part, compensated by her independence and freedom. She can appear in public and go for shopping. She entertains guests and attends to their comforts. The women of the hills do not, however, content themselves with marrying once or twice according to Reet but, as every subsequent Reet adds to her attraction she must marry as many times as she can find new husbands willing to pay for her."

He further states that, "while a woman is free to leave her husband at her sweet will she has much liberty in choosing her friends and companions to have gay time" (1975:77). Considering women as inferior, the Todas do not allow their participation in ritualistic performances. They are not even allowed to cook food where milk is used. In spite of their being debarred from sacred dairies and ritual ceremonies, they are otherwise treated kindly. They are never made the target of any social contempt. Over and above it is said that the Toda women are pampered among Indian tribal women. The Kinnaura and Bhot women of Kinnaur and Lahaul are said to be very hardy and capable of undertaking strenuous duties. They are treated with respect and understanding. Freedom of women is of a great magnitude among the Nayars. The worth of her rights and privileges can be calculated from the group being matriarchal and matrilineal.

The Ways of Marrying

Marriage, as discussed in the introductory part, being a very decisive factor in calling a union of men and woman as polyandrous, needs to be seen in broader perspective at macro level. This would establish whether a link between man and woman, for sexual or cohabitation purpose, is marked by the performance of any marital ritual. Some variation, in rules in regard to whether brothers would join a common wife or she would join group of husbands, is marked. Some groups have a provision of giving choice to the wife, when she gets married to one, for co-husbands and there are others in which she almost compulsorily and automatically becomes wife to all. The eldest brother, among Jaunsaris, controls marriage. According to Majumdar (1962:72):

> "It is the eldest brother who marries the wife or wives, and it is through him that his brothers have access to the common wives. In principle and in practice, all the brothers form an inseparable group as 'fraternal husbands' in the name of the eldest brother. The wives, on the other hand, join the union individually, one after another, in the same way as is usually found in the polygamous system, except that the single husband is substituted by the polyandrous group of husbands."

The Khasas of Jaunsar-Bawar have a ceremony and after its performance the brothers become husbands or *Khawand.* They are stated to be ascribed the recognition of husband even if they are not present at the time of ceremony. As observed by Saxena, the eldest brother, among Jaunsaris, goes through marriage ceremony with the bride and the other brothers, *if-so-facto*, become her husbands. In respect of the inhabitants of Kanaur valley, Parmar (1975:65) writes that, "one of the brothers, usually the one who is the bride's equal in age, goes with some of this relatives to the bride's house on the day fixed by the Lama. There they are well entertained and the Lama solemnizes the wedding by reciting some *mantras*. Next day they return to their own house with the bride richly dressed and adorned. After a religious ceremony, the bride's right hand is held by all the brothers who are deemed to have married her." In case of Bashar polyandry, the bride washes the feet of all the bridegrooms. The latter tie *paju*, the pieces of muslin cloth round their caps. And this marks the completion of marriage ceremony. In case of Ladakhis, the bride, after she is brought to the bridegroom's house and bridegrooms are made to sit at a place in the kitchen. Then they are all made to eat in a common plate. This is followed by the putting of Goras on the heads of all the brothers. The ceremony confirms all brothers as common husbands of the same woman. The eligibility of younger brothers, for becoming husbands, is considered when the eldest marries.

In the wedding ceremony of Lahulis, the offering of locally prepared cake entitles the brothers to behave as co-husbands. A very interesting account, where mother-in-law's sanction is involved, has been given by Parmar for the polyandrous Lahaulis of Chamba Lahaul. Parmar (1975:65) mentions that, "while the bridegroom brings the bride home, his younger brother accompanies the bride on her ceremonial return. The younger brother presents a rupee to the girl's mother and this establishes his rights as a second husband. More than two brothers are not allowed". For the polyandry of Sirmur, he further writes that "A woman is married with elaborate ceremony only to one brother. She may be married to the eldest, youngest or any other bother. That depends on the particular circumstances of each case. If they are all at home, a wife is brought for the first time to the eldest brother. But the determining factor is the *Lagan* (auspicious star). If the *Lagan* does not suit him, the wife is brought in the name of the brother whom the *Lagan* suits. But if she was in fact meant for the eldest brother, the ceremonies would be performed in someone else's name while she would be considered the wife of the eldest, to the youngest, or to any other brother, she becomes the wife of all the brothers and all of them have equal right of access to her as is the case among the Todas" (Parmar 1975:89-90). In his *Fraternal Polyandry in Malabar*, Aiyappan explains how Iiavans marry. Only the eldest brother goes to fetch the bride from her house. Then, in the bridegroom's house, the ceremony of 'drinking milk' is performed. The bride and all the brothers are made to sit in a row and each given sweet drink. This declares them all as co-husbands of the common woman. The society also accepts it so. An exactly a similar performance is done in Thandan marriage. The bride and all the bridegrooms are served coconut milk. The drinking authorises husband-wife relationship. Among the Kammalans of Cochin, as reported by Gait, all the bridegrooms together participate in the marriage ceremony performed on the occasion.

In case of the Pannikans and Kaniyans of Cochin, all the brothers join the bride and sit at one place. Then they are all ceremonially served a sweet preparation which announces that the bride would be the common wife of all the brothers. The Toda wedding, as in case of most others, is also marked by a simple ceremony. In presence of the members of bride's family any of the brothers gives a piece of cloth to the bride. The act marks the wedding ceremony.

Arrangement for Sharing Wife

Another interesting element in the study of polyandry is in regard to the arrangement for sexually sharing common wife. In order to avoid confusion, in the matter under reference, means have been devised for access to the woman in a way that all kinds of clash in the programme is avoided. The common husbands, as also the community at large understand as to who can approach when and where to the common wife. There are accepted signals and signs which permit or prohibit entry to the common wife's place. The same also point as to which of the brothers is with the wife at a particular moment. The wife's role is no less important in the matter. Among the polyandrous families of Jaunsar-Bawar, even the talking with the common wife, by the younger brothers, is avoided in the presence of the eldest brother. In respect of Bawar area, Saxena has given that the different brothers have been given days for consorting. The younger husbands cannot have sex relations with the common wife in presence, in the house, of the eldest husband. In his absence alone, the sex act is done in the house. On many occasions the fields are also used for the purpose. The privileged position of the eldest brother is duly recognised by the Jaunsaris co-husbands. Saxena (1962:21) has pointed out that "all the wives have to share bed with the eldest brother turn by turn, and so it goes on in the strict order of precedence among all other brothers."

Likewise, the sex arrangement with the common wife, in case of Sirmur polyandrous families, has been explained by Parmar (1975:91) when he states that "Far greater tact has, however, to be exercised in adjusting the relations of the husbands and in not giving any of them a cause for complaint or jealousy. At times, the practice is to keep ones shoes or cap outside the room where a husband and his wife are sleeping. That would indicate the sexual possession of the wife by the particular husband." Among the Lahulis, the woman's favour is equally distributed and all have equal sexual right over the common wife. Sexual unions are said to be tactfully arranged. Among them has also been the practice of leaving a hat or beads at the door when indulging in sex with the common wife. Among the Ladakhis, as I was told, the eldest brother enjoys more rights over the common wife. Normally, the younger brothers, as co-husbands, keep away when the eldest is present in the house. The same privilege is passed on to the next eldest when the eldest brother is away. More time is spent in the company of the eldest husband, and the common wife does so in a way to avoid jealousy of others. Colder climate of Ladakh curtails sexual privacy. In colder months, all brothers sleep with the common wife, in the same room. There is no regularly established roster of sex relations with the wife. Sometimes the wife decides as to who would sleep with her on a particular night. The eldest brother may also decide about it. As the other brothers also sleep in the same room, the cohabiting couple keeps a Ladakhi table in-between as a gesture of privacy. Like the Ladakhis, the Toda woman, in a polyandrous wedlock, also, many times, decides as to which of the husbands would sleep with her on particular nights.

Regulation of sexual intercourse is more on an understanding between plural partners. There are no specific signals for the purpose. When the husbands live separately, more so in case of non-fraternal polyandrous marriage, the wife manages to live, for a month or so, with each husband by turn. This may be resembling the system among Nayars of Kerala where the common wife arranges sexual intercourse, by turn, with various husbands, living in different places. A signal system, among a group of Kerala polyandrous people, has been reported by Aiyappan. In his book, *Iravas and Culture Change* (p. 101), Aiyappan has given that, when one husband was with the common wife, it used to be the custom that he leaves his knife etc., on the door frame of the bedroom to signal his presence there to the others". However, for the same groups of Thandans and Kammalans, Peter gives a slightly twisted version. According to Peter (1963:220), "It was usually the woman who decided with whom she should spend the night; the others then stayed out on the verandah or in another room. Even in the older generation, anything remotely resembling the leaving of a knife at the door was never done. The husband who did not wish to be disturbed when he was with the common wife would leave his clothes lying about in the neighbouring room or in the verandah as a signal to his brothers. An old Thandan woman confirmed this".

Determining Fatherhood

For a child born of a polyandrous union, it becomes difficult to ascertain biological paternity. Many times, even the mother may not be able to say anything in the matter. At the same time, some of the polyandrous groups themselves do not bother to know as to who is the father of the particular child. But there are others who care for it and have devised methods of determining, at least socially, the paternity of the children born of a common wife but different husbands. In some cases the co-husbands divide the children among themselves. Others consider every child belonging to every husband and, thus, all husbands have equal right over the children. Srivastava, in his paper entitled, "Adivasi Jaunsar-Bawar Ke" (Sarita 1975:23-24) has for Jaunsaris, stated that "the social fatherhood is recognised because the real father is not known. Accordingly the eldest son belongs to the eldest brother. The second belongs to the next elder and then the same sequence is followed". In general, a child calls all brothers in wedlock as *Baba* or father. But whenever there is a need of making distinction, it is done on the basis of occupation that a particular father follows. One who looks after the goats is called *Bakrawal Baba* and so on. Among the polyandrous people of Sirmur, paternity is not at all bothered for so long as all brothers stay together. But in case of separation, the wife as well as the children go with the husband by whom she was actually brought.

A similar situation has been reported for Kinnars where the younger brothers, as Saxena pointed out, have no rights over the children. For Bashar, Parmar made mention of conventional methods for ascertaining the social paternity. The common trend is that all the husbands are recognised as the father of every child but making a distinction of elder and younger; for instance *Teg Babach* or the elder father and *Gato Babach* or the younger father. When the common wife is asked about the father of any child, she always and in all cases, refers to the eldest husband. But in the event of division of a polyandrous family, it is the wife who names the fathers of various children. But in case of the lower classes of Bashar, as Parmar points out, the husbands determine paternity for the children through the casting of lots. The Lahulis consider all their children as the joint property. As such it is not bothered to determine the social fatherhood. The mother, at times, may have some knowledge of it. In Ladakh, the children, born of a polyandrous union, call all husbands of a common wife as father. But they do make a distinction of the elder and younger ones. Children are not specifically assigned to particular husbands. However, more claim over children is said to be of the eldest husband who is designated as *Bap* (father). The others being referred to as *Chhota Bap*. While referring, the children are explained as belonging to the eldest brother. Like some other groups, the children, among the Thandans and Kammalans belong, collectively, to all the fathers. They are not specifically allotted to the individual father. The ceremony of 'Bow and Arrow' is performed among the Todas to confer social fatherhood to the child. In the seventh month of pregnancy, the eldest husband offers a small bow and arrow to the woman. This makes his assume child's paternity. The same stands true even for the subsequent children unless some other brother repeats the performance. In case of the latter, the paternity would be assumed by the next man who performed the ceremony in the later stage of common wife's pregnancy. As part of actual performance, a niche is cut in the trunk of a tree and a lamp placed there. The villagers, assembled on the occasion, tell to the expectant wife to share at the lamp. This is followed by the husband's handing over a miniature bow and arrow. Normally, the first two children belong to the eldest husband. Then in case of the third or fourth pregnancy, the second performs the ceremony and assumes father's title.

Reasons for Origin and Growth of Polyandry

The structure of the institution of polyandry is based on multidimensional foundation. Its rise can be explained on multifarious bases including social, economic, historical, political and demographic/biological ones. Not all aspects are equally responsive in all the groups having the custom of polyandry. Also the one applicable to group 'X', may not be so in case of group 'Y'. However, some uniformity in case of at least the Himalayan polyandrous groups can be marked in respect of some common base. There, too, it may not be true when viewed in the situation of diverse bases. Reasons for the origin and growth of polyandry have been viewed in two different but related perspectives: one in the form of general views about the custom, and second the specific reasons in case of specific polyandrous tribe or caste. Some experts have explained the origin of the custom of polyandry on the basis of certain advantages which people could derive out of it.

In the opinion of Rockhil the cause of polyandry lies in the desire to transmit an estate undivided. Polyandry is also attributed to the shortage of women by Rivers, Liviton, McLennan and Westermarck. Others have challenged the argument. A pure social base for polyandry was put forward by Herbert Spencer. It was, according to him, the 'greater family and greater social cohesiveness', consideration that led to the adoption of polyandry. Prince Peter explained the sociological and economic reasons in support. He brought into this fold elements, like prestige, attendance in court, woman care, peace, harmony, solidarity, economic protection, poverty, protection of estate and property, hard economic conditions, limiting heirs to property, labour supply, bride price, population growth etc. Peter (1963:566) feels that 'difficult and austere economy is perhaps the most convincing of all the reasons preferred as an explanation of polyandry". He summarized the causes into social, economic, historical and demographical dimensions. Li Yu-i came out with personal reason in support of polyandry. He feels that the brothers will not quarrel if they have one wife. Parmar has explained that the custom originated from extreme poverty coupled with scarcity of land and women. His explanation further involves that it did help curb fragmentation of holding and partitions of families. Further, Parmar, while summing up, gave psychological (traditions), biological (scarcity of women and birth to more male issues), and economic (undivided estate) reasons. Chatterjee and Jha gave scarcity of females as a reason. Cunningham, Trebeck, Risley do not agree to the point. Risley's idea that "no correlation exists between the disparity of sexes and polyandry may be true in a society where individual tendencies have a free scope but where such is not the case it has some correlation as brothers may easily share a wife in such society" (quoted by Parmar 1975:111). A geo-economic base, as a reason in support of the origin of polyandry, has also been explained. With more members in family, environments can be better exploited. To maintain cooperation and unity among the brothers, the polyandrous trend was boosted up, is another view-point. Female infanticide is another cause given for the introduction of polyandry.

Polyandry has also been described as a stage in the development of sex relations between man and woman. In the beginning, according to McLennan, marriage was not known and the earliest form of marriage was polyandry. Such a development did take place before any historical explanation came forth. Scarcity of women, more so because of female infanticide, was given the cause for such a development. Monogamy and polygyny, in order, then followed polyandry. Some, however, never agree to the view and take it as mere speculative. The wishes of the women, the desire for offspring, travels of the men away from home, disproportion of the sexes and economic motives have been given as the causes of polyandry by Westermarck. According to Peter (1963:553), "Charles Darwin places polyandry as second in his scheme of development after polygyny and monogamy, and before promiscuity, which is followed by polygyny and monogamy in recurrence. Robertson Smith explained polyandry as a stage on the way from promiscuity and matriliny to monogamy". This subsequently paved way for the recognition of paternity and kinship. Others like Herbert Spencer are of the opinion that polyandry can crop up at any stage of development and in the evolution of the institution of marriage, it should not be looked upon as a stage. But that polyandry is a stage in the evolution of marriage was stressed by McLennan and thus associated with Morgan in the matter. Within the frame of his formulations, the earliest form of marriage was nothing but polyandry.

Apart from the general views described above, there are specific ones in respect of individual group. According to Majumdar (1962:3), "the Khasas claim the earliest origin of polyandry in the Jaunsar-Bawar region. It is from the *Pandavas* that they trace the origin of their prevalent polyandrous system of marriage". *Pandavas* mythology supported Jaunsaris polyandry. Five Pandava brothers namely Yudhisthira, Bhim, Arjuna, Nakula and Sahadeva married Draupadi, a common wife. In addition to polyandry as a persistence of ancient cultural tradition, there is also the scarcity of women in Jaunsar-Bawar. But Saxena has discussed that disparity in sex ratio may not be a cause because others, with the same position in the district, do not practise polyandry. Rather, he brings in an economic reason in support. According to Saxena (1962:6), "the hardships of economic life have completely influenced the social life and customs of the people, who have been forced to adopt a system of family life in keeping with the demand for joint labour within a village. The practice of polyandry is the outcome of this demand. In a region where nature is extremely hard to exploit, it is difficult for an individual to maintain his independent family in modern sense of the word. A Jaunsari woman can, thus, be conveniently looked after by a group of brothers who own her as their common wife." Saxena himself, however, mentioned of another version. The contact of the Rajputs and Brahmans with Doms, who may be regarded as the aborigines of Jaunsar-Bawar and were polyandrous, was responsible for their adoption of polyandry. And this process was greatly helped by the force of circumstances, such as geographical isolation and economic hardships of the region (Saxena, 1962:22). In case of the people of Jaunsar-Bawar, the element of inheritance is also said to have some say in the matter. All brothers have some claim to parental property, but then the additional share is given to the eldest. He has a choice in the selection of agriculture fields and other household articles. The system makes others join the eldest in marriage.

One of the chief reasons that led Lahaulis to find for polyandry include the avoiding of division of small land holdings which people possess. With this custom they could keep the holdings intact and inherit the same undivided. Another cause, in support, is said to be the avoidance of quarrel among women. Their belief is that the sisters-in-law, with separate husbands, cannot possibly pull on together in a joint family. Joint stay of brothers is possible with a common wife. It has further been reported that the Lahaulis resort to polyandrous marital relation to keep up the family name.

In case of Ladakhis, the non-fraternal polyandry is said to be practised when the bride remains childless for quite some time. It may also be done to get additional hands to work in the fields. The rule of primogeniture is stated to restrain brothers to share a common wife and live together. The version given by Cunningham is different when he says that the Ladakhi Bhotias borrowed the institution of polyandry from Himalayan Kshtriayas where it was present since the time when Pandavas espoused Draupadi. Borrowing polyandry as a cultural trait has also been reported in case of Dards. The latter led to the adoption of polyandry in imitation of Ladakhis. It was because of culture contact and geographical proximity that the custom, with many other traits, was internalized by the Dards.

As in case of Ladakhis, for Kinnars too, the rule of primogeniture is greatly held responsible for the introduction of polyandry. The younger brothers were left with nothing to fall back upon, and rather were made to join the eldest brother for economic, as also the social purpose. Among other responsible factors for continuance of polyandry in Simla hills are included disparity in the proportion of sexes and maximum population pressure on land per square mile. Even the progeny was proud of having more number of fathers. The woman considered it as a privilege to be the wife of many husbands. May be that she received more care under such condition. Writing on Sirmor polyandry, Parmar (1975:89, 97) states that, "the economic factors are said to be responsible for its institution. Land under cultivation is extremely limited and rocky. It would become difficult for the family to carry on if partitions were effected and land divided and fragmented. It would be uneconomical to cultivate it. It has been observed that polyandry prevents sub-division of property and maintains it as an economic holding. It not only restricts population and makes it possible for the poor to get a joint wife for the management of the household but it also helps the solidarity of the family whereas separate wives lead to disputes between brothers and result in the disintegration of the group". For polyandry of Himachal Pradesh and the adjoining Uttar-Pradesh hills, the cause of 'tradition' has also been explained. "While polyandry has been found to be due to scarcity of women and land and a desire to leave an estate undivided, tradition has played no less significant role in sustaining custom."

The Pandava brothers had a common spouse and when her father raised an objection to the union of his daughter with five husbands, Yudhishthira told him on the authority of old practice that they had to take the path which their forefathers had followed. Now this region is associated with the life and exploits of Arjuna who conquered it and indeed the people of the area are divided into two sections: Shathis and Pashis, after the Pandavas and Kauravas. The Pandava tradition has determined the moral and social attitude of the people, lending them support in adhering to polyandry inspite of the gives and reproaches of monogamous people of the plains (Parmar, 1975:146).

It is categorically stated in the Punjab States Gazetteer, Bashahr State (1910:6) that "polyandry was in former times directly encouraged by the state which imposed penalty on partitions. If the brothers divided moveable property one half share of the whole was taken over the state and divisions of immovable property were refused official recognition." Even Parmar has stressed, for Bashahr State that the administration encouraged polyandry and imposed penalty on partitions. The society too, to avoid partitions, enforced rights of the eldest and youngest brothers. Parmar writes that the eldest brother gets one good field extra and the youngest the ancestral house, if the brothers think o separating. In case of living separately the others would be the losers, and as such it is preferred to live in polyandrous union.

In respect of Nayar polyandry, the views of Iyer and Chattopadhayay are frequently mentioned. As Chattopadhayay puts it the Nambudri Brahmins had the rule of primogeniture. Mostly the eldest brother, among them, married and the rest contracted union with Nayar women. The reason, based on religious tradition is given by Iyer. Accordingly, Parasurama pronounced his commandment to the Samathan and Sudra castes to gratify the desires of the Brahmans, ordering them to put off chastity and the cloth which covered their breast and declaring that promiscuous intercourse with three or four men in common was devoid of the least taint of sin. For Kandayans and Nayars, it is also mentioned that they had to spare one man from each family for the army of the king or the chief. Then the other brother was made to take care of the wife of man who left. The kind of military obligation, stated above, has, thus, been attributed as a cause of polyandry among these people. In still another explanation, it is believed that Thandans and Tiyas of Kerala brought the custom of polyandry from Ceylon where they actually originated. And for Kandayans of Ceylon two major reasons for polyandry are given. One is the poverty because of which they cannot afford independent family. The other is applicable to the rich section who give political reason. They speak for the system as it helps them keep wealth and influence concentrated in their hands. Then the Kerala castes and tribes are also stated to practise polyandry to avoid the situation of quarrel among the brothers. A Kerala proverb meaning 'where four breasts cannot agree, two heads can', may provide support to the explanation.

Birth of Toda polyandry, according to Rivers, can be attributed to 'severe struggle for existence'. It is presumed that when Todas came to Nilgiri hills, there were very limited sources of food. They had to, then, struggle hard for existence. One means of adaptation, under such conditions, was the adoption of the practice of female infanticide. This was, in consequence, followed by polyandry. The number of women considerably declined. Peter, for Todas, gives tradition/myth as a base for polyandry. "Terkish, according to Peter (1963:267), it seems, married an ordinary Toda called Puth who, after his death was deified. With him, the mother-goddess of the Nilgiris had thirteen children, eleven boys and two girls. None of these children married, except two of the sons, Podzovordjen and Podjovorj, these polyandrously to an ordinary Toda woman called *Notirsh*. She, too, after her death, became a goddess, now well-known to all Todas. From this polyandrous marriage of the gods, Kwoten, the man-god who ran after Terkosh and was eventually carried off by her was born. He married Muturpani, a Toda woman and not a goddess and had two sons by her, Koltawutn and Kshorwutn of whom there are still descendants alive today".

Peter, proposing his explanation as 'anthropological theory', highlights the elements of cooperation, affection, solidarity, unity, etc., as supporting pillars to the polyandrous structure. These elements, according to him, have relevance to natural environmental conditions. According to Peter (1963:568):

> "Polyandry is initially due to the fact that certain peoples find themselves living in a difficult and insecure natural environment which imposes upon them a strenuous economic and social organization. This necessarily takes the form of a very great interdependence between the men in the society, who, in order to work either fields or herds of animals have to put the good of the community before their own selfish and individual aims. Great solidarity between them is thus, cultivated; they repress their natural aggression to a marked degree, and develop feelings of interdependence and of love for one another to a much greater extent than other people living in more secured environmental conditions. The balance of love and hate which exists normally in every individual is thus upset in favour of affection between these men, who come to look upon their unity as the supreme social ideal to be attained. The unity and solidarity of the sibling group is thus enormously intensified, far beyond the usual requirements of the average nuclear family elsewhere. Fraternal polyandry becomes the rule with these people. On the very good excuse that close association between males is essential and jealousy must, therefore, not be given a free reign, incestuous desires find considerable satisfaction in the fact that access to a sister-in-law is possible. Such practices become socially acceptable, because the community is in need of close cooperation and solidarity between men. Polyandry is thus, near incestuous form of the marital institution, correlated with excessive economic and social pressure on the nuclear family of people living in difficult natural or social environment."

Polyandry and Change

In regard to their attitude to polyandry, people can be classified into two schools of thought: one that treats it good and the other that discards the same, considering it as bad. Those subscribing to the later school have, directly or indirectly, always condemned the custom of polyandry. Instances are available of such doings as conscious or unconscious. Planned and intentionally regulated legislations were, at certain places, enacted to curb the practice. Situations of culture-contact also led to its decline. Economic growth was another factor responsible for the degeneration of the custom. Some from within the polyandrous group themselves realized to do away with the custom. Under various influences, put together, it can be inferred that some change in attitude to and practice of polyandry has been noticed. The details involved in specific cases can be discussed as under.

Though not free of the element of controversy, it has been discussed about the Kerala polyandry that the foreign influence undermined it. The custom confronted some downfall when the new order started replacing the old one. The new circumstances do not favour one woman's marriage to many men. The great deal of cultural change which hit at some of the fundamentals of social and economic structure also partially led to the decline of polyandry in Kerala. Some people who once practised polyandry but then gradually abandoned it, now look at the custom with abhorrence and resist any move for polyandry. In regard to Nayar polyandry, Peter (1963:92) has stated that "Since the beginning of the 19th century, British rule on the coast of Malabar brought about such social and economic changes that the traditional pattern of Nayar matrimony disintegrated and disappeared". Kathleen Gough, however, does not support it much. Rather, she is of the opinion that the disappearance of polyandry among Nayars is not because of European criticism but because of the 'collapse of the military organization and the return of young Nayar men to help in managing the land in their own villages'. Disappearance of Nayar Militias also led to the fading away of the custom of polyandry.

In Kerala, the enforcement of legislation against polyandry has had its own say in the matter. Polyandry in north Cochin was declared illegal vide the Cochin Makkathayam Thiyya Act of 1940. As part of the Act, all polyandrous marriages, performed after the enforcement of Act, shall be treated as void. In his book, *Iravas and Culture Change* (p. 103), Aiyappan throws light on the changing trends of Irava Polyandry. As he puts it, "The differences in occupations and income and the development of new sexual standards are two active forces that one sees in operation against polyandry. The old ways are no longer fashionable, and are even despised and considered to be primitive and barbarous. The women, too do not want to be shared any longer by a number of brothers, and prefer to return home or refuse polyandrous marriages rather than be joined in wedlock in the traditional manner'. The accounts given in respect of Iiavan polyandry indicate that the traditional fraternal polyandry has assumed some new forms. The brothers, having one wife, may bring in another wife and sharing her also. Apart from such rise of polyandrous form, the brothers, at times, divide themselves into groups for the purpose of marriage. Some brothers may withdraw from the original union and go in for a new common wife.

Among the Ladakhis, the working of polyandrous system has been hampered and affected because of the growth of a different kind of social outlook among the people. Many of those who have sufficient experience of situation outside Ladakh, through their travel outside Ladakh or otherwise, and also the educated ones, look down upon the custom. They explain the institution of polyandry as undesirable and outdated. People were encouraged for such an attitude for various reasons. Outsiders described the custom as bad and immoral. Froncke, a Moravian missionary treated Ladakhi polyandry as something disgusting. He told to the people to replace the custom by some better form of matrimony. Even the 'Code of Tribal Custom of the Ladakh Tehsil' condemned the custom and rather suggested for its discontinuation on the ground that it did not hold morality. Also of relevance is a note given in *Amrit Bazar Patrika* (March 16, 1952). The note entitled "Poverty, Mass Ignorance and Social Evils in Ladakh" gives that "Two social evils, ugly and venomous, are eating into the vitals of Ladakh Buddhists. One is the custom of polyandry. . . the other the very common use of *Chang* (beer). Polyandry has undermined the powers of increase of the people. The only way to do away with the evil is to improve conditions in the land so that the development of resources of the district bring enough wealth and strong public opinion against polyandry". Some of the informants are bitter about the situation.

> "Lobsang To Tok, an informant of Peter, complained bitterly of the 'immorality' of young people in Leh. He said that polyandry was no longer desired by the younger generation, and that this was all due to outside influence from Indian and Turk traders from Sinkiang, and from European missionaries and travellers who were perpetually speaking against the time-honoured custom of polyandrous matrimony such Ladakhis had always practised and were introducing the 'bad habit' of monogamous marriage" (quoted by Peter 1963:361).

Polyandrous people, who live in comparatively more isolation have a greater continuance of the custom. There it exists as a very integral part of local culture and where people take it as a moral arrangement of matrimonial alliance. But where the culture-contact situation involves the severity of social interaction with outsiders, the custom is ridiculed and gradually the people start either hiding it or do away with it. In regard to the polyandry among the Jaunsaris, Saxena is of the firm opinion that the impact of modern civilization has strained people of the polyandrous custom. Even some eminent persons from outside propagate against the custom. Likewise, for Simla hills, Parmar (1975:148) states that "In places which have been brought within the pale of modern civilization by railways, or where education has spread, polyandry is giving way to monogamy for the simple reason that the introduction of railways and modern communications has meant an improvement in the financial condition of the people and a change in their outlook. The latter helped reduce the influence of polyandry". The decline of polyandry is also, at times, the result of organized social movements. More involved in such venture were some social workers. The organized efforts, initiated around 1911, against polyandry in Himachal were intensified by the Vidya Prabandhani Sabha, Simla, especially when its Secretary, Thakur Surat Singh, a social reformer, seriously devoted, around 1925, for the eradication of polyandry. The pamphlet entitled "Himalayan Tragedy of Marriage', brought out as a part of campaign, had wide impact causing awakening among the people. Speeches of the people strengthened the move. The earlier esteem under which polyandry was rated got a setback. Many people got into a new fold of vision, and what they had been practising for centuries was taken as something degrading.

However, the persistence of polyandry has, in spite of such circumstances, been there all through with varying degree. Like the one in Himachal Pradesh, an organization known as Kashmir Raj Bodhi Maha Sabha, was formed for Ladakhis. One of the demands of this association formed of non-Ladakhis, submitted as a memorandum to Grievances Enquiry Commission by the President of Sabha around December 1931, was for the abolition of polyandry and the law of primogeniture among the Ladakhis. The Government, in return, sanctioned allowance to social reformers and religious preachers who were then considered major force to mould public opinion against polyandry and sex liberties. The Polyandrous Marriages Prohibition Act, 1941 was also promulgated by the government. With such forces operating around, some Ladakhis had to relent.

Apart from the 'patch-form' reasons for the institutional growth of polyandry, given earlier, a more systematic explanation, as attempted by me, can be put forth. It gives a wider coverage, in chain form, to the conditions, growth and sustenance of the custom of polyandry. It appears that the single and isolated reason does not explain for all polyandrous groups. My explanation merges a group of considerations together to make it more sound and applicable to wider polyandrous groups. It would be correct to say that the frame of this theoretical explanation is more closely applicable to Himalayan and Toda polyandry, and comparatively less so in case of the tribes and castes of Kerala. At the same time, such an explanation sounds more befitting than any other analysis in the context of total matrix of Indian polyandry. It does, to a great extent, channelize into a single stream the view-points, which otherwise appear so stray in the context of the diversity involved in the different polyandrous groups. The sequence or order of arguments is to be looked into two but related perspectives. It may be termed as two phases in the rise of polyandry. Correlation between interpretations involved in various categories, under each phase, is of a logically positive kind. From the gamut of explanations, given in the following paragraphs, it may be taken that polyandry has been as outcome of adaptability. Such an adaptational theory of polyandry also hints at the fact that the people made conscious efforts to develop this kind of marital relations. I have stressed on the same theory in my earlier paper entitled "Ladakhi Polyandry—Reinterpreted, published in *Indian Anthropologist* (1978: vol. 8, No. I). Under the current academic venture, however, the explanation has been further stretched by adding some more elements in the two phases as given in Table 1.1.

TABLE 1.1: Polyandry as an Outcome of Adaptability

	Phase in sequence		Positive stimulants/devices
1.	That led people to relise of the custom	(a)	Impositions and limitations of natural and man-made mini resources; hard and inhospitable geographical conditions; physical isolation.
		(b)	Growing anxiety against fast population growth; female infanticide; dedication of boys to monastery.
		(c)	Feeling of threat of insecurity to women.
		(d)	Need for resource protection and their maximum exploitation.
		(e)	Urge to inherit undivided estate; of whatever order it was.
		(f)	Necessity of living together unitedly.
		(g)	Obvious advantages which people then anticipated from a custom like polyandry.
(2)	That led people to create devices/ means which could sustain the custom	(a)	Providing for typical marriage ceremonies.
		(b)	Devising of befitting ways of sex relation; granting of sexual liberty.
		(c)	Evolution of a suitable land tenure system.
		(d)	Reinforcement provided by religion and its organizations.
		(e)	Maintenance of stress on recognition of myths and traditions.
		(f)	According prestige and recognition to polyandrous marriage and family.
		(g)	Recognition by the state and the administration thereof of the custom.

A systematic analysis of the contents of this paradigm would be more revealing to explain the origin, growth and continuance of the custom of polyandry. Very limited resources with difficult topography, mountainous region, undulating terrain, rocky and poor soil, very small cultivable landholdings, insufficient produce, condition of food scarcity, primitive technology and means of production, in some places scarce rainfall and scarcity of fodder, natural rigours, absence of alternative additional economic means because of comparatively more isolation and inaccessibility must have made living mighty hard. Indigenous resources were not found sufficient for people's existence. Land and livestock, within limitations, were the chief sources on which the people then could depend. At the same time, they could not have thought of any major improvement or expansion of resources. My presumption is that such inhospitable conditions, at some stage, exerted great amount of pressure on human beings to recourse to some alternatives, more conducive to smooth living.

Such state of affairs might have made people bother for their growing number, and at the same time realise that any faster increase in their number would never be supported with so meagre resources and with that kind of technology. Then alone, they might have thought of reshaping the system in the context of resources limitation and increase in population. To meet the situation of scarce resources and poor means of production, it is quite likely that the people might have thought of restricting their rate of population growth through the introduction of polyandry. There is every possibility that the people realised that polyandry would cause reduction in the number of procreating agencies, and hence a check in population expansion. Striking of such an idea might have guaranteed people survival under the conditions of scarcity. Limiting population could have also been partly achieved, by a few, through female infanticide. This process, too, could create favourable conditions for the rise of polyandry. The other means to contain population, and to which people resorted was the dedication of boys to monastic institutions where they led a life of celibacy. Similar to the need of controlling population, to cope with typical kind of living conditions, the system of polyandry must have also been desired keeping in view certain other important requirements of the people under those conditions. One such could be to tackle the problem of insecurity to women. The people should have felt that at least one man must always stay with a woman to provide her adequate protection and to look after her comforts. And that she should not be left alone when her husband went out for cattle grazing or to serve in king's army. As the man had to stay away for longer durations, it might have been thought proper to leave behind the husband's brother to look after the wife. In order that the brother, who stayed back for woman's security, could live cordially with her, the people thought of granting him sex privilege with the woman. For such purpose, the polyandrous system could be most befitting and suitable. Similarly people must have found this kind of marital relation and family as most appropriate to meet the necessity of existing resource protection. It could be better done by living together, as is possible in a polyandrous family. With more hands, people could exploit the resources better.

The small cultivable landholdings needed to be kept intact and protected against fragmentation so that they remained economically viable. This could again be achieved through polyandrous system wherein the brothers had to live jointly. There could then be no possibility of land fragmentation. Instead, it encouraged joint living which also proved of great help in case of the herders. More and better care could be taken of the livestock. Then the system ensured cooperation meant to live a healthy and happy life. In addition to the above considerations, the system of polyandry would have been adjudged suitable enough to meet people's urge of inheriting undivided estate. The keenness for the latter was again to keep it economically viable under the typical geo-economic conditions. In tune with the people's desire for an economical living, the system got preferential treatment and support from masses. All shared the common house, kitchen and other things which proved economical to the family.

At the same time the feeling that in comparison to any other kind of joint living, staying together in polyandrous family could be more conducive to the maintenance of unity and healthy intra-family relations in the best possible form, could be held high through the system. Because of the interest in common wife, and because of her and her eldest husband's say, things remained normal. An atmosphere of submissiveness, cordiality and cooperation prevailed. Even at present, the dependability, especially on the common wife and the eldest brother, among polyandrous families, is of the kind where the younger brothers subscribe to the prescribed norms set by the persistence of traditions. Then the appropriateness of polyandrous system could be again observed in the division of labour required and desired for handling of the means of production and for better exploitation of resources. People, somehow, could anticipate that a better kind of division of labour was possible in case of polyandrous families than others. And the same could subsequently prove of more economic advantage, especially by providing sufficient manpower to attend to agriculture, animal husbandry and other indoor and outdoor activities.

At the level of technology, then prevalent, things could be done better when more hands attended to them. Those still in favour of the custom continue to announce of such advantages. Thus, the people adapted themselves to particular kind of situation and requirements by coining polyandrous form of marital relationship. The adaptation was between man, society and environment.

Considering polyandry as a sufficiently adequate means of adjustment to particular situations, the people thought of strengthening it through various sustaining devices. These involved social, economic, religious and other cultural elements. Considering it as something very important in the matter, special kinds of additional marriage ceremonies were thought out and resorted to. These, for various groups, have been explained in the relevant section. Once all the brothers join in the ceremony, alongwith the common wife, they get the recognition as husbands. Normally the bride remains least perturbed on undergoing the ceremony for being shared by more than one husband. Rather, she feels that her doing so ensures definite security under the circumstances. Sexual relationships within polyandrous union were given a new deal through the induction of certain new norms to make the custom of polyandry more acceptable and established. In addition to such relationships between the common wife and various husbands, certain sex liberties were granted to those who failed to marry. Premarital and even extra-marital sex relations, in most of the polyandrous groups, became a thing of tolerance and without any significant stigma associated with the same. People granted recognition to the wider horizons of sex permissibilities.

Another very strong measure, taken by quite a few groups, to sustain the custom of polyandry was evolved in the garb of an economic compulsion. They came out with the rule of primogeniture in order to keep up the polyandrous marital form. The eldest son was made more or less the sole repository of family property. Rest of the brothers depended upon him. In the absence of adequate means of support, the other brothers could not afford to have individual wife. In case they thought of division in the family, the major share had to go to the eldest son. It was then rather preferred to share the eldest brother's wife. When a girl, in the absence of sons, inherited land and other property, she, after marriage, in many cases, was joined by her husbands. Simultaneous to the social purpose, the primogeniture system of inheritance also helped prevent fragmentation of land holdings which people desired to maintain for economic viability. Religion and religious organizations were also taken help for the sustenance of polyandry. People devoted to the social custom in the name of religion. This largely happened in case of Buddhist people of upper Himalayas. With the trend, the community and monastery relationship became more intimate and interdependent. The surplus females, who could not marry because of polyandry, were made to join monastic nunneries. The females put up the least objection for their devotion to religious life by becoming nuns. In the absence of such an arrangement for absorbing the surplus females, there could arise some kind of social problems in society. The adjustment responded favourably to the promotion of polyandrous system and to the maintenance of order in society. The people felt obliged to the religious order and its call.

Many continue, even today, to dedicate their children to the monasteries. They all lead to the life of celibacy. It was almost made a tradition to spare at least one child to join lamasery or nunnery. With such an adjustment, for boosting up polyandry, came the idea of putting extra stress on the recognition of certain myths and other cultural traditions. The latter solidified the faith of people in all generations in respect of the custom's upkeep. After being socially internalized, the idea trickled, as part of positive valuation, and the people then never felt anything bad of the custom. Most of such myths and traditions were, directly or indirectly, rooted into some aspect of religion. At the same time, the people made polyandrous custom as a very integral part of their social system. In addition to declaring it as a preferential form of marriage, the people accorded great deal of appreciation to such a social institution.

The polyandrous families, and the members thereof, got socially superior status. Gradually it became an accepted virtue, so much so that the tradition-oriented parents exert, even now, upon their children to go in for polyandrous unions, considering it as prestigious. Apart from what the society arranged to adapt itself to the urgent requirements, by making some additions and alterations in its socio-economic system, and apart from what the religious order contributed in the matter, the state and its administration also came out with rules and regulations to promote polyandry. This was also done keeping in view people's desire. Official provision was, at many places, made not only for the recognition of the custom but also to directly or indirectly punish those who thought of going against it. Enactments for encouraging polyandry proved helpful for its maintenance and persistence.

As already mentioned elsewhere in the paper, the custom of polyandry is, in most of the groups, towards a constant and faster decline. This kind of trend has more prominently been marked during the last, say, forty years. The causes of decline, already explained too, can be classified into two major categories, correspondingly affecting elements of the two phases: Firstly, those that minimized the realization of such a custom, and secondly, those that weakened the sustaining devices or stimulants. The causes were promoted essentially by the human agencies, mostly of the non-polyandrous outside people, who outrightly condemned, and are still doing so, the centuries-old custom. The root causes for the rise of polyandry, as described minutely in the two interconnected phases, are being hit (as discussed in the section on change in polyandry), directly or indirectly, mainly by the outsiders and partly by some of the polyandrous people themselves as an influence of outsiders. But so long as the elements, responsible for its origin and growth, survive, in any form, the custom would persist in one way or the other. When the former get vanished, the institution of polyandry may come to the state of extinction.

2

MATRILINEAL DESCENT AND ITS EXEGESIS

For smooth functioning of social organization, a society has to follow a particular descent set-up. This may be defined from a typical principle followed by the social system. It can be either unilineal, which follows single factor, or bilineal, which is double-factor based. Matrilineal system operates on the single factor using mother's lineage or descent. But then matrilineal descent is guided by certain permanent features, without which this will loose its real character and may be weakened in the long run. These features maintain and perpetuate the matrilineal descent groups. Theoretically they constitute rule of matrilineal descent, the exogamy and division of functions and authority on the basis of sex. From these permanent features emanate certain other related features. Matrilineal descent is closely associated with matrilocal residence, that is, where residence after marriage is wife's house, and matriarchy which upholds the dominance of female kins in decision-making and resource control. This clearly speaks of female and her kins in administration and authority over the members of the descent group in case of matrilineal descent order. It is clear from these features that a lineage or clan, in order to get status of descent group, should own property. It should have a head and the members of the lineage should gather from time to time for ceremonial, ritual, administrative and legal purposes. It should act as a corporal unit and hold the property jointly. The matrilineal descent group should assert authority over the male and female equally as both are important for its perpetuation.

Matrilineal system is widely reported among certain communities of the world. In ancient Indian literature matriliny has been referred as *Nari Rajya* (female kingdom) which finds prominent reference in great Epic, *Mahabharata*. It is stated in the Jaimini Bharata that there was Nari Rajya in north-east at the time of *Mahabharata*. During the great *Aswamegha Yagna* (horse sacrifice), Arjuna the Pandava prince, along with the sacred horse, reached Nari Rajya, where a woman ruler, Pramila, ruled over the country. Arjuna married her and then proceeded to Manipur. It is very likely that the Nari Rajya of *Mahabharata* was the present matrilineal society of Meghalaya and its border population, especially in Assam. The matrilineal system is still prevalent in some parts of north-east and south-west of India. In north-east Indian matriliny is reported among Khasi, Jaintia and Garo tribes of Meghalaya state. Hill Lalungs, Rabhas and Kachari (Dimasa) of Assam also practise matriliny to a limited extent. It is also reported among Nayars, Mappilas and Tiyyars of Kerala state and its adjoining areas.

The most important factor, besides others, contributing to the origin of matriliny seems to be economic in nature. Technology, division of labour, organization of work groups, control of resources, types of subsistence activities and the ecological niches in which these activities occur must have been supplement to horticulture and primitive cultivation in order to pave way to matriliny. The primitive method of cultivation allows more important role to woman which is denied to her in advanced technology because the women's role, then, as food producer, becomes insignificant and secondary. This situation of important role might have led to plot-ownership by women and a whole network of relationship, might have resulted out of it, which had more prominence for women in important fields. The simple economic activities and women's property interest find a functional fit in matrilineal system, which results into the association between women in charge of production and matrilineal kinship system. The advanced and complex industrialized economic system does not seem to find a fit in matrilineal set up. As Nakane (1975) reiterates that in small aboriginal communities the women make more important contributions to domestic work as well as economy because in these societies economic and political status differentiation is hardly developed. Whereas in more advanced economy and industrialization, with more complex division of labour and areas of specialization, the women are kept in background. Here women have to play secondary role and are normally subordinate to male role. Hence advance economy, with women's secondary role, does not fulfil the prerequisite for matrilineal set-up which tends to disappear with plough cultivation and vanishes with industrialization.

Now, let us see upto what extent the matrilineal communities in India are retaining the matrilineal descent system. The most important feature of this system is that in matriliny the descent is traced through mother only. A child is born into mother's clan and initiated in the group through matriclan. The matrilineal communities claim to be descendants of some female ancestress. Patriclan is taken care of at the time of marriage for exogamy purpose but the person is known only by the matriclan which is the prerequisite for matrilineal descent system. In matrilineal system when a man marries he produces children for his wife's lineage and not for his matrilineage. These children are assigned to woman's lineage. If they are not assigned to mother's lineage the system looses its identity as matrilineal. Hence the allocation of child to the mother's group only. Knowing fully the limitations, the father can only be a source of tenderness of his children. His authority over his children is limited and curtailed due to the fact that he will not be succeeded by his children in lineage or property group.

Bride-price in matrilineal system does not change the allocation of children from mother's lineage to any other group. Payment for the bride-price mother's does not give husband any extra power to have authority over his wife and children in matriliny. Among Mappilas, bride-price (*Mahar*) is fixed for the wife, it is to be paid to wife by the husband in case he divorces her. But this concession does not alter the system of allocating the child to mother's lineage. The children belong to mother's clan or lineage only among the matrilineal Khasi, Jaintia, Garo, Hill Lalung, Nayars and Tiyyars. A Garo child is born in its mother's clan (Machong) and gets affiliated to one of the five larger groups known as Chatchi, to which its Machong is affiliated. Among Khasi and Jaintia it is the *Kur* (mother's clan) to which a child is affiliated. Among Hill Lalungs the descent is traced through mother. The ritual of Kush-Singa signifies a man's formal breakaway from his natal clan and his child's formal initiation to his mother's clan. The Dimasa Kacharis and the Rabhas use both matrilineal and patrilineal descent with a stronger bent towards the latter in recent times. Mappillas retain matrilineal descent system with introduction of orthodox Sunni-Muslim Law into the marriage institution. Even if the child is born in the man's Taravad, the child is affiliated to mother's lineage only.

In general, matrilocal residence is practised among matrilineal communities. Here the husband shifts to his wife's residence after marriage. Among Garos the husband stays in his wife's house (*Nok*) which is matrilocal in nature. The Khasi husband shifts to his wife's residence (*Iing*). A Khasi mother weeps over the marriage of her son as he has to leave her forever and go to his wife's house as it is a matrilocal residence. A Jaintia husband is a privileged visitor, every night, in his wife's house. A Nayar husband is also a privileged visitor to his wife's Taravad. Among Hill Lalungs the residence, after marriage, is wife's house. A Mappilla husband joins his wife's Taravad and a Tiyyar husband sometimes joins his wife's Taravad or his wife joins his Taravad. War Khasi also practise matrilocal residence. A Khasi husband moves to his wife's residence after marriage. It may be the *Iing* (ancestral home) of *Ka Khadduh* (the heiress), or a new house if his wife is a non-heiress. The Iing of his wife, who is heiress, may be housing few generations of matrikins. Among these must be heiress, her unmarried daughters and sons, the divorced or widowed brothers, old parents of the heiress and the would be heiress with her husband and children. Here woman is the head of the house. In case of a non-heiress, the husband constructs the house for his wife on the land given by the wife's mother. Even here the wife is the head of the family, inspite of the house built by the labour of the husband. A Garo Nok consists of *Nokna* (the heiress) who inherits the house, her husband, unmarried daughters and sons, the would be *Nokna* with her husband and children. The other daughters and sons are married out. Among Garo and Khasi every one, except the heiress daughter, has to leave the parental house after marriage. The non-heiress daughter is given a plot of land, for house construction, by her mother. The husband builds her house on this land by the material help extended by the wife's mother.

The next important feature of matriliny is inheritance of property by females. The female ultimogeniture is exercised by some societies. The others choose any of the daughter for property and ancestral home inheritance. Among Khasi there is clear-cut demarcation of descent and property inheritance in female line. A Ka Khadduh is the youngest daughter in the family. The ancestral house as well as a lion's share in other property go to her. The other daughter too gets a plot for house construction and some cultivable land. But a son, normally, does not inherit any movable or immovable property among Khasis. He is supposed to join his wife's house and work for her in all economic pursuits. Ka Khadduh stays with her parents last of all. She is obliged to look after her old parents and widowed or divorced brother. If there is no daughter in the family the wife adopts her sister's daughter to inherit property. Garo choose any daughter for the role of Nokna. It is obligatory on the part of Nokna to marry her father's sister's son in order to inherit ancestral property and house. A Nokna has to look after her aged parents, unmarried sisters and brothers and divorced or widowed brothers. Here, husband of the Nokna is the head of the family who manages his wife's property with the help of *Chra* (maternal uncle and other maternal male kins of wife). If at any stage the Nokna is found guilty of not fulfilling her obligations, she can be disinherited by the joint consent of Chra, and the next daughter can be made the Nokna. Traditionally the ancestral house and fields go to the youngest daughter among Hill Lalungs who allow to inherit her from mother.

Among Jaintias too the youngest daughter inherits ancestral

property's largest share. Other daughters get plot of land for making hut only. Among War Khasis the ancestral property, except the parental house, is equally divided among all the daughters and sons. The man, after marriage, also shares his portion of property and uses its income exclusively for himself. But this property cannot be inherited by his children, and after his death it is retained by his natal family collectively. A Nayar Taravad holds property in female line collectively. All the matrikins stay together and get material help from natal Taravad whose head is a female. Among Mappillas too property is inherited by females. A husband is supposed to work for his wife's Taravad also. But he has to look after his mother and sister's Taravad first among Nayars.

The main structural characteristic, in the context of male authority, in matrilineal system, is that the group placement runs through female line but the line of authority runs through men. The male kins of female exercise authority in all matters pertaining to family and beyond. Though the property owner is female but the property is managed by her brother or uncle whose decision is binding to all. The woman, as sister or niece, looks to her brother for any initiative in religious or economic matters. He performs, and presides over all ritualistic functions in the family. He is the authority in his sister or niece's house. This position will be held by his nephew who will be next authority. In Garo matriliny, group placement is through female (heiress), but the authority of management is vested in males. Here the husband, and not the brother, is the manager of property. Char is, of course, a strong and final authority but husband is equally strong in authority.

So we find that the headship of family goes to the male among Garos. For the perpetuation and functioning, the matrilineal group depends on retaining control over both male and female as the line of descent and authority go parallel. In general, the male-held statuses have authority over female-held statuses among matrilineal groups. There are many fields of authority including economic, political and religious. These give special allocation of statuses to the person performing the connected roles and activities to them. The two fields, descent and property, are occupied by females but the control and authority fields, and the statuses attached to them, are vested in males. This makes the female and children of the concerned group subordinate to the male authority. Looking to the traditionally prescribed role of male and female in Khasi and Jaintia society, it sounds that the male-dominated roles are of authority. The religious head, Lyngdoh, is always a male. The political head, Siem, is never a woman. The female is head of family and inherits property but the management of the family and property matters is in the person of her brother or uncle who are males. A man continues to be a person of authority in his natal home even after marriage. According to Majumdar (1955) in the capacity of *Pante* (member of the same Machong) he is expected to settle his Machong's affairs. He often participates in discussions about the affairs of his wife's Machong and his opinion is given weightage. A man, even after marriage, among Hill Lalungs is called upon to help, whenever the sister has any difficulty in managing her affairs regarding the management of land or settlement of disputes over division of land among the sisters, in the capacity of *Borjela* (mother's brother). Among Nayars and Mappilla the group placement is through females as the children belong to mother's group and descent but authority runs through male line. Karanavan is the authority in Taravad. He manages all the ritualistic, economic and marital affairs of his sister's Taravad. No decision can be taken, nor any decision implemented, without his consent. He is the final authority and females of his group look to him for advice. The male-held status controls the female-held status.

Matrilineal descent group should be exogamous as one of its basic prerequisite. It should be exogamous for marriage purpose but endogamous in relation with the wider unit of which it is a member. On the smaller and lower level it should be exogamous to bring in the marrying members from exogamous group only. Among Khasi, clan exogamy is strictly followed. There are many clans defined for marriage exogamy. Strictness about clan exogamy sustains on incestuous act which is taken as the most ghastly sin by the Khasis. The offenders of this act, at one time, were punished severely. Their heads used to be shaven in typical design and they were excommunicated. They could not construct house in the same village nor could they come and live in Khasi community. The clans are clearly defined for marriage purposes. Though preferential marriages are not so strictly favoured these days, but clan exogamy is strictly adhered to. Among Garo a Sangma cannot marry a Sangma; neither a Marak can marry a Marak and they are more strict about the same motherhood which is always exogamous for them. The persons indulging in incestuous act were termed as *Ma'dong* (one who married his own mother). Among Garos cross-cousin marriage is largely preferred by Songsarek (non-Christians). Whereas the Khasis have no special preference for this type of marital alliance and it is totally prohibited among Lalungs. Among Garos a cross-cousin is generally preferred in case of *Nokna*. The other daughters are under no compulsion to abide by such binding but clan exogamy is strictly and religiously followed by all. It is their belief that incestous act will bring misfortune not only to the family but the clan, and the village will also suffer the wrath of God due to such forbidden relationship. Besides preferential cross-cousin marriage among Garos the girls are given freedom to select their own partners for marriage. Under no circumstances the marriage proposal should come from boy's side. Under the matrilineal system women's place is in the home as they are regarded essentially as home makers and home keepers and this requires their permanent presence in the house. As the daughters are to inherit the property and look after their parents, they are allowed the freedom to choose their mates. But clan exogamy is strictly adhered to by all.

More freedom in choosing marriage partners is given to women in most of the matrilineal communities. The proposal of marriage may come from any side of either the boy or the girl but it is entirely on the girls discretion to accept the offer or not. Among Khasis, the woman chooses her husband, keeping in view the clan exogamy. They have no preferential marriage. Among Lalungs the girls are free to choose their marriage partners. They meet the boys on the occasion of festivals when many village youths and damsels come to celebrate it. There they get chance to choose the partners of their choice and then parents normally agree to their likings if it is according to clan exogamy rule. Among Nayars a female is entirely free to choose her husband and leave him whenever she feels like it. The fluid nature of marriage among the matrilineal set-up is the impetus to easy divorce and remarriage which is possible because of more freedom to women in this field.

In matrilineal set up the male members can be of three kinds in the context of authority line. In one category are those who are already in authority operation action; second category of males is of those who are going to take over from the first category, in the coming future; hence they are important and are must for the group in order to perpetuate it; the last category of males is of those who are not going to get a chance to perform authority role. They cannot succeed to those positions in their life time. Among Khasis matrilineal descent group the authority role is exercised by the eldest brother or the maternal uncle of the heiress. He is the authority and manager of the Iing. The maternal uncle is the current authority in the household, hence important to it. In the event of his death, he will be succeeded by his nephew (sister's son) only. This can also happen in case of former's incapability. One of the nephews may get this role and others may be asked to prepare themselves for the same role in case the first is incapable to function properly. The third category of males is of those in marrying affines (husbands) who are not going to get the authority role in their life-time. In case of Khasi's, the husband of the heiress comes in this category. The same husband may be in the authority role in his natal Iing but in his wife's Iing he is deprived of this role and status. In Garo matriliny the headship and authority of the Nok is vested in the husband of the heiress. He comes in the first category of authority line. The second category of males, in the context of authority, in Nok, is of the successor of the first category of male *i.e.* the next Nokrom. Among Garos the Nokrom is invariably the son of father's sister. The father's nephew is the next authority male in the Nok. There is no third category of males among Garos in the sense of Khasis as the Garo husband of an heiress daughter exercises more authority than his Khasi counterpart because of the headship of the family vested in his person.

Likewise there can be three categories of women, in matrilineal social group, in the context of property inheritance. The first category comprises of those females who are holding the property at present time; the second category holds those females who are going to inherit the ancestral property and house after the death of the present property holder; the third category of females consists of those who are never going to inherit property from mother. Among Khasis it is the youngest daughter, invariably, who is going to inherit the ancestral property and house. She comes in first category. The second category comprises of the nominated heiress and third category of females consists of the non-heiress daughters who are married out and have to earn their livelihood themselves. They do not get any share in the ancestral house and property. Of course they are given a plot of land, to build their house, by mother. Among Garos the first category of females consists of the women who are the owner of the Nok and ancestral property. She is the present property holder. The second category of females, in property line, comprises of those females who are nominated as heiress to the ancestral property. Among Garos it is the choice of the parents, with the help of the Chra, to decide about the heiress daughter. One of the daughters inherits the ancestral house and property. The third category of females are those non-heiress daughters who are not going to inherit the ancestral property or the house. They have to shift to their new house which is constructed on the plot allotted to them by their mother. They have to start afresh with their husbands. This third category of females also get a plot of cultivable land. As they do not get much share in ancestral property the Garo and Khasi non-heiress daughters are normally in pitiable conditions. They live in pathetic condition whereas their heiress sister enjoys the ancestral property.

The deprivation of authority, in the case of males, and property, in the case of females, of third category persons makes them the potential source of strain in matrilineal system. The females, in this category, are under no obligation of their natal Iing to abide by any restriction and they develop deeper and stronger marital ties as the husband is the defacto head of the family here and maintains his wife and family. On the other hand the third category males have tense relations with the male authority in the family. This results in clash of interests between husband and brother of the female when the husband demands woman's loyalty towards him, an act which goes against the matrilineal descent system. This clash of interest, due to deprivation of authority in male line, is more pronounced among Khasis and among Garos, where the husband, being the manager of property, is in better position.

The matrilineal system brings the consanguine kins closer and together but lessens the cohesiveness of the conjugal family. In almost all the rituals and occasions it is the brother and sister or niece and uncle who have to take decisions together. The uncle or brother is an authority in his sister or niece's family. All the discussions are about brother-sister, nieces and nephews. The husband, in this talk, feels outcast. He, being of different clan, is never involved in family rituals, as the wive's clan members alone can partake in them. Although the husband works very hard in his wife's field or orchards, throughout the day, yet he is deprived of sympathetic treatment from his wife who is mostly busy in serving her uncle or brother.

There is hardly anything of common interest between a wife and husband, except sexual partnership, among Khasis. The husband is sure that his wife's family does not care for him as they have their own organization of wife's brother, uncle, mother, nephew and nieces of Kur to work with. This matter of fact, among Khasis, tends to weaken the conjugal family. On the other hand the consanguine family must function as unit in order to retain the matrilineal nature of descent system. In his turn a husband is supposed to sort out the problems of his natal Iing where he is an authority and moreover he is wanted and welcome as consanguine member. The conjugal family among Khasi and Jaintia communities appears to be of secondary importance in social relevance due to in-built emphasis given to Kur. When husband feels neglected, in this arrangement, he goes to enjoy better treatment and welcome at his sister's place, or to some other woman who gives him more attention. Lover's relations and illegal marriages are common among Khasis due to the social network where woman's strong stability and men's fluid nature, in terms of residence are prominent. The repeated action, of such kind, results in divorce with ultimate consequences. Though a Khasi woman often experiences psychological and emotional setback, due to her husband's absence from the house, she is not much perturbed.

The divorce is hardly a catastrophy for her as she is holding a key-point in the whole network of the social system and is well secured in her organization. She can afford to be careless for the husband who has no authority in her Iing. Her children also do not give much respect and importance to father as he is not given respect by the mother or maternal uncle even. They also give more importance to maternal uncle who cares for his nephew and nieces and is authority in their mother's house. This all tends to strengthen the consanguine family but weakens the conjugal one. Although the consanguine family, among Garos, is close-knit but the conjugal family is also substantially strong as the husband here is vested with the authority over family. This institutionalization of authority in husband makes his position strong and he exercises authority over the male and female in the family. That does not lessen the authority of the maternal uncle as there is categorically defined balance of matrilineal and patrilineal line of authority in Garo social system. Here co-residence of the married couple is the crucial factor. And it does not weaken the cohesiveness of conjugal family. Among Garos a fresh mate is readily supplied in case of death or some permanent physical disability to carry the normal married or family chores. Here husband hardly thinks of divorce because the Chra and Mahari of both sides always reconcile. The marriage is maintained by the cooperation of two local lines, each of which represents a localized lineage group. The pressure from both lineages keeps a necessary balance between consanguine an conjugal families. The cross-cousin marriage, as preferential form, is again a contributing factor for this cohesiveness. Cross-cousin marriage signifies the political importance of the maternal uncle, as lineage head, among Garo matrilineal system (Nakane, 1967). Among Nayars husbands are only visiting in the night and hence are hardly consulted or invited for the family decisions by the *Karanavan* (maternal uncle) who looks after the property line and is the authority in the family (descent group). A husband is only supposed to give some token gifts on special occasions to his wife in order to retain the marriage (of special kind) which is called *Sambandham*. If he fails to present these gifts the marriage (*Sambandham*) is taken as broken automatically. A husband, among Nayars, is not supposed to maintain his wife as she gets everything from her natal home (*Taravad*). A husband is considered nowhere in the important family affairs. The wife may have many husbands simultaneously. Similarly, a husband may visit many wives. A Taravad may have three to five generation of kins but a husband visits wife's Taravad only due to right of sex with his wife. All men are supposed to work for and help their mother, sisters and are not to develop deep liking for wife, resulting into conjugal family as a week point. In such a close-knit and secured structure, and the fluid nature of *Sambandham*, the conjugal family remains weak among Nayars.

In order to maintain the matrilineal system, women's ties to their husbands should not supersede those of the descent group. Marital ties are supposed to be weaker than the descent group ties in order to maintain the matrilineal system. The institutionalized strong, intense and long lasting solidarity between husband and wife is always discouraged in matrilineal system. The strong bonds between married couple may weaken the system. Schneider (1961:17) rightly remarked that—

> "the institutionalization of very strong, lasting or intense solidarities between husband and wife is not compatible with the maintenance of matrilineal descent groups. Where stable marriage is a normative element such that there is a strong and consistent pressure on all husbands and wives to be firmly bound to each other, this will constitute a source of strain on the matrilineal descent group."

In the institution of matriliny a potential conflict remains forever between bonds of descent and the bonds of marriage. Both try to pull in different and contrary directions. Husband and wife, in matrilineal system, always try to have interest in their respective descent groups which is more important to each partner. This demands that bonds of marriage should not be stronger than the bonds of descent as this, in the long run, will go contrary to the interest of matrilineal system. In this regard Schneider rightly pointed out that "greater the priority accorded to the bonds of marriage, the weaker the bonds of descent and the lower their priority" (1961:18). Therefore, in order to maintain matrilineal system, and looking to the necessity of both men and women for the system, the ties between wife and husband should not supersede the descent ties. And as the men are also imperative to execute the authority role in their natal group, the marriage ties cannot be accorded priority over descent group to the extent that one fails to fulfil his duty in his natal group.

A husband, among Nayars, was always discouraged to allow his property share by his wife. Although earned separately by his own efforts, acquisition of husband's wealth by wife could pull the husband away from his natal Taravad, resulting in his weaker ties for descent and stronger ties for his married life. A man was praised if he caredless for his wife and children and spend his life in caring more for his mother and sisters or nieces. On the other hand the man, in his natal Taravad, acts as authority and his descent ties are stronger than his marriage ties where he is totally neglected as a member of different lineage than wife's. Likewise, among Khasis, the man is always an authority, to some extent, in his own group. The brother or maternal uncle has first to fulfil his duty to his sister or niece's family. His own married life is to be given a second priority. The first preference is given to his own group of birth. Then his sister or wife are also needed to continue the matrilineal descent which should not be deemed by the upper hand of marital relationship.

Hence the marital ties are to be curbed in priority of descent ties in order to maintain matrilineal group. A man of authority is significantly bound to his Iing by the stronger ties of economic (management), religious and social responsibilities as well as by sentiments, although he forms an independent domestic unit. As reiterated by Nakane (1967:133) "Such a man with two household, the family of orientation and of procreation says 'one leg is in my sister's house and the other is in my wife's and he feels more at home in his sister's. Khasi men whom outsiders often regard as hopeless in their social position, thus enjoy the highest status in their Iing". This clearly proves a man's preference for his sister's house to the one of wife. Whenever he feels like, he spends nights in his sister's house and does not visit his wife, resulting in an unstable married life. And such behaviour, on the part of husband, is because he carries a feeling of an outsider in his wife's house where the wife, and not he, entertains the outsiders and discusses various matters with them. If uncle is present, then the wife will just entertain with service and he will talk to the guest. The husband is left out of all such entertainment even when he does hard labour in wife's field or trade. He will hardly be asked to participate in family conversation which is invariably centred upon nephew, niece, uncle, sister and brothers only. Such a detachable attitude of husband is the core of maintenance of matrilineal system and without which the members of descent group will not be coherent.

But marriage with a non-heiress, among Khasis, gives the husband more opportunities to develop stronger, stable and long lasting ties of marital relations. The elder sisters of Ka Khadduh build their new houses with their husbands. Due to the economic pressure, and absence of any adult male member of matrilineal descent, the husband becomes defacto head of such home which is mostly built upon his labour. In such a case the wife and husband, who are both detached and cut off from their natal Iings, come closer and develop strong and stable emotional ties in their married life. Here the marital ties supersede the descent ties, causing potential strain in matriliny, though for a short period only. In the next generation when this neolocal residence assumes the forms of an organised Iing, the same tense relations between husband of Ka Khadduh and her brother will prevail and the husband will be the sufferer. The brother will be the authority over sister's property and his married life will again suffer due to this authority role in his Iing. Thus, we find that though there may be little relaxation of priorities of married life on descent ties but after a period the same situation prevails and matrilineal descent group is retained.

Among Garos the situation to judge the priority never becomes so serious as to threaten the special matrilineal descent group. The most outstanding structural element in Garo matrilineal descent group is that the property group is formed by the cooperation of two local lines, each of which represent a localized lineage group, and hence weakened in solidarity. To maintain the matrilineal descent group, as a prerequisite, both men and women are necessary and the authority role should vest in men. The authority role, among Garo, is not vested in maternal uncle alone but is shared by the other lineage person also, that is, the son-in-law who heads the Nok and manages the property though with the help of Chra and maternal uncle. The relation between Chra and son-in-law is not strained to the extent that one surrenders one's personality in favour of other. Both the lineage ties go simultaneously to maintain the Garo matrilineage. Nokna and her husband have membership of their respective natal Nok. The husband retains his loyalty to his natal Nok, and exerts his authority there, in the role of Chra. But his loyalty to his wife's Nok is equally appreciated as he has to, with his labour, improve the economic status and at the same time he enjoys the status of head of the Nok.

A Garo husband demands full attention of his wife in matters of sex and other day-to-day works. Thus, among Garos the matriliny is retained by marriage as well as descent ties with equal priority. Among War Khasi the institutionalization of strong everlasting and stable ties between husband and wife is more pronounced due to the difference in rule of inheritance. Among them the property sharing by males keeps them more attached to their natal family. The economically sound position of a man makes his position, in the wife's house also, as one of welcome. And his authority is also more prominent in his wife's house as the same is reflected in daily life. A husband is given due respect and at the time of meals the upper portions of rice, which is taken as the best, is served to him by his wife (Das Gupta, 1983). Here, the wife is equally under the authority of husband, and to the authority of her matrikins which may become the source of strain in matriliny. The husband, as the custodian of property, may command more authority over his wife and children. But this ambivalence, in War Khasi matriliny, is curtailed to some extent by the rule that the property of father cannot be inherited by his children or wife. This property is jointly held by husband's family and cannot be distributed among sons or his children. The man can use it as a source of income as long as he is alive. After his death it is retained by his sister's (heiress) family who gets the ancestral house in addition to equal portion of land.

Here we find that in order to retain matriliny, where both men and women are necessary and authority is with male matrikins, the ties of marital group become strong but do not supersede the descent group ties, a unique feature of War Khasi matriliny. The problem of priorities of ties is solved by institutionalization of certain alienation in regard to the husband among Khasi and Jaintias. Here husband is not allowed to inherit or share the property and the children belong to mother's lineage only, which does not allow the ties of marital bonds to supersede the descent ties. Hence descent ties priority remains in favourable position. The males of matrilineage have the authority to manage and handle all the rituals concerning religious, political and economic life. A husband's presence, by and large, is nowhere necessary and demanded. He cannot dictate his wife to his wishes or authority as he belongs to a different descent. The husband has to remain under the authority of matrilineal kins of his wife. An economically independent wife will not subjugate to the husband's authority who may try to alienate her from her traditional role of heiress or property owner. There is almost constant tension and friction between the husband and his wife's brother over the authority. This results in a frail marriage bond and more separations establishing priority of descent ties over marital ties. A Mapilla husband divorces his wife, on her request, otherwise his life in a matrilocal house, surrounded by his wife's kins, would be intolerable (Gough, 1961). Here too the priority of marital ties do not supersede the descent ties. The wife, who is owner of property, is economically secured and her brother being the authority, his presence is a source of constant strain for the husband. Likewise the authority of a Tiyyar husband is considerably curtailed due to the priority of descent ties over marital ties. Institutionally the Karnavan is the authority in Taravad and wife owns property. With this specification of authority a husband is under the authority of matrikins of the wife which shows priority of descent ties in matrilineal system. Though the man in the status of husband is left with no authority in matrilineal set up but he is equally important in the status of brother or uncle in his own descent group where he exercises significant authority. This dual personality poses special problems for matriliny as husband's attachment to his own descent group cannot be withered completely. This attachment also establishes priority or descent ties over marital ties.

As men have to keep rather loose marital ties, in order to help their sister's family, it becomes obligatory on the part of women also to live with weak marital ties in order not to supersede the descent ties which should be given priority in the interest of coherence in matrilineal system. It is very likely, in the family, for men to demand wife's loyalty which may ultimately cause strain in descent ties resulting in its weakening. This weakening of descent ties may go contrary to the interest of matrilineal system where the bonds of descent through sister and brother is more important. Hence women's priority of family life should not supersede the priority of descent group if matriliny is to succeed. If women, due to strong ties between husband and wife, are lost to the descent group it may not perpetuate in pure sense as women for the group are equally important for inheritance. Hence, priorities should be grouped so that more importance always goes to descent ties. The husbands as in-marrying affines and non-heiress sisters as out-marrying affines may try to draw their mates from the descent ties. As they are detached from their natal groups, both try to make some base emotionally as well as economically. But this tendency is controlled to some extent, by the inbuilt infrastructure in the system. Here the husband is allotted a secondary position as he is not allowed to be recognised in management and authority. The wife's loyalty is based on descent priority and not on marital priority in case of heiress among Khasis. Though the non-heiress daughter, in her neolocal residence and with husband as property manager, develops priorities which supersede descent ties to some extent but she also cannot ignore her descent ties completely. Time to time her brother or uncle, who is manager to their heiress sister, may remind non-heiress sister of her obligation to the ancestral Iing and social performances. The husband of such woman is also mindful of ancestral Iing's demands. The plot of land, which is being used for cultivation by the daughter and her husband, belongs collectively to her mother and is distributed to each person by the manager who again belongs to the ancestral Iing. Hence the daughter and her husband are, to some extent, under the supervision of ancestral Iing, even if they are economically independent. Ritualistically they depend on the ancestral Iing, hence the importance of descent ties.

The non-heiress daughters, among Garos, are free to some extent, from the obligation of cross-cousin marriage. This is due to their non-inheritance of ancestral property, and this attitude helps accord priority of marital ties over descent ties. But they are not totally devoid of descent obligation as they get a plot of cultivable land, from Jhum land, and house from mother for their living. This Jhum land is distributed among all the village families, by rotation, by the Nokma (village head and husband of *Nokna* of the chief clan of village). This way the daughter, though economically independent, is still to observe adherence to village and descent ties in order to have her share of land for cultivation each time. At the time of birth, death and marriage ceremonies the wife leans heavily on her Chra and descent group people without whose permission nothing important can be decided. Hence we find among Garos and Khasis the marital ties are subordinate to descent ties where bonds of brother and sister are more important than the bond of wife and husband. And it goes in the interest of matrilineal setup. However, it causes strain in case of non-heiress daughter who give more priority to marital ties, in order to establish themselves, in the beginning.

The status of mother and wife are more important, than a husband and father, in matrilineal social set-up. The husband is required to regulate the sexual behaviour of wife and produce an heiress and an heir for descent and authority line respectively of the concerned group. In some communities his services are not required even for maintaining his wife, as she gets everything from her natal house. In others, his job is only to supply food to the family. The biological importance of father is deemed to such an extent that he can be forgotten in polyandrous matrilineal groups. Here father and mother have the weakest link as husband and wife. The relation between a father and child is to be built up formally right from the start in such group, unlike mother and child who have spontaneous bonds. The child, who is initiated into mother's descent, develops love and regard for maternal uncle instead of father. The strong bond between mother and child and weak between father and child makes the status of husband less important. The father cannot exercise any significant authority in showing interest in the welfare of his children. He can only show tender love but no authority is left with him to implement this matriliny. Role of mothers is significantly glorified in most of the origin legends, and the importance of authority of husband and father is substantially limited in matrilineal descent groups. Father's secondary role does not allow the child to follow him to the extent that he is lost to his descent group. Right from beginning a child learns to respect mother, grandmother (maternal) and *Kur* (mother's lineage).

The relationship between father and child, in a matrilineal society, may be of some authority and positive effects. As a father he may socialize the children to some extent but it is not allowed to go contrary to the interest of matrilineal descent group. Consequently the authority and guidance sphere of father are well specified. This creates tension between a man and the matrilineal descent group as far as the control over wife and children is concerned. The bonds of positive affect, which may develop between father and child, in matrilineal society, are of significance. Here, using his authority, as a father, over his children in direct opposition to the maternal uncle, the father can draw children to his side. If a father is of politically significant position and has a sound economy, due to his personal labour or otherwise, he may try to draw his children, especially sons, to his favour. And the sons may easily fall back to his position and authority. This goes certainly against the interest of matrilineal descent group and is a positive source of strain in the system.

Father may divert children's (sons) loyalty to his own group. His political position and economic cooperation with son may attract the son to his group and thereby threaten the matrilineal descent group which may loose male members for authority in its own interest. As both, the male and female, are necessary for the success of matrilineal set up, it cannot afford to loose the sons (matrikins) from its fold. This keeps father's authority curtailed to maximum limit.

Matrilineal descent, associated with matrilocal residence, poses a secondary status to the husband. A husband, among Khasis, cannot inherit property and he cannot exert pressure in decision-making. Even in case of non-heiress wife the husband cannot claim to the wealth accumulated with his own hard work. This automatically goes to wife and children. He remains a non-entity among the wife's matrikin in the house. In case of divorce, which is easy to get and so common due to fluid nature of marriage bond, a Khasi husband has to leave his wife's residence and go back to his mother or sister's Iing. A woman, being in privileged position because of matrilineal descent and inheritance and matrilocal residence, is seen living secured and happy with her own kins, whereas the husband has to leave his property and children and go away alone. However, a widower can stay in the same house if he marries the younger sister of his deceased wife. But even this concession cannot be utilized in case of heiress who has no younger sister, being the youngest daughter herself.

In old age the plight of a widower or divorced husband is more miserable as he may not be of more use physically. Unless he remarries some woman, he tends to live alone and helpless. The children, in Khasi house, give more respect to mother and maternal uncle rather than to the father. This is because in matriliny the husband has secondary role to play and the property is managed and headed by maternal uncle rather than the father who does not own any property. Thus, in Khasi matriliny the more secured the wife is, due to matrilocal residence the more insecured a husband remains in case of heiress wife. Among Garos the matrilocal residence poses a little different picture. Here the husband/father enjoys better position as he is the head of the family, and has more say in property management inspite of the wife being heiress of the ancestral house, land and the property. The son-in-law, among Garos, is invariably a cross-cousin. Right from beginning the father of the daughter keeps alert to reserve his sister's son who would marry his daughter. This boy will then take after him, as the head of his family where his daughter is heiress. There is a close and tender relationship between a maternal uncle and his sister's son as former is in the status of would-be father-in-law to the latter.

Among Garos it is a usual system in village relationship as most of the sons-in-law belong to one lineage and the daughters belong to another. The son-in-law can see many familiar faces, among villagers, who have come from his village as son-in-law. This fact derives support for the son-in-law, who is also husband and father, in case he is ill-treated. All the sons-in-law, together, with their Mahari, put pressure on the wife and on the in-law's Mahari, for proper treatment to them. A husband who heads the family, is consulted in all domestic and descent matters, though his opinion is not binding upon the Chra. He is equally important to the descent and property group. His children and wife give him due respect. Even the mother-in-law treats him with regards as he would be her potential husband in case he takes over after her husband's death. Thus, we find that among Garos a husband enjoys considerably high status due to the structural network, in spite of there being the matrilocal residence. In case of death of a wife the husband need not leave wife's residence as the Mahari of wife is obliged to supply another mate for him. The same holds true for the widow and a mate is arranged for her also. The marriage, among Garos, is, thus, not a personal arrangement but deeply involves two lineages, that is, of the husband and wife. And it is obligatory on both the Maharis to continue the relationship, once established, by supplying the fresh mate each time the occasion demands.

In the event of some conflict between wife and husband, the Mahari of both sides try to reconcile both the parties and then punish one who is found guilty of misconduct. The divorce and separation, therefore, do not take place that easily as it is not considered a personal matter but involves both the Maharis of husband and wife. This expresses the stronghold of husband in his wife's residence, as a rule, and his stable position thereof. But if divorce takes place, the husband has to leave the wife's house.

War Khasi matriliny practises matrilocal residence as a rule. But here again we find the husband in a somewhat better position than that of the Khasi husband. This is due to property sharing by the males also. Here property is equally distributed among male and female children, the ancestral house going to the heiress daughter exclusively. Though the husband joins, after marriage, wife's residence, he owns some property in his parental place. From time to time he looks after this property and the income from the same belongs to him. Hence he is not entirely at the mercy of his wife. Though surrounded by matrikins of his wife he enjoys higher status. The wife and children also give more respect to husband and father. The serving of the upper portion of rice to husband shows the respect given to him by the wife. In case of divorce or death of wife a War Khasi husband has to leave his wife's residence. He goes back to his natal home, but not as a pathetic figure like Khasi husband who has nothing to fall back. Economically sound position of a War Khasi husband gives him more respect and better status in his wife's residence. The somewhat better position of a War Khasi husband does not in any manner minimize the status of wife in her natal home. Jaintia too practice matrilocal residence but here the husband is usually a privileged night visitor. During the day, the husband works in the field, orchards or any other economic pursuits in his natal home. He sounds as outsider to his children who are deprived of his filial affection and guidance most of the time. His wife too gives him only little attention because her matrikins are there to guide her. Hence, the husband does not command an important status among jaintias. Neither he wholly maintains his wife nor he is a source of love to children. He is hardly consulted in family or property matters, hence his status is relegated to secondary position due to inbuilt structural ambivalence.

Secondary position to husband, due to matrilocal residence, is prominent among Nayars also. The husband, who is a privileged visitor, cannot assert himself in matters of family importance. The Karanavan is vested with authority in almost all the matter concerning political, religious, ceremonial life etc. It is on the discretion of the Karanavan that a female is obliged to have a husband from her own caste or one from a higher caste (Namboodri Brahmin). Hence a husband is chiefly left on the mercy of Karanavan and his sister who happens to be the wife. In case the husband stops sending the necessary obligatory gifts on special occasion, the marriage (*Sambandham*) is taken as broken and it is the husband who has to stop visiting his wife's residence. Wife may have fresh marriage relations but a husband remains as an outsider for her and her matrikins. Among Mappillas too it is husband who leaves the wife's house, after divorce, and not the wife who is well secured, surrounded by her relations, and who owns the house and property and to whom the children belong.

In matrilineal societies certain changes are, of late, visible resulting into the disintegration of once much guarded system. Under economic changes, and due to other sources of strain, the matrilineal system is gradually changing, more so in terms of its disintegration. The elementary families are emerging, replacing the former types as the key kinship group. A narrow range of interpersonal kinship relationship in respect of economic cooperation, residence, socialization and legal responsibility links itself with other elementary families. The degree of this change greatly varies from society to society but the pinch of exposure to the economic pressure is essentially felt by all.

In the process some of the matrilineal societies have switched over to more patriliny practices and some are in the process, practising both to their interest. There are still others where matriliny continues to dominate, though signs of change are visible there too. Apart from economic pressure, the pressure at the level of ideas, through acculturative influence, is also resulting in disintegration of matriliny. In this regard Nakane stated that "in general among the Garo, to become Christian means separation from all traditional ways of living. This attitude often results in an apathy against all aspects of old culture" (1967:88).

We find that change of ideas have practical implication on economic ways among Garo matriliny. When one changes over to wet cultivation, certain other things follow. For instances this economic change does result, in many cases, in change of residential pattern. As already discussed, in the body of this paper, the wet cultivation encourages greater cooperation between father and son, and the father is enthusiastic about handing over this cultivation to his son rather than to his son-in-law who maybe ignorant of the techniques of wet cultivation as he belongs to the village practising Jhum cultivation alone. This tendency supports the disruption of traditional inheritance and succession structure. As the son, in this case, inherits the land, he may not like to leave it, and move to live in his wife's house somewhere else. Rather, he prefers to bring his wife to his father's residence, and hence switching over to partilocal set-up. The son may marry a girl from the same village practising wet cultivation and, thus, ignore the basic rule of cross-cousin marital alliance which supports the Garo matrilineal descent system. Simultaneously, this may have other repercussions. The wet cultivation culminates into private ownership of land, hence a person practising wet cultivation has to abandon his rights on the village Jhum fields in order to retain his portion of wet cultivation. Consequently he is cut off from the village economic organization centred upon the institution of Nokma. This enthuses isolation from certain cultural moorings. When this wet land, owned by Nokma, is inherited by heiress daughter, it will create significant difficulties. The wet land will be inherited undivided by the Nokma leaving thereby no share for other daughters who will face economic difficulty after marriage. So, the economic change, born of wet cultivation, does have considerable adverse impact on traditional succession rule.

Stronger ties of cooperation between father and sons tend to develop due to the private ownership which goes contrary to the interest of matriliny. In this arrangement sons are more attached to their father than the lineage people. And the pressure of maternal uncle and his authority is considerably reduced. On the other hand the paternal authority increases and his management prevails over others. The majority of wet cultivators even become keen, and try hard, to get a son for property inheritance. They do not want their daughters and son-in-law to take over the hard earned private property. It is widely thought that there is great risk in letting the females succeed to this land as they have to rely upon their husbands who may be ignorant of the new technique of wet cultivation and , thus, may not get much out of his land. They prefer their sons, who are well familiar with the new techniques, to succeed to this land instead of the Nokna and the Nokrom. Undoubtedly this tendency tends to change the traditional Garo social organization. It may ultimately lead to a new type of organization reflecting adversely on the matrilineal system, paving the way for partilineal system in the long run.

Property inheritance by males is institutionalized among War Khasi matriliny. This might be the extension of male's role in spheres other than domestic. Some of the local customs support the dominant position of the husband. This is reflected in serving of upper portion of cooked rice to the husband, as also in consulting father and maternal uncle in day-to-day living and for approval of marital alliance. The father's authority in decision-making and in other major spheres of War Khasi life may be due to culture contact with the plain people, and the consequent acculturative influence. However, the trend is an indication of weakening matriliny with a definite tilt to a social organization where male members inherit property. Among Khasis the husbands of non-heiress daughters set-up their own economic base which detaches the wife from her natal household and grows stronger ties between husband and wife. The strong husband and wife relations are detrimental to matriliny and it may pave way for patriarchy and patrilocal residence in many cases. More economic opportunities in Shillong have proved disastrous to matriliny among Khasis.

The role of women in political and religious arena is customarily never recognised among matrilineal societies. The customarily weak political and religious position of Khasi women has been exploited by male member in their own interest. All the politically important positions were held by males. *Siem*, the political head; *Lyngdoh*, the religious head and other village officials were never the women. Thus, all the important statuses have customarily been held by males among the Khasis. And male-held statuses had authority over the female-held statuses. As an instance, although the women inherited property, as the custodian of ancestral wealth, she had to look to her brother or maternal uncle who enjoyed the sole authority of management of this ancestral property. The weak position of woman could easily be manipulated by men whenever the new trends of pressures exerted in the shape of political, economic or technological advancement.

The rise of new economic trends is giving blow to the matrilocal residence. As the cultivable land has become scarce, due to the continuous fragmentation, and the yield is not sufficient the men are resorting to other means of earning, including employment. For employment many men shift to other places and towns where invariably the wife has to join the husband and go for neolocal residence. In such cases the father tries to hand over his property to the sons only. This tendency poses threat to matrilineal system to some extent, but not wholly as many people try to adhere to old system of matriliny. Likewise due to wet cultivation among Garos the economic dependence and cooperation between a father and sons have increased considerably. The father, in many a cases, is reluctant to hand over the land under wet cultivation to the son-in-law who may be practising Jhum cultivation in his natal group. It is felt that the latter may be unfit to carry forward the new type of economy, and rather may jeopardise the wet cultivation which has been generated with so much of labour and cooperation of his father-in-law and brother-in-law. Within this background it is desired that a son should look after the land. He even brings his wife to his residence rather than going to live with her in her parental home. He prefers to choose wife from the village practising wet cultivation. This goes in favour of village endogamy and contrary to cross-cousin marriage which has been so fervently practised by most people. The trend is causing setback to matrilocal residence in particular and matriliny in general. Neolocal, in the beginning, converts into patrilocal pattern after sometime in case of most of the politically influential persons and other elites. Economic pressure also leads to neolocal and patrilocal residence in matrilineal systems.

Thus, we find new economic and political trends playing vital role in causing change in matrilineal character of the system. The Rabhas, Kachari and Lalungs, who have lately been in transition from matriliny to patriliny, were once practising matriliny only. Now they are either practising both the systems loosely or have tilted more towards patrilineal system and patrilocal residence, mainly due to economic factors. The surrounding local impact, in terms of acculturation, should not be forgotten in this matter, though economy is definitely a decisive force. Change of residence pattern from matrilocal to patrilocal is reported among the Lalungs. Here men do not leave their house after marriage, hence wives have to join them in their houses. As the man lives in his own house the children also belong to his clan and not to mothers (Shyam Choudhury and Das, 1973). This change of residence, among Lalungs, is ascribed to many factors. The most plausible factor in this change process was economic in nature. Those who owned more land did not want to leave it and join wife's residence in order to add more working hands in their fields.

With the development of market economy, and land being no longer always held under total communal ownership, the changes in matriliny are significantly visible. Land tenure, based on private ownership, and male inheritance are resulting in social stratification and new political structure adjustment which are giving jolt to the system based on kinship priorities, the core of matrilineal system. Due to new economic trends, sharply different from those of primitive economy, the matrilineal system is loosing ground in some of the communities. It is, however, still practised more fervently among the communities where economic advancement is not yet a threat to vanish it completely. Although the cracks are clearly visible in this amazon of matriliny we can still hope of higher status for women here.

3

SHIFTING CULTIVATION
A Way of Life

Nature and man have always been very intimately connected. In spatial as well as temporal context they could almost be treated as inseparable. This has been true in spite of mutual challenges each could get confronted with the other. The struggle in respect of man-nature relationship does speak, to a large extent, of many elements of culture and their variation the societies uphold. All through historic and pre-historic times the human-beings have exploited their immediate environment for survival. The type of technology used for subsistence also varied as per the requirement of human group as well as the connected environment. And in tune with technology could evolve many patterns of social structure and values, beliefs, attitudes etc. The later remained less elaborate and differentiated in the event of primitive technology. However, more elaborate social and cultural institutions grew with the progressive evolution of techno-economic and techno-environmental praxis. The whole process, when carefully screened, suggests of looking at man and his society in adaptation with nature. The background of adaptation of human society to the surrounding environmental conditions is, thus, the key, among other factors, to understand human organistion and the underlying cognition in terms of norms and value complex. The environment is not merely geographic in nature but also includes social atmosphere. Natural and social variations, some times in conjunction with significant historic events, support cultural diversities of large magnitude.

Even the contemporary global situation continues to bear variations in levels of human societies and their respective life-ways. In the present exercise the author deals with a specific issue marking hundreds of tribal communities in a large part of the globe. Such communities are of shifting cultivators. These populations have also been dealt as slash and burn or swidden cultivators. This section of human society represents a pre-settled agriculture stage. Though they represent a stage above the hunters and gatherers most of them supplement their economy of shifting cultivation by procuring additional food material through hunting and gathering.

It may be stated that shifting cultivation is reported among certain communities of Borneo, Thailand, New Guinea, Africa, Latin America, Myanmar, Indo-China, Sumatra, Philippine, India, Sri Lanka, Korea etc. How much is the magnitude of this kind of economy is well high-lighted by Edouard Saouma, a one time Director of the Land and Water Division of the F.A.O. In his foreword of the *Soils Bulletin* (No. 24) of the F.A.O. Saouma mentions that 36 millions sq. km of land are under shifting cultivation. It represents 25 per cent of the total cultivated soils of the world and 250 million people, nearly 7 per cent of mankind, are fed from these lands. According to one estimate nearly 2.6 million tribals in India practise shifting cultivation. However, the practice is most popular among North-East Indian tribes, exception being the Apatanis, Angamis, Chakesang, Monpa, Sherdukpen and a section of Garos, among whom settled cultivation has become popular. It is estimated that in North-East India (comprising Assam, Arunachal Pradesh, Manipur, Meghalaya, Mazoram, Nagaland and Tripura), the *Jhum* (shifting cultivation) covers about 26,96,000 hectares of land. According to an ICAR (1983) estimate, nearly 4,92,000 tribal families are engaged in shifting cultivation. And at one point of time only 16.8 per cent of the total area under shifting cultivation is cultivated. This works out to approximately 1.07 hectares per family. Shifting cultivation is also widely reported from Andhra Pradesh and Orissa. In the context of *Jhum* cultivation in North-East, a more detailed account has been provided by Datta (1988 : 1) according to whom "*Jhum* in North-East is below 3 per cent of the total geographical area whereas total area under *Jhum* is below 15 per cent. Though not very accurate in nature, it is suggested that 43.2 per cent families in Arunachal Pradesh, 30.17 per cent in Manipur, 20.42 per cent in Meghalaya, 61.72 per cent in Mizoram, 77.88 per cent in Nagaland and 11.31 per cent in Tripura are practising shifting cultivation". Slash and burn cultivation (*Podu*) is again widely reported in Andhra Pradesh. In his book *Tribes of India : The Struggle for Survival*, C. Von Furer Haimendorf (1985) mentions that "in the districts of Khammam, West Godavari, East Godavari, Visakhapatnam and Srikakulam the slash and burn cultivation is still, the main method of tillage of a number of tribal communities and is carried on side by side with plough cultivation wherever the tribals are in a state of transition between the two systems. Konda Reddis continue to practise *Podu*. In East Godavari district, particularly in the hills of Chodavaram Taluk *Podu* is the predominant form of tillage. Whereas the Reddis of Godavari region use only digging sticks for the cultivation of their *Podu*, in Chodavaram the Reddis dig over their *Podu* with iron hoes. The largest areas under *Podu* cultivation to be found in Andhra Pradesh are in Srikakulam district. There most of the hills in the blocks of Sitampeta and Bhadragiri are covered with the typical patchwork pattern of current *Podu*, abandoned *Podu* fields, and secondary jungle. The tribals most dependent on *Podu* cultivation are the Saoras of high hills where level land suitable for plough cultivation is very limited or non-existent.

According to National Commission on Agriculture (1976) some 13,55,300 acres of land are under shifting cultivation. But then the actual area under direct use as actual or potential swidden plots would be atleast five times or roughly 7 million acres, as reported by Mahapatra (1988) who in the same breath, further mentions that the swidden cultivation is overwhelmingly practised by the Scheduled Tribes, whose number is estimated variously. For Kaith (1956), 109 tribal communities, 5,28,940 households and 26,44,200 population are involved in swidden cultivation. Mahapatra (1988) has demarcated two regions of swidden cultivation in India. First of these is constituted of Central Indian comprising the states of Andhra Pradesh, Madhya Pradesh and Orissa. The second region is marked by North-East India, comprising the states of Assam, Tripura, Nagaland, Manipur, Meghalaya, Mizoram and Arunachal Pradesh. Mahapatra further asserts that the pattern of swidden cultivation is basically different between the two regions, while in Central India usually the swidden is cultivated with a hoe digger or even with a plough as among the Hill Bhuiyan and Juang of North Orissa, in North-Eastern India usually mixed seeds are dropped in holes made with a digging stick, more in common with South-East Asian practice. Further while assessing the extent, nature and direction of dependence on Swidden cultivation as a principal mode of subsistence in different parts of India. Mahapatra (1988 : 7) states "All the Scheduled Tribes of Nagaland, except the Angami and Chakesang who depend on terrace cultivation, depend on swidden cultivation. In Mizoram almost all the Scheduled Tribes, while all the tribes of Arunachal Pradesh except the Monpa and Sherdukpen pastoralists and the Apa Tani, resort to swidden cultivation to subsist. In Meghalaya the Scheduled Tribes combine swidden cultivation with horticulture. In Orissa the Dongiriya Kondh carry on swidden cultivation alongwith horticulture, whereas the Saora have terrace cultivation, horticulture and some root cash crops, apart from swiddens."

Slash and burn cultivation has been known by different terms. Banerjee, Sachchidananda, Bose and Burman have given a long list of local terms used for shifting cultivation. In Assam and Tripura it is known as *Jhum*, in Bihar *Kurao* and *Knallu*; in Gujarat *Waler;* in Orissa

Penda, *Bewar* and *Dahiya*; in Nagaland *Tekonglu*; in Tripura *Hookuimong*; in Arunachal Pradesh *Adiabik*. Among some other terms are *Toila* and *Koman* in Orissa, *Dhipa* in Madhya Pradesh, *Gudia, Bajda, Sarba, Dogar, Chara* or *Podu* in Southern Orissa and parts of Andhra Pradesh, *Lankapadsenad* among the Koyas of Orissa and Andhra Pradesh, *Bogma* among the Garos and *Lykgkhalum* or *Shyrli* among the Khasis of Meghalaya. Term like *Jhum* is commonly used by the tribals of various states in North-East India.

The shifting cultivation, though a surface level phenomenon, has been conceptualized.in different forms. This is true in spite of largely common characteristics and similarity in many elements of operation. In his article "The Study of Shifting Cultivation", published in *Current Anthropology*, Conklin (1961) writes that "any continuing agricultural system in which impermanent clearances are cropped for shorter period in years than they are followed constitutes shifting cultivation". In common English parlance shifting cultivation is equated to slash and burn method of cultivation. In F.A.O. paper (1957) shifting cultivation has been defined as "custom of cultivating, clearing, scattering in the search for natural vegetation and of abandoning them as soon as the soil is exhausted, and this includes, in certain areas, shifting of households in order to follow the cultivator's search for new fertile land". With certain dimensions of commonalities with the above explanations, Mahapatra tried to elaborate the format of shifting cultivation. In 1953 Mahapatra adopted the following definition of swidden cultivation:

> "Impermanent cultivation on hill slopes, or slightly level land, after cutting, and burning the vegetation for rotation cropping for one/two or at best three years, and then abandoning the swidden plot for recuperation."

It may be mentioned that there are many characteristics or features of shifting cultivation. Many of these are commonly reported in various areas of shifting cultivation, though all of them may not be reported everywhere. First of these is the allotment of plots. Since the swidden areas are owned at community, village, tribe, clan or lineage level, the plots to be cultivated are allotted according to some set pattern and conditions locally suitable. This is followed by the feature of slash and burn operation of vegetal species. This is usually done peior to the onset of rains. Families cooperate in the venture of preparing fields of sowing as part of this operation. As yet another feature the swiddeners keep the plots fallow for many years in the interest of regenerating the forest. This also helps restore the soil fertility. Such a pattern is guided by the population pressure and number of members in a family. Sometimes it may be decided by the community at large. Another important characteristic of slash and burn cultivation is represented by its being area extensive and labour intensive. As a matter of fact it requires many hands as labour input and, that is why the swiddeners have a preference for larger families. There is more dependence on human resources to manage for higher labour requirement. Commonly reported are various forms of cooperative labour and reciprocity beyond family members. The higher dependence on human labour is largely attributed to the fact of not using drought animal in shifting cultivation. In fact the topography and terrain of hills and forests, where slash and burn cultivation is done, restrain the use of drought animals and the plough. The tools and implements used in shifting cultivation speak of a very simple and primitive technology. But then they do speak of human adaptation to typical environment in which the people operate. The swiddeners technology is represented by axe, digging stick, hoe, scrapper etc. The families usually shift to the site of plots to look after the crops and to protect them from various animals. The division of labour is well defined on the basis of age and sex. Men take to cutting and clearing of trees and other vegetation and women go for sowing weeding etc. However, there is absence of rigid group specialization. Many experts on shifting cultivation have argued that such a cultivtion is well in adaptation to soil type and biotic resource. Man seems to be in harmony with nature. The natural environment does not pose for alternative opening for the people. This retains the subsistence or non-surplus nature of swiddeners economy. The element of profit is missing. At times some root crops (turmeric, ginger) or oilseeds are exchanged for paddy. The forward trading has not been there. In the absence of large food stocks, people take help of communal granary in moments of food crisis, specially in the lean months. This is also the time when middlemen and money-lenders exploit the crisis situation of shifting cultivators. The typical natural conditions prevalent in swidden areas have also made people strike a balance at supernatural level. Such cultivators have devised taboos, myths, rituals, spirits, gods and beliefs of the kind having bearing in the specificity of environment. Thus the swiddeners not only claim harmony with nature but also with the supernatural forces.

In addition to what characterised shifting cultivation/cultivators, as highlighted in the above paragraphs, Mahapatra has given yet another account of major features of the swidden economy. This is systematic and runs as per the following paradigm :

(1) Land for swidden cultivation was traditionally owned by the village, clan or lineage, and an individual household could

cultivate as large an area as was commensurate with the needs of the household, manpower available and the area of the mature forest in the fallow zone, available for cutting the swidden;

(2) Capital investment was minimum and within the means of each household to be renewed or replaced when necessary;

(3) Swidden cultivation is never a mono-crop culture. A large variety of crops is grown—at least a few varieties of cereals, legumes (beans and pulses), root crops, leafy and other vegetables, cotton and one or two varieties of oil seeds (as in Orissa and adjoining Andhra Pradesh);

(4) Since the crops ripen at various times, during the eight month cropping season, there is at no time the risk of total crop failure, whether due to drought, or excessive rainfall in a region of uncertain monsoon;

(5) These crops together provide them with a more balanced diet than those from the lowland or terraced fields of permanent cultivation which yield usually only one crop, paddy;

(6) Swidden cultivation and dependence on forest resources like roots and tubers, fruits, flowers and leaves, animals, fishes in the hill streams and timber etc. are interwoven in the life and economy of people. In other words, swidden cultivation is invariably supplemented by food gathering, hunting, fishing and use of other forest resources in day to day life;

(7) The forest and the abandoned swiddens provide the people with fodder, fuel, timber, thatching material etc. for their survival system;

(8) Because of the insufficiency of food crops raised in the decades of the 20th century, swiddeners have resorted to day labour for construction works, forestry, or some times plantation labour in far-away regions;

(9) Apart from the incipient stratification with the dominant first-settlers descendants and the immigrant households, having differential command over scarce land resources like terraces, gently sloping or flat land for permanent agriculture, as in North Orissa (Mahapatra, 1960) and from the so-called "chiefs" among some Naga groups or slave-owing masters in Arunachal Pradesh, who also worked along with their slaves, there was no scope for developing a true 'leisure class'. Polygymous households with more wives as working force came in handy for working larger swiddens in North-East India" (Mahapatra, 1988 : 11, 12).

As against plough or permanent cultivation, the shifting cultivation is marked by certain additional operations to which the people have adjusted so well. In the first instance the villagers go for the selection of site. It is not that any part of the forest is selected at random for the purpose. The chief, council of elders or clan or lineage head decide of the site considering the contiguous nature of forest and its vegetational maturity which is so essential a pre-requisite. Mainly the forest with matured vegetation is declared fit for slash and burn cultivation. The plots are then allotted to individual families. If the area is under joint ownership the allotment is followed by the demarcation of field boundaries. Subsequently the swiddeners get engaged in cutting and clearing the jungle. This too is not done haphazardly. Useful species of trees are spared in felling operation. These may be fruit trees or those bearing oilseeds, tasar etc. In many instances the stems of the trees are retained and not cut. They are believed to check soil erosion. The cut vegetation is then left for drying. And once the lot is dried, the whole thing is set on fire. Thus the felled vegetation is reduced to ashes. When the fire extinguishes, the people at times resort to the spreading of ash.

Simultaneously then arises the necessity of making a temporary field hut. This specially happens when the field is away and when it requires constant watch for crop protection. Staying on the field, in crop season, also saves time and the labour input also increases. Once the field is ready for sowing, some of the swiddeners demarcate a part for vegetable gardening and the rest is spared for raising other kind of crops. While sowing some go for broadcasting of seeds and others plant the seeds into holes made with a digging stick or pick. In certain instances the dibbling of major crops is not done and the seeds and the manure, formed of ash, may be forked in the soil. Sowing is labour intensive and various families cooperate in this endeavour. Once the seeds germinate and the plants are in the growing stage, the hazardous operation of weeding is needed with frequent time interval. This operation is rather difficult because of multi-crop pattern used in the same field. And it is all the more so in heavy rainfall areas where slash and burn cultivation is practised. At this stage people stick to watch-hut as the crops need constant protection against wild animals. For multi-crop pattern, largely resorted to by the swiddeners, and for quite a long crop season, the harvesting of crop is usually not done in one lot. The last to be harvested is usually the major crop and which takes more time to ripe. The minor vegetable or other crop may ripe in between and their produce may be procured and used accordingly. The process keeps the family members increasingly engaged.

The next operation involves the transportation of harvested

produce. Because of the distance, undulating and zig-zag terrain and lack of mechanical means of transportation, the process of transportation is quite cumbersome and time consuming. The produce is mostly transported on human head/back. The operations of sowing and harvesting are accompanied by various kinds of rituals marking man's relationship to nature and superorganic and the same is reflected in native ideology. It may be mentioned that some of the major operations, outlined above, get deleted in the second and subsequent years of cultivation in the same plot of land. Further, it would be worthwhile to mention here that some minor kind of variations may be noted in swidden cultivation operations in different regions and among different tribes. After using the field for a few years, and especially when its soil fertility is reduced, people shift to the next site. During this period of fallow the natural vegetation starts growing again and gradually matures over the years and finally the site is again used in the cycle of shifting cultivation.

Shifting cultivation has always been a debatable and controversial issue in the eyes of botanists, forest experts, anthropologists, agriculture scientists, economists, planners etc. Some express themselves as pro-shifting cultivation and other react as antagonists. To some it appears as very primitive method of cultivation with all its attendant drawbacks. These specially pertain to its economic dimension. To them slash and burn cultivation involves the wanton destruction of forests and leads to severe soil erosion. Over and above the yield is poor. Further shifting cultivation being land extensive and labour intensive demands for more manpower. It causes resource degradation and is hazardous to soil and fertility. Studies on shifting cultivation in Meghalaya state support that Jhum paddy cultivation is mixture or alone is an unremunerative enterprise with very low returns. The crop yield registering around 6 quintals per hectare was found miserably poor (ICAR, 1983 : 25). Quite close to the above is D.N. Borthakur's (1976) observation. In his paper on improving productivity of Jhum Cultivation...", Borthakur argues that "shifting cultivation has been rightly held responsible for crippling the economy of the people of the region, that is, North-East India". While proposing for alternative systems of farming for increasing productivity in swidden land in North-East India, Borthakur points out that swidden cultivation is the outcome of age-old tradition and thus has become the way of life. While conceiving change or improvement in the Jhum system, the improved technology should be such that could cater to the needs of the people and is easily accessible and acceptable to them. Considering shifting cultivation as economically backward enterprise, Alemchiba Ao mentions that among Ao Naga there is some move torwards terrace cultivation and a reduction in the area under shifting cultivation. But the mentions that "shifting cultivation by slash and burn method is by far the most important type of agriculture" (1966 : 54). On similar lines, but in a different tone, spoke Walflang. Considering shifting cultivation as a big problem, Walflang writes :

> "Agriculture, absorbing more than 72 per cent of the working force, in the North-Eastern region, is still in its primitive system especially in the hills where *Jhuming* is still popular. Perhaps since the beginning of the plan itself the problems of Jhum cultivation has dominated the mind of each plan but till today no satisfactory solution has been supplied to this effect" (1978 : 114).

Many factors mark the backwardness of the North-East region but the most prominent, in economic sense, of these is taken the Jhum cultivation. Out of such a cultivation people do not get enough for survival. For instance, in Mizoram, where the Jhum is extremely popular, people do not get yield sufficient for the year. The argument seeks support from surveys carried out in predominantly Jhum villages of Mizoram. In Lungdou, a Mizo village, "more than 80 per cent inhabitants depend on Jhum cultivation alone for their livelihood with little or no independent source of income. The total yield of the Jhum land is, more often than not, insufficient to meet their annual family needs. In general the economic backwardness of Mizoram state needs no emphasis. Over 90 per cent of the total population still depend on shifting cultivation of a Jhum type. The Jhum products are not sufficient to supply even three months requirements" (Laitunga, 1981 : 65; 1982 : 18, 22). Though expressing serious reservations Datta (1988) also mentions of vast literature on shifting cultivation in North-East region which suggest of the important drawbacks of it. These include deforestation, soil erosion, primitive technique, low productivity, low income and less scope for providing social amenities to the shifting population. And as such shifting cultivation cannot co-exist with programmers aimed at eradication of rural poverty and tribal development. As mentioned earlier the deforestation is largely attributed to shifting cultivation. In this regard David Spurgeon writes :

> "While commercial logging does remove the best trees, the greatest harm to the forest is caused by the practice of shifting agriculture. This practice annually destroys ten million hectares of high forest and cause a steady decline in the fertility of the land... In the past the soil fertility returned to abandoned areas over a period of 25-30 years, as a result of natural processes. But as population pressures

increased, the cultivators returned to their abandoned sites much sooner and the period of natural bush fallow was progressively shortened" (1982 : 11).

But many experts do not digest this explanation. They bring in many other dimensions of interest and for which they have sought support from their empirical studies. One such pertinent observation is in regard to *Podu* cultivation in Andhra Pradesh. According to C. Von Furer-Haimendorf (1985 : 77):

> "The argument, often put forward by forest officials, that *Podu* cultivation is inherently wasteful and detrimental to the preservation of forests is nevertheless not without flaws. In the areas inhabited for centuries if not millennia by shifting cultivators, there are some of the largest natural forests, whereas the expansion of intensive plough cultivation has nearly everywhere led to a disappearance of forests. This becomes obvious in many parts of Andhra Pradesh. In Adilabad, where Kolams and Naikpods were prectising *Podu* cultivation and even the plough cultivating Gonds frequently shifted their fields and then allowed forest to grow up on the abandoned land, there were vast stretches of forest as late as the first decade of the twentieth century. The same applies to the tribal areas of Warangal and Khammam, and in East Godavari District, the habitat of the *Podu* cultivating Knoda Reddis, there are some of the most extensive areas of natural forest in the whole of southern India".

Hangover of the views of 19th century forest officials and botanists regarding shifting cultivation continued to widely prevail even up to the mid-fifties of current century. They denounced it as primitive agriculture practice which interfered with the eco-system of the region causing thereby degradation of the environment. After the end of British regime in 1947 some of the Indian experts tried to import a new thinking regarding shifting cultivation, though the diversity of views continued to mark the scene. On the basis of his studies on shifting cultivation D.S. Nag (1958) approves the argument of Jacks and Whyte whose opinion is rather interesting. According to them "It must be admitted that no agricultural system except shifting cultivation has yet been devised that will ensure lasting stability and fertility to tropical forest soils under human management". Within the changing purview of views the National Commission on Agriculture (1976) recommended, among other things, that "shifting cultivation should be regulated, contained and replaced as expeditiously as possible by resorting to Agro-Sylvicultural methods apart from other methods... The main approach to the solution of the problem of shifting cultivation should be by permanently settling the shifting cultivators and weaning them away from the practice of shifting cultivation."

In spite of various drawbacks of shifting cultivation, as highlighted in the preceding paragraphs, some specialists express a different opinion. Directly or indirectly they hold a positive opinion about swidden cultivation stating that this could be the best instance of human adaptation to particular kind of environmental conditions. And the terrain and topography of regions where shifting cultivation is practised is not replaceable. Therefore, the only thing left to the experts is to suggest for modification in technology of such a cultivation to increase the yield of swiddeners. It would be of very much relevance to quote Jaganath Pathy at this juncture. Shifting cultivation, according to Pathy (1988 : 4) "is based on irreplaceable knowledge accumulated through centuries. It harnesses solar energy through the forests and is efficient in recycling biomass and organic manure. Compared to modern agriculture, it is very low input and energy efficient system and that too mostly in the form of family labour. Soil and forest management being crucial to shifting cultivation, may communities construct contour bunds in swidden, grow non-legume nitrogen fixers, leave boles of larger trees and fruit trees undamaged, manage sacred groves, do not disturb steep slopes before sowing, and entertain several taboos to protect forest resources. Shifting cultivation is a mixed cropping system of cereals, pulses, oilseeds, vegetables and perennial crops, at once."

The multi-layered cropping with extensive root system conserves soil nutrients, while the spatial distribution of different crops along the slope and the sequential harvesting maximises the use of the light resource. This ensures conservation of precious soil minerals and checks damage through pests. It helps in more even distribution of a family labour, and is in insurance against total crop failure. When the fallow phase is about ten years, it gives reasonable economic returns to the cultivator. A study noted that the carrying capacity of Mizo hills is three times that of the population density and twice in case of Abujhmar hills. But in Keonjhar hills, the population density is about three times of its carrying capacity. Crucial is fallow period. A longer fallow is adequate for survival of both cultivators and the forests. It may be mentioned that some more studies have supported the viability of shifting cultivation. They have gone even to the extent of explaining its commercial nature. This specially applies to the cash crops grown by the swiddeners, though it does not seem to be a widely reported feature. But in certain belts the shifting cultivators are said to be self-sufficient. Though in a generalised way Burman and Sharma have given their version of slash and burn cultivation which carries lot of meaning in it though it is open to empirical review:

> "In most parts of the country, shifting cultivation has been found to be in existence for quite sometime, mostly in cash and commercial nexus. For instance, along with cereals and millets, many of the tribes of the North-East grow cotton for sale to cutivators from the plains. Chillies and vegetables grown by the shifting cultivators of Manipur, Tripura, Nagaland frequently find their way to the market. Ginger and turmeric grown by shifting cultivators of Orissa have extensive market in the plains. Even in the pre-Independence period the shifting cultivators of Arunachal had to supplement their sources of livelihood by entering into a trade channel, linking the plains of Assam with Tibet" (Burman and Sharma, 1970 : 150).

In certain areas of shifting cultivation in Orissa, the economic picture is stated to be quite attractive, so much so that even the non-tribals of a particular category are said to have gone for it. Such an explanation otherwise does not seem to be in tune with many other reporting on shifting cultivation, where the picture given is of a different kind. For instance, the cause of poverty and economic backwardness in Mozoram is attributed to their shifting cultivation. But for Fernandes and Menon (1984, 1987) the shifting cultivation in Koraput district of Orissa has become a profitable investment particularly in view of the good price that is fetched by oilseeds and pulse grains. In some cases the money-lenders from outside have appropriated tribal lands and are using the same for shifting cultivation, not for survival but for commercial purpose. In continuation to such observations are general policy statements which justify shifting cultivation. Attributing it to steep and undulating topography, physico-social environment, their population, community based land tenure system, limited crop cycle and a rainy season, some favour the practice. M.D. Chaturvedi (1953) stated that "the notion widely held that shifting cultivation is responsible in the main for large scale soil erosion needs to be effectively dispelled. The current approach lies in accepting it not as a necessary evil, but reorganising it as a way of life, not condemning it as evil practice, but regarding it as an agricultural practice evolved as a reflex to the physiographical character of land" (Bhowmick, 1980). In the post-independence period more assertions, on similar lines, poured in. They provided for rethinking and new look to the practice of shifting cultivation. It was in 1957 that M.S. Shivaraman, the then Adviser to the Programme Administration of the

Planning Commission, observed :

> "It is a mistake to assume that shifting cultivation in itself is unscientific land use. Actually, it is a practical approach to certain inherent difficulties in preparing a proper seedbed in steep slopes where any disturbance of the surface by hoeing or ploughing will result in washing away of the fertile top soil. The tribal people, therefore, take care not to plough or disturb the soil before sowing. The destruction of weeds and improvement of tilth necessary for a proper seedbed are achieved with the help of fire. In most of the interior areas, where communication is not developed and sufficient land suitable for terracing is not available, Jhuming alone can be done for the present and as such every effort should be made to improve the fertility of the Jhumed field" (Bhowmick, 1980 : 9, 10).

Since North-East India is predominantly a shifting cultivation area, some more observations have been made on this situation. And a few of these favour the continuance of the practice for various reasons. According to Sharma (1980 : 4) "The most remarkable feature of shifting cultivation is that almost all varieties of cereals and vegetables are grown in one Jhum field which is impossible in case of wet plain land". Likewise writing on the Tangams of Arunachal Pradesh, Bhattacharjee speaks of the advantages of Jhum, stating that :

> "In it cropping area is very large and so is the total yield. There is seldom any wholesale crop failure. If one crop fails there is always a subsidiary one for the people to fall back upon. A farmer has only one field on the average to tend at a time. The incidence of pests and diseases is also very low. The heavier part of the work such as the clearing of the forest, the burning of the debris and the fencing of the fields are done collectively. The pressure is not heavy. Fields do not monopolise the whole time of the farmer making it... a dead and dull routine. It keeps human spirit alive and fresh" (1975 : 37).

Finding no alternative to Jhuming in the steep hills inhabited by the Nagas, and with no scope for further innovations, people argued for it's retention and continuity. And this led to the adoption of the Naga Jhum Land Regulation, 1946. The Regulation, encouraging shifting cultivation and peoples' expertise thereof, gave absolute rights over the Jhum lands. However, the Regulation was subsequently replaced by the Naga Forest Act, 1968 and the Nagaland Requisition and Acquisition Act, 1965 which authorised government control in terms of absolute rights over forests and land and their acquisition. It may also be pointed out that to check soil erosion from Jhum fields some tribals use indigenous methods. At more delicate points around the field, people use stumps of wood as an embankment. People also allow some trees to grow to a certain height along with thin canopy of boughs. The arrangement helps retain the soil in the rainy season.

On the basis of strength and weakness, as analysed by various authors referred above, of shifting cultivation, some versions have been given and the same need to be highlighted. And these provide a picture of what is being done to the practice of shifting cultivation, as also what needs to be done. A clear picture, it seems, is yet to emerge. However, a precondition to consensus of ideas, demands for a detailed account of what has, of late, been proposed. This would help pave way for a perspective planning in respect of shifting cultivation which is so widely prevalent and forms such an important issue in this age of science and technology. In regard to the shifting cultivation in Andhra Pradesh, C. Von Furer-Haimendorf (1985 : 78) writes :

> "The Government, which in the past eight years has pursued a very effective policy of tribal rehabilitation, recognises the part Podu is playing in the economy of such tribes as Saoras, Jatapus and Konda Doras. Relatively small plots have been assigned to tribals on patta on the assumption that the occupiers augment the yields by crop grown on Podu fields. Whereas in Adilabad the Forest Department has fought a relentless battle against Podu cultivation and ousted innumerable Kolams from the valleys and hills they and their forefathers had inhabited since time immemorial, in Srikakulam only limited areas have been declared reserved forest, and the majority of hill slopes are open for Podu cultivation. Here the government has accepted the fact that the tribesmen have an inherent right to the hills and valleys of their ancient homeland, while in the forest areas of Adilabad the tribals were at best tolerated, but often ruthlessly evicted from land claimed by the Forest Department without regard for the Kolams long standing occupation."

Such a categorical statement, however, does not involve policy statement. But it does speak of the plight of practice and the tribals thereof. The abstraction, to be made, has been left to the readers. However, the state of mind is an indication of the fact that Haimendorf's attitude is pro-tribal and the connected practice thereof. Though focusing on the shifting cultivation in the hills of North-East, Dutta's position is close to what I commented on Haimendorf above. What should be the way out is his assertion, though close on wheels. Dutta (1988 : 7) further states:

> "We should reorient our analysis of shifting cultivation and instead of deploring the practice right and left our technological scientific knowledge should be diverted to make the system as much productive as possible. Further by gradually opening of newer opportunities surplus members of Jhumiya families should be absorbed in economic activities outside Jhum. Moreover the positive spirits of Jhuming should be preserved by and accommodated in any alternative agricultural model. The egalitarian spirit should be strengthened and if possible cooperativisation should be encouraged."

When Jhuming is labour-intensive the point regarding surplus members and their diversion to other economic activities is to be taken with a pinch of salt. However, to enrich the yield the proposal for new technology and scientific procedures is worthwhile and this is what many other experts have proposed. Not entering into this arena, Pathy talks of the diversion from shifting cultivation, mainly emanating from internal pressure. Some of the tribes have already switched over to some extent, to terraced cultivation. In many instances the fallow lands on steep slopes, not earlier used for shifting cultivation, have also been brought under swidden cultivation. The mixed crops pattern under shifting cultivation as also been, at certain places, readjusted for better. However, the paucity of land for terrace cultivation continue to be there. Further instances of modified form of shifting cultivation have been reported. Writing on Jhum in North-East India, Ramkrishnan (1983) has stated :

> "At higher elevations of Meghalaya only the lower branches of the sparsely distributed Khasi pine trees are cut, instead of the whole tree. Further, unlike in its typical form where the slash is burnt in situ and the seeds are dibbled directly into the soil ash complex, here the slash is placed in parallel rows running, along the slope topped over by a thin layer of soil forming the elevated ridges alternating with highly compacted soil of the narrow furrows. The dried slash is thus subjected to a slow burn with crops being planted only on the ridges. Here organic fertilisers may be used. One of the reasons why only branches are lopped in high elevation *Jhum* is due to sparsely distributed pines and the slower regrowth under cooler climate and more acidic soil".

Yet another dimension pertains to the environmental impact of shifting cultivation. The impression from one corner is that soil erosion and deterioration are accelerated by the practice of shifting cultivation.

On the other hand there are reports and stuies which denounce such a generalisation. Quoting a U.N. Study Team report (1967) and Sixth Five-Year Plan, Ministry of Agriculture (1981), Roy Burman gives a very revealing account of this front. The account precisely amounts to his saying that soil erosion and deterioration are over magnified in terms of shifting cultivation. Such an environmental impact is not the major issue. While emphasising on this viewpoint Burman quotes a U.N. Study Team report (1967). Though the study pertains to shifting cultivation in Thailand, it has its general implication. The study assets; "Contrary to widespread belief, the shifting cultivation as practised by the hill tribes does not lead to any grave soil deterioration. Under this system soil erosion is rare and we have as yet not observed any serious accelerated wash off or gully erosion". The matter does not end here as Burman further observes. "Replacement of shifting cultivation by a system of sedimentary, agriculture, on the slopy soil would under the present conditions, almost inevitably lead to a grave soil deterioration and to accelerated erosion. Terracing for crops other than the most remunerative would not be an answer, because the cost would be too high and further more, because most soil in the area do not lend themselves to a simple system of terracing. As a logical proposition it has been stated that the U.N. Study Team observation is a probable part answer. But one can go further. According to official statistics out of 175.00 million hectares of land in the country with environmental problem 3.00 million hectares are under shifting cultivation. Thus shifting cultivation accounts for less than two per cent area which have been delineated as environmentally problematic. And yet whenever the problem of soil erosion is discussed, shifting cultivation is mentioned first. One wonders why" (Burman, 1988 : 26).

Claims and counter claims of various forms, as referred in the previous paragraphs, are indicator of the fact that the practice of shifting cultivation is not as simple as it overtly appears to be. There are many polemical dimensions in terms of version given about such a practice. And the same need to be reviewed on a common platform to be shared by experts of diverse streams connected to shifting cultivation. But what can be abstracted at the current juncture is well summarised by Mann (1987) though it specifically pertains to North-East India. And since then the picture has not drifted much. Though many attribute, as per Mann, the economic backwardness of the tribal North-East belt to *Jhum* cultivation and its attendant drawbacks, including poor yield, deforestation, labour intensiveness and area extensiveness, there seems to be hardly any viable alternative to this practice in view of the terrain and topography characteristic of the region. Even the Seventh Five Year

Plan (Vol. II, p. 342) has categorically mentioned that no viable alternative to shifting cultivation has yet been found. Agricultural scientists and other experts are working hard towards either adding to or modifying the traditional form rather than doing away with it altogether. It is increasingly being realised that *Jhum* cultivation should be improved upon with the help of modern technical know-how. Settled cultivation, except in some patches, may not be possible because of the constraint of the peculiar terrain and topography. Evne the sociologists and social anthropologists specialists of society and culture, are in favour of scientific improvement in *Jhum* cultivation, rather than its total replacement which, even otherwise, does not seem to be possible. Within this approach the tribal inhabitants would not only improve economically, but would also not drift away from many traditional elements of their culture connected to shifting cultivation. Further the practice of shifting cultivation is not independent of many other connected areas of economic structure. These also need to be reviewed prior to any intervention in the practice. Else, the effort itself may be interfered. One of such important areas related to land ownership pattern and the system of allocation of fields. These have been in vogue since centuries and any intervention may meet opposition if not procedurally tackled. As the control of land and forest form an important arena it needs to be reviewed in macro perspective. The leadership holding it may not entertain any interference as the latter would amount to imbalance in the existing pattern, norms and the values thereof. Though pertaining to the micro situation of Warmoung, an Ao Naga village the explanations of Burman and Alemchiba regarding ownership and allotment patterns of *Jhum* land are quite elaborate. Basing on this study Burman, in his paper "Shifting Cultivation : A Closer Look" states : "In the village a number of contiguous blocks have been demarcated for generations, where shifting cultivation is carried out by rotation. A cultivation is shifted from one area to another in a regular cycle, everybody knows which area will be cleared for shifting cultivation, after which slight adjustments in the size of the area are however made according to availability of working force and other considerations.

The *Putu-menden* or Village Council makes the adjustment and declares how much land, and which are to be cleared in each block in a particular year. Generally in each block, the various clans and households have plots of their own. These plots belonging to clans are frequently demarcated by hill sides, stones and streams. But sometimes there is no clear land mark to demarcate the plots, in such cases boundary quarrels break out among the various clans from time to time. In each block in addition to clan land and individual family land, there is also some village common land. If a particular household does not have any land of its own, or is not able to get some clan land, for cultivation in that block, it is assigned land from the village common land. Thus the village comman land serves as a security-cushion against destitution. The control over the clan land vests with the eldest male member of the clan. He has the right to choose the best plot, but he cannot deny to others their reasonable share. Sometimes some individual or clan has surplus land to spare. Individuals who are in want of land, take the same on lease from such an individual or clan" (1988 : 16). This micro situation apart the communal ownership of land is reported in many other regions of shifting cultivation. The individual households carry on their cultivation activities on the plots allotted to them or otherwise selected. The right to cultivate is by and large of usufruct nature, devoid of individual ownership. And under such a condition a household may even cultivate a different plot at same time phase. As a general understanding the plot can be retained so long as one is serious of his operations in it. Even the usufructary right ceases if the plot is not used effectively. But because of economic pressure the plots are, in general, fully utilised within the limitation of their technology and as such the change of plot is not reported in higher frequency. People are, in many cases, quite conscious of the nature of plots and hence the corresponding choice. This is usually at the state of mind of a *Jhumia*. At the same time the households are specially particular of the maintenance of good plots. In many areas of Nagaland and Manipur the tribals go for contour bunding to check soil erosion. For this purpose they fix logs of wood across the slope. When people can differentiate plots on the basis of their nature, and once they import so much labour to retain the soil, they may not be keen to shift. It would be of interest to point out that in his study of Pongchaw, the Wancho tribal village of Arunachal Pradesh, Schchidananda (1985 : 22) states that each field has a name which is drawn from the nature of the soil or its location. A few of such names include :

(1) *Kham man*—this name is given to the field which has rich harvest, there is so much to carry on head that the hair begins falling;

(2) *Chuinam*—the field with poor soil and resultant poor harvest is given this name. Those who cultivate such a field are often short of food and have to depend on a kind of wild vegetable called *Chuinam*;

(3) *Loakkho*—mean pushing down of an elephant. The land with steep slope bears this designation;

(4) *Ju-sap*—the land highly infested by rats which damage the crop;

(5) *Gung hingi*—the harvest in such land is so poor that the people sometimes return with empty baskets; and

(6) *Abaio*—high land where previously birds used to chirp loudly.

In addition to economic dimension of shifting cultivation is its social-cultural relevance. The agriculture and other hard scientists and even the economists keep silence over such a dimension. More concerned on the issue are the social anthropologists who are the specialists in such a field, and who express more concern as the tribals form their special field of interest. Social organisation, religion and certain components of ideological structure of the tribes do appear in the explanations of social anthropologists concerning shifting cultivation. Any move on shifting cultivation cannot keep such areas isolated. It may further be mentioned that such cultural elements are as old as the swidden cultivation itself. And as usch they have become integral part of the overall system. As shifting cultivation is labour intensive the tribals need more hands to work on it. This necessitated exchange of labour. The pattern of exchange crystalised over the years on the lines of reciprocal cooperation. This paved way to social division of labour, an important aspect of social organisation of tribes practising shifting cultivation. The communal ownership of land further enthused such a provision. The arrangement even reflects on the nature of interpersonal and inter family relations which are so well adjusted in tune with swidden cultivation. Human adaptation of this kind led to the rise of egalitarian adjustments and their persistence. As such in the regions of shifting cultivation the tribal psyche is characterized by egalitarian ethos. The cooperation as a requirement of shifting cultivation ecology serves as a required strong impetus to the strong linkages and bonds among the people. The system is so well knit that even the deprived family and the physically handicapped persons are also taken care of. Shifting cultivation as the earliest form of agriculture continues to be predominantly practised by the tribals. And as such it has become a way of life with them. In terms of nutrition people are at an advantageous position as they grow so many varieties of crops in the same field and they consume the same. On the left over of the produce, which is not taken proper for human consumption, survive their livestock which further adds to the nutrients obtained from shifting cultivation field. Further the class structure and shifting cultivation are also connected.

In this regard the observations made on the basis of a field study of *Podu* cultivation in Andhra Pradesh are quite revealing. According to this study Fernandes (1988 : 5) writes :

> "In the case of the poorest sections, all their cultivated food came exclusively from shifting cultivation since most of them were landless. The proportion changed as one climed up the class ladder since also the land onership pattern changed with it. In other words, there is a direct link between the position of the class, land ownership and *Podu* cultivation. The poorer the class, the higher the extent of dependence on it".

As already stated the economic dimension should not obscure the social and cultural implications of shifting cultivation. In this regard Mann (1987 : 169-171) provides the most elaborate account, though his observations are essentially confined to tribal North-East India. For him "numerous elements of social and cultural life seem to have originated (and are also sustained) with various operations of Jhum. Certain parameters of social organisation and religion have a strong bearing on shifting cultivation. Many activities related to mundane life as well as the supernatural world, as conceived by the tribals, are inseparable from certain phases in the Jhum cycle. Thus, Jhum cultivation is to be seen as an integral part of the wider social-cultural nexus. Jhum cultivation being labour intensive, the tribals need more manpower. This is why large families are preferred as the size is believed to be to their advantage in terms of Jhum yield. Studies on Mizos (Goswami, 1970) support the argument that a large family is an asset. Even the Daflas, among whom the land is community owned and is available in plenty for Jhuming, there is a widespread belief that with more working hand in the family there would be more yield. To acquire these working hands in the family, they prefer to be polygynous: the wives are additional hands and assure even more working hands through procreation. We find here, then, a connection between shifting cultivation and polygyny. Those who are comparatively better off among the Daflas prefer to have more than one wife as additional hands forming chief input in shifting cultivation. In addition to polygyny, there is yet another aspect of marriage connected to Jhum. In the case of the Padams, the wife's first visit to her husband's house is normally around the time when the Jhum fields are harvested.

Apart from family and marriage some social positions, clearly defined among certian tribes, are also significantly relevant to shifting cultivation. In some cases the chief distributes the Jhum land and his decision is corroborated by the people. He also enjoys certain other privileges. Among the Lushais the Ramhuals have been the advisors on Jhum cultivation. Enjoying a high social position in the village, a Ramhual can exercise, his choice in the selection of fields for Jhum cultivation. As experts the Ramhauls suggest the belts to be cut each year for Jhum. They are accepted as more knowledgeable as far as the suitable slopes for Jhuming are concerned. Likewise, among the Wanchos, the Ngopa and the Anupa are the experts who perform rituals while selecting the new Jhum lands. They occupy socially significant positions. The Ngopa makes use of a special kind of bamboo. He puts it in the fire and makes his calculations as part of the omen. The Anupa determines the particular selection by examining an egg.

A large number of festivals and other festive activities associated with joy, merriment, drinking feasting etc., are linked to Jhum cultivation. Among the Mizos the celebration of *Mimkut,* or the maize festival, after the harvesting of Jhum crops, was quite popular. Singing, dancing and drinking rice beer marked *Mimkut.* The occasion also demanded paying homage to the departed souls of the community and part of the harvest was consecrated to them. Jungle cleaning, as an operation in Jhum, was followed by the festival known as Chapchar Kut. The biggest festival which the Mizos celebrated was Pawlkut, the harvest festival. With plenty of grain at hand, people kept up the spirit of gaiety. Such festivals, however, did feel the impact of Christianity and they are now a mixture of tradition and modernity. Similarly the Aos celebrate Maotsu, an important festival celebrated aftger the Jhum fields are sown. People also connect this festival to the fertility of the earth and expect a rich plant growth. Before setting the Jungle to fire in order to prepare the Jhum land, the Zeliangroungs observe the festival of Meleyingi. The celebration goes on for about six days. On the last day in a gay and festive mood, the village elders set the jungle on fire. Kukjong, a very popular festival of the Tangsas, is also rooted in Jhum cultivation and is celebrated prior to the clearing of jungles for the Jhum fields. A celebration on a large scale, it continues for six days, during which the men and women of the community participate in singing and dancing associated with the occasion. To start with, a community hunting expedition is organised. The party members return on the third day with their game. In the meanwhile the women, who stay behind, prepare beer. A grand feast is then organised and everyone participates in it. Feasting and dancing continue for another two days. This is followed by the clearing of jungles. Among the Angamis, according to Dasgupta and Das (1984 : 38), "The principal community ceremonies of Terhengi and Sekrengi are of great significance as the Terhengi marks the completion of the argicultural year and the Sekrengi has for its object the preservation of health. Another ceremony, Gnongi, marks the completion of the sowing of Jhum land. The ceremony of The *Krangi* marks the transplantation of the paddy. Likewengi ceremony marks the beginning. *Lideh* marks the opening of the rice harvest."

Some of the tribals also perform certain religious rites which often involve sacrifice as part of *Jhum* cultivation. As the origin of such rites lies in the *Jhum* itself, people cannot easily afford to ignore them. These are necessary in the interest of the protection of crops and for better produce. It is believed by many that the supernatural forces can be propitiated through such performances. In other words, the *Jhum*, basically an economic activity, is inseparable from certain elements of religious life as well. The sacrifice of a white cock is reported among the Tangams as a necessary part of the process of Jhum cultivation. The Tangams recognised a malevolent spirit popularly called *Yahang* and the big trees are believed to be the abode of this spirit. In order to prepare the *Jhum* fields these trees need to be felled. In other words, the residence of *Yahang* is destroyed and there is every chance that the spirit may be offended and cause harm to the tribals and their crops. To prevent this, the Tangams attempts to appease *Yahang* by sacrificing a white cock. The widespread belief is that the spirit is pacified with this act and does not, then, hinder in any operation associated with the *Jhum* cultivation. The Tangams believe that if this sacrifice is not performed, the malevolent spirit may become revengeful and cause harm. Likewise, in the interest of *Jhum* cultivation the Aos, more so the non-Christians, perform certain religious rites. Of these the two important ones are connected to the clearing of jungles and the prosperity of crops. For the prosperity of crops, and to avoid injury, the Aos sacrifice a cock or an egg, an act that is accompanied by prayer. In another rite an egg is offered at a place of worship near the field itself. This is followed by a token reaping, in the belief and hope that the harvest would give a rich yield.

The above explanations are support to the fact that *Jhum* cultivation is intimately linked to the traditional social-cultural milieu of the people in various forms. Therefore, any attempt to discontinue it or even curb it would directly interfere with the life, culture and social organisation of the people, which have, over the centuries, survived as instance of adaptation to natural environment. In terference, other than improvement in *Jhum* cultivation, would cause imbalance in vital areas of life and culture. And this would be contraty to the policy of planned integration of tribals. The integrated perspective of *Jhum* cultivation demands for an improvement in *Jhum* practices in the light of latest knowledge in the field of agriculture. It would help improve the economy of the people, but, at the same time, the associated social fabric and cultural values must not be ignored so that the people's faith in the same is not shattered. Balanced development of tribal people will provide fillip to their smooth, integration, thereby protecting what is best in them as way of life. Unwanted impositions would rupture their ecosystem and the cultural network.

4

DORMITORY SYSTEM AND MODERNIZATION

To maintain cohesion and coherence in the society certain structure is maintained. One such structure is inherent in the youth dormitory system among certain tribal communities of North-East India. These dormitories are of two types : one for young boys, where only the males are allowed to join, and the other is for girls where they sleep and entertain their lovers. The dormitories have been given different names among different tribes. But in most of the cases the underlying functions are common.

The customary name for youth dormitory of the Ao Nagas is *Ariju* or *Arichu* and its members assist the village council in administration. "The *Ariju* is an institution for the adolescent boys. After completing the age of 11-15 years all the boys have to go to *Ariju* to sleep there at night. Early in the morning they return to their respective houses and busy themselves with their household works". (The Report of the Law Research Institute, 1979 : 31). Existence of youth dormitory is also reported among other Nagaland communities. According to Bareh (1970: 84), "All the Naga tribes have dormitory organization known as *Morung*, a sort of the bachelor's club where boys are gathered to spend the night." Likewise youth dormitories are reported among Wanchos of Arunachal Pradesh. A dormitory is locally called *Pa* (*Pavu*). A village may report of several *Morungs* (youth dormitory) depending upon the population size. On an average each *Morung* serves 50 to 60 houses. The largest *Morung* is referred to as *Pavu (Pavnu)* and the smallest as *Posa* (Pavsu).

The boys' dormitories are actively functioning among the Hill Lalungs too. This institution, among the Lalung, is called *Samadi* (Bordoloi, 1972). Likewise, the bachelor's dormitories are reported among the Rengma, Angami, Tangkhul, Khamti, Tangsa, Nocte, Sherdukpen and Apa Tani tribes. Among the Nocte a bachelor's dormitory is called Poh and is organised on sound principles to fulfil its functions (Nair, 1985). The institution of bachelor's dormitory is known as Terang or Farla among Karbi, Anglong and Nodrung among Dimasa, Mishings call it *Mimber Yame* (Bordoloi, Sharma, Saikia and Das : 1985). Among Tangsa the normal age for marriage is considerably high and the girls and boys choose their mates through dormitory. A girl is free, in her choice, to entertain any boy of her liking.

In North-East India the existence of female dormitories is reported among some tribal communities including Noctes, Adis (Padam, Minyong, Boris, Pailibos, Ramos etc.), Gallongs, Tangsa, Zemi Naga, Ao, Konyak, Tangkhul, Khamti, Sherdukpen etc. The institution of dormitory was far more popular in the past. Of late it is towards speedy decline. More so it is true in case of female dormitories. However, we still come across the reminiscent of glorious past of this mighty institution among some of the chivalrous communities of today. As in case of some other institutions, we cannot exactly locate the birth of the institution of female dormitory, though it certainly has association with its male counterpart, that is, male dormitory. The female dormitory, with its explicit functions, can certainly lead us to the idea of its inception in the first place and then to its maintenance and prevalence, though in declining form, till this day.

Although the girls' dormitories emit a very important function but not much attention is given to the architectural design of the same. They are very simple structures, mostly square in shape, whereas the male dormitories are the finest examples of architectural display among the communities wherever they are reported. Many a times no special building, as female dormitory, is constructed but some virgins are housed together in the house of a widow or any other old woman, who has surpassed her romantic age. The maintenance of these houses is not given much attention although they have been repositories of culture and its transmission. On the other hand the male dormitory is rendered all the necessary assistance in the form of labour, food, expertise and training. At the same time the male dormitory is, most of the time, tabooed for female and rarely the females are allowed to enjoy festivals of grand nature. The buildings of youth dormitories, by and large, display craftsmanship of superb expertise, in native sense, depicting various aspects of native human and eco-systems. Figures of animals are carved outside as well as inside of the dormitory. They are the museums of specimens of cultural heritage and trophies. Besides cubicles and fire places there is kept a large wooden platform on which the men sit and relax.

In general it is taken as privilege to work for bachelors' dormitory. Every able-bodied person is obliged to help in the construction of its building as it is done on cooperative basis. A celebration marks the completion of Morung among the Noctes. Separate land is allotted, by the chiefs, to the Morung and its earnings stand for its maintenance and sustenance. Morung is an important Wancho institution. It varies in size and number as per population variation. The chief has the privilege of controlling the biggest, Morung; while the smaller ones are under the control of chief's brothers and sons. A chief gets some share of game killed or fish caught by the members of the Morung under his control. The construction and maintenance of the dormitories are essentially the responsibility of its members, though the villagers cooperate in the venture. The maintenance of log-drum, in the dormitory, is also essential as it is played on different occasions conveying different meanings. The inaugurations of the Morung and the installation of log-drum are great occasions for the entire village and are celebrated with a community feast. On such occasions, in the case of *Pavu (Pavnu)*, the chief's families of the allied villages are also invited (Law Research Institute, Gauhati, 1979). Youth dormitory, among Karbi Anglong people, is known as Terang or Farla. In some interior areas it is also called *Jirkedam*. Bordoloi, Thakur, Saikia and Das (1985 : 45) report that "the dormitory is generally constructed in a central place of the village with timber posts and thatched roofs on a raised bamboo platform. The inside is decorated very nicely with their own artistic sense. There is a hearth in the centre of the house and during winter the members of Farla sit around it to get rid of cold".

The functional aspect of the youth dormitories helped their construction in a great number. As already made clear in the above explanations, the most important aspect of the boy's dormitory is that it is meant only for young boys and till they get married. No female entry was, in normal course, allowed inside the dormitory meant for males. The reason being their pious nature which could defile by female entry. Female entry into male dormitory could distract the youth from their main functions of guarding and helping the village and could fail in their defined mission. The manifest function of boys' dormitory basically was to provide a guard-line to the village. The boys had to remain prepared to save the concerned village from any attack by enemy, fire or animals. They had to stop the enemy as well as warn the villagers of the enemy's approach. The dormitory was organised on the corporal basis which provided a strong opposition to the invader. According to Dutta (1984 : 373) "The Noctes have a well organised Morung (bachelor's dormitory) for men which in the good old days were centres of training the youth in the art of fighting, venue for holding meetings and discussion of the villages and guard houses to protect the village from outrages and accidental damages. Now-a-days the Morungs are centres of recreation and sleeping houses of the bachelors". It may be mentioned that the function of training the youth in the art of fighting does not hold much relevance now as the present conditions are different than what they were before. But the other functions of dormitory are still recognised.

One of the underlying causes, among many others, to the existence of youth dormitories is the requirement of privacy for sleeping purpose. As most of the houses in the tribal belt are single-roomed or otherwise small ones, the young boys and girls are desired to sleep apart and away from the parents. Any time after the age of seven or so the boys and girls go to sleep in their respective dormitories. In this regard Majumdar (1984: 315), while discussing the case of Garos, reports that "the grand old bachelors' dormitories are no longer there. But anyway, the spirit of the dormitory is not entirely lost. Even now, at least in the village, they continue to think that it is improper for the boys to sleep in the house where parents and sisters sleep. Even a single boy will have an improptue house near the house of his parents, which will be used as his bedroom and which goes by the name of Nok-pante, the same name as they used to apply for the grand bachelor's dormitory".

The youth dormitory is joined by all the young boys and girls. In villages the dormitory membership of a child is, sometimes, decided at the time of birth itself. This specially holds true for Zemi Nagas. Bordoloi confirms that "as a customary rule as soon as a boy or a girl crosses the age of eight, he or she has to sleep in his or her dormitory at night and is never allowed to spend the night and at home. As one Morung is not sufficient to accommodate all the youths of the village, that is why each Zemi village is found to have more than one Morung. They have got a Morung system which is unique by its own nature. In Zemi dialect the boy's dormitory is called *Hangsenki* while the girl's dormitory is called *Leosanki*" (1983 : 1).

While the girls' dormitories are mostly open to boys, the girls are rarely allowed inside the boys dormitories. The girls can enter a boy's dormitory only on some special occasions marked by singing, dancing, feasting etc. Otherwise, most of the time the boys dormitories are a taboo for girls. Whereas the girls' dormitory caters for boys' entertainment, besides other important functions. The girls' dormitories are the main meeting ground for boys and girls more so in the night. According to Roy (1966 : 194, 197, 198) "The Moshup or bachelor's dormitory for boys is very important institution in Adi society. The Rasheng or the dormitory for girls is erected in each village on the same principle as the Moshup. The Rasheng, a small hut having one square room with a fire-place in the centre is constructed by experienced old men. Moshups and Rasheng are central institutions where boys and girls get practical training in traditional mode of life. Here the boys and girls are allowed to find their way into the mysteries of life, in addition to the social and communal life, to the mysteries of sex."

Presentation and perpetuation of traditional art, skill, dance, myths etc., and training in sex and other mysteries of life are also allocated to the institution of youth dormitories. Among Tangsa, as reported by Nair (1985 : 98), the "girls' dormitories (Loops or Likpyas) are functioning in full vigour even today. Unmarried girls of the village spend their nights in these loops. Initial steps towards courting take place in the loops as the bachelors are free to spend their evenings in these virgin houses". The Sherdukpens are also stated to have youth dormitory to the benefit of boys and girls. The later get, through dormitory activities, practical training and orientation in different life-ways. For Nair (1985 : 121), "The dormitory institution among the Sherdukpen provides young girls and boys with—opportunities for initiation into the mysteries of sex and selection of marriage partners. The system is also responsible for perpetuation of the fine arts of the tribe". The girls' dormitory is taken as a place for meeting and enjoying for boys and girls. The female dormitories are also reported among the Khamtis and these discharge some important functions. Nair writes that the "houses of virgins and bachelors' barracks play an important part in the pre-marital sexual understanding of Khamti society. Each village has its dormitory for the young unmarried girls at one end. The girls are sent to the dormitory when they attain puberty. A girl who becomes an inmate of the girls' dormitory never sleeps at her home until she is married. The virgins' house is a sacred place, and is in charge of old maidens who have outlived the age of romance. Nobody dares to outrage the modesty of the girls. The morality of the Khamti village is, therefore, high" (1985 : 62).

An institution, similar to youth dormitory, is reported among the Mishings. This is called Mimbir Yame and it works to collect funds for festival celebration and to render help to the needy ones. Thus, the Mimbir Yame have different functions than the meeting platform for young boys and girls for the sake of sexual gratification only. In this regard Bordoloi, Sharma, Thakur, Saikia and Das (1985 : 59) state that "among the Mishings there is a benevolent organisation of the young men and women in a village called *Mimbir Yame*. The literal meaning of the term is 'young women and men'. Unmarried girls and boys above the age of 12-13 years become the active members of the body. Discipline and tribal etiquette are taught here and the discipline is maintained by some specially elected officers. The members of Mimbir Yame render help to any villager, in need, in respect of erecting house, weeding paddy etc., in exchange of nominal remuneration. The money, thus received, is used for celebrating 'Porag' festival". A similar kind of organisation, called *Patang* (gang) works among the Apatanis (Haimendorf, 1962). All the young boys and girls of the village together form the members of this group. They render help in cleaning the fields, preparing the field boundaries, transplanting besides constructing houses for which they get remuneration in the form of food and drink by the owner. Here we find the village youths and damsels being the members of the workforce without whose help much of the work may not be accomplished. In almost all the community works their help is sought after. Likewise, among the Mizos if a person fell sick during harvest season, he was looked after by the members of the youth organisation and was taken to the next village and ultimately to the medical care unit by young people. Though rugged individualism is taking place of the older community feeling, still some reminiscents are left of the same. The girls too help in this venture collectively asking for monetary or material help to give forward to Church so that it can be used for welfare purposes.

Besides being a resting place for the night the female dormitory has multiple functions to observe. This is the main orientation centre for the young members of the community who learn of the cultural traits through imitation. They get opportunity and guidance to prepare themselves for later life. Here the girls and boys meet and after sizing up each other choose the right life partner. In the female dormitory they learn the secrets of life which are cherished by all of them. The dormitory, in general, is the foremost institution of socialization among certain tribal communities.

While writing on girls' dormitory among Padams and Minyongs, Sachin Roy mentions a number of functions. "The Rasheng or the dormitory for girls, according to Roy, is erected in each village on the same principle as the Moshup. The Rasheng, a small hut having only one square room with a fireplace in the centre is constructed by experienced old men who in return are supplied with rice and Apong. The Rasheng members help in collecting the raw material" (1966 : 197). The size and shape of the dormitory are designed, for specific functions and reasons, by the experienced people. The latter get food and rice-beer (*Apong*) as remuneration. This building is made on the lines of *Moshup* (bachelor's dormitory). A girls' socialization, after adolescence, is dependent largely upon the training she receives in the dormitory. Not only the training in traditional art and craft but also the socialization in other life-ways forms part of the dormitory activities. In this field Moshup and Rasheng play very important part as central institutions. In this regard Roy (1966 : 197, 198) elaborates that "after adolescence, a girl really starts her romantic life and in the Rasheng she starts her courtship which leads her to choose her mate in future life. Young boys from different Moshups come and join the girls in the Rasheng in the night. A girl is free to entertain any boy of her choice. Older experienced girls teach the younger different types of dances, their traditional songs and heroic myths. The younger members get training in spinning and weaving from their mothers but more from their senior Rasheng friends".

While writing on the youth dormitory (Morung) among the Noctes, Parul Dutta (1978) reports about the existence of separate girls' dormitory. In villages where there is no separate morung for girls they sleep in the house of a widow or widower. In some villages, according to Dutta (1978: 50, 146), separate girls' morungs (Janso Pang) are run. A girls' morung is smaller in size than a boys' morung and is square in shape. In villages where there is no separate morung for girls, the girls generally sleep together in groups in the houses of widow or widowers. Boys and girls from different clans meet in such places". It is clear from the above statement that though the boys and girls are granted freedom to meet each other in girls dormitory but they have to adhere to the rule of clan exogamy which cannot be ignored. P.T. Nair (1985) also reports of the presence of girls' dormitory among the Noctes. Some married girls also sleep there. For Nair (1985 : 80), "The Nocte way of wooing and courting commences at their dormitories. Their larger villages contain a number of *Poh* (bachelor's barracks) and *Yanpo* (virgin houses). The Yanpos welcome boys at night and there is no objection to their staying there for the whole night. A certain number of married girls also sleep in Yanpo where they are visited by their husbands, till they beget a baby". A girl continues sleeping in the female dormitory even after her marriage and is visited by her husband till he builds a house of his own, or till the girl begets a baby, whichever is earlier. In this sense dormitory also serves the purpose of bridal home, though temporarily.

The dormitory system for girls lends freedom to them in smooth socialization and internalization of culture traits more relevant to them. The girl enters the dormitory, usually after the puberty stage, and starts getting necessary training useful in later life. She learns various cultural traits of her tribe. These include singing, dancing, myths, weaving etc. This she does in the company of her inmates. It is rightly said that a girl learns weaving and spinning from her mother but more from her dormitory inmates. Socialization of a girl gets strong impetus through dormitory activities. Besides proficiency in traditional art, a girl learns, by practice, the art of love. The pent-up psychological tensions are released which leave the girl in her natural self. The freedom of mixing with opposite sex in the dormitory has been helpful in avoiding the abnormal sexual behaviour among the tribal girls and boys. It keeps them disciplined and a girl's moral and character are generally high.

The girls dormitory has helped preserve the higher age of marriage for girls. This is very important practice, and rather a prerequisite for a healthy marriage and motherhood, the tribals have been keeping up for long. Normally the girls start their romantic age in dormitory and carry it for quite some time. They size up their life partner which is again an indication of their maturity of mind and weightage to their ideas and choice which is telling contribution to their status in society. Among Tangsa the normal marriageable age for girls is about twenty and it is due to the fact that the girls' dormitories are running there in full swing. Even after marriage the women remember their dormitory days with nostalgia. If the freedom of choice of marriage partner is snatched away from the girls, and they are given in marriage against their will, the age of marriage may lower down as has happened in some other societies. With forced marriage the status of women certainly gets setback, which is not desirable.

Almost every villager owes, in terms of duty, towards bachelors' dormitory in some form or other. Care is taken to project its image in the grand way highlighting its manyfold functions. Bareh elaborates the special features of the youth dormitories among Naga villages. According to him, "Morung is a vital corporate village institution as a centre of the village ceremonies, arts, music and folk-songs and field of training to young men in undertaking duties for the village welfare. Boys over eight to ten years of age, till their marriage, are its members. It is thatched, walled with wood. At the porch, along the oblong wooden posts as in Rengma style, there are carved images like Mithun's skull. Angami Morung is a mechang type where a porch particularly is more elevated. The young men pass their nights in the Morung at a cubicle of solid plank" (1970 : 84). The most important item of Morung is the log-drum. For Ghosh, "The Morung is also a guardhouse of the village. So there is the big log-drum nearby. The drum is hollowed out of a big trunk like a canoe" (1979 : 71).

The boy's dormitory has been providing the venue for holding the village meetings where elders discuss the socio-religious and political matters. In the context of political function of the Morung, Haimendorf explains that "today, the morung are still the principle exogamous units and the men cooperate in some economic activities, but the political structure of the village based on the close interaction of the five Morungs has largely been replaced by different and wider alignments. In accordance with the administration system, common to all parts of Nagaland, each village has a village council which consists of the nominees of the morung, the headman (Gaon Bura) who are now as they were in British days appointed by the district officer and as an ex-officio member the chief (Ang) of the village" (1973 : 4).

Further, the bachelor's dormitories function as the main schools for imparting training in martial arts. The senior members of the dormitory teach the younger entrants a variety of arts like singing of heroic songs, dance, use of bow and arrow for hunting purpose. All possible guidance is rendered for an overall socialization of the young entrant to make him responsible youth. The bachelor's dormitory, according to Roy, is the best institution for imparting training to develop "spirit of responsibility, alertness and habit of taking risk in the face of danger" (1966 : 194).

Community feelings are also promoted through bachelors' dormitory and these enthuse a combined task force to meet any eventuality. For instance *Samadi* (Bachelors' dormitory) is actively functioning among Hill Lalungs of Assam and has helped enthuse community specific ethnocentricism. The admission of boys to Samadi is done in batches after every five years. This system is well organised under the supervision of village headman. The youths take responsibility of office bearers and get upgraded after five years when the new batch joins. While discussing the importance of dormitory among Hill Lalungs, Goswami (1972 : 10, 12) states that:

> "dormitory system is built-in mechanism in shifting hill cultivation economy both for coordinating the activities of individuals and other social units as well as for perpetuating a smooth functioning of their society. The shifting cultivators have no room in their homes where they can entertain or lodge the guests and unknown visitors. The village dormitory serves all these purposes. Shifting cultivation needs the occasional help of a number of individuals than what an individual family can provide. This situation is overcome by extending an invitation to the work-group of the dormitory. An outstanding feature of the village dormitory is to keep the inhabitants of the village united in their thoughts and actions through collective participation at the public rituals through the agency of the youths of the dormitory".

The roles of bachelors' dormitory, such as imparting training to youths, providing guard line or task force for village and displaying of trophies marking heroic deeds are so important to some communities that they cannot do without it. For example Zemi Nagas (Bordoloi, 1983) have more than one dormitory for accommodating the village youths. Likewise, besides bachelor's dormitories there are found dormitories for females among some of the communities. These are used by unmarried girls for sleeping and entertaining the unmarried youths (though married man is not taboo) in the night. The girls' dormitory provides the healthy entertainment and normally the relationship of boy and girl, developed in the dormitory, culminates into marriage. The young men and women size up each other and then choose the life partner speaking for equality of status and maturity of mind. Most of the marriages take place at mature age which itself is a healthy state of affairs.

While further elaborating the functions of dormitory we come across a very important event. This is elaborated by Bordoloi (1983 : 6) when he states that "when a Zemi girl is married to a Zemi of another village, all the youths of her village, irrespective of Morungs, have to go to the village of her husband and work in the Jhum of her husband for one season from the beginning of cutting jungle to harvest. In return the husband of the girl has to offer rice beer and a pig to the youth. If he is rich enough he has to offer a mithun for the feast". Here we find the cooperation rendered by the dormitory youths to their counterpart to help them settle in their new home after marriage. This gesture of friendship, even after one ceases to be the member of the dormitory, goes a long way to establish oneself as a responsible member of society.

In spite of the important functions of dormitory it is steadily on decline among most of the communities. The reasons in support are the formal education, alien civilization and spread of Christianity. The grand old dormitories have stopped functioning in traditional way. But they are being preserved because they serve the purpose of sleeping houses for the bachelors and maidens separately. The very motive of entertainment by girls' dormitory is defeated in this way. The boys cannot visit girls' dormitory. Writing on this aspect Ghosh (1979 : 71) states that "at present as a result of Christianity, education and civilization, the olden system of Morung or bachelors' dormitory has fallen into disuse. But still the trail of tradition is manifest in the fact that the Morungs are now used as sleeping houses of the unmarried men and women - some are used by men and some by women separately". Of late, youth dormitories, among certain tribes, have received a severe setback. For instance there is reported sharp disappearance of Morung from Ao community. Among others, one reason, accounting for this trend, lies in conversion to Christianity. However, some remanants of Morung system do persist, though in new garb. In this regard Alemchiba Ao (1966 : 23) states that "though the institution of *Areju* (bachelor's dormitory) has disappeared from the village, pale substitutes of Areju and the age group system still continue. There are at present two dormitories, one for the boys and another for the girls under the control of the Church. For each of these dormitories, an honorary superintendent is appointed by the Church. The main function of these dormitories is to ensure segregation of unmarried boys and girls". Free mixing of young boys and girls in pre-marital stage is denounced by the Church and military principle of youth dormitories is overlooked. Development work and modern education are also the reasons for decline of youth dormitories in Karbi villages. Bordoloi explains that "this traditional institution is now gradually dying as it fails to withstand the onslaught of rapid changes brought about by development works including spread of education" (1985 : 47). Likewise the *Nodrong* (bachelors' dormitory), among Dimasa Kacharis, has almost lost its functional significance. In the absence of awareness among the young generation, about the utility of these institutions, the latter may meet its inglorious death.

The very purpose and aim of dormitory, that is, mixing of young men and women freely, is defeated by all encompassing impact of Charistianity, education and modernity. They denounce the old way of wooing and choosing the marriage partner by the tribals, hence underrating of dormitories and more so of girls' dormitories on immorality ground. An excessive collapse of dormitory system is also reported among the Mizos. But then survival of its certain ramifications is reported. For instance, both the boys and girls mix freely and opt for love marriages, though arranged marriages are also common. Though the age-old dormitory system is almost a thing of the past among the Mizos, the boys and girls continue to meet in the girl's house. They start courting after the age of thirteen and fourteen. Laitunga (1982 : 30) joins to state that "after taking evening meals youngmen enjoy their leisure time by courting girls. While a number of boys are sitting round a girl in her house, she should not make any sign by which boys may learn whom she loved. Otherwise no other boys except her lover would pay a visit to her. This will adversely affect her position in society because the quality of girl is, traditionally, assessed on the basis of the number of courtiers she has. The girl hardly goes out of her house in the night without having companions or escorts". This clearly indicates of the freedom of women in mixing with opposite sex though the old grand dormitory is replaced by girls' house. This system of courting is well recognised as 'Nula Rim' among the Mizos. In this pursuit the parents, by and large, encourage the girls and help them choose their life partners.

The winds of change due to modern education, consequently despising their own cultural values, is contributing in a big way in the dismantling of the institution of dormitory. The school buildings are being erected in place of grand old dormitory buildings. The winds of change seem to be working in rivalry, and not in cooperation with the older institution, importing irrepairable loss on the tribal psyche and social life. A vacuum seems to be widening between the old and the replacement and the harm is beyond comprehension. Taking the harmful repercussions in view about the demolishment of youth dormitories, to give rise to modern educational institutions, Elwin (1959 : 194) cautioned while reiterating that "if it is possible to work through them, instead of in rivalry to them, not only will the schools be more attractive but many psychological conflicts will be resolved". Elwin professed to build the new institutions in collaboration and cooperation of the old one to ease out the tension and bring in the smooth change for tribal social life. According to the policy forwarded by Elwin (1959 : 246) "the school hostels are not allowed to function as rivals of dormitories, for the administration is alive to the fact that the disappearance of the dormitories would mean, as it has meant when they have disappeared in similar cultures elsewhere, a general weakening of tribal discipline, a decay of recreational arts and an increase of sexual promiscuity".

Like Elwin, Alemchiba Ao showed great concern over the decline of dormitory system. Explaining in depth the importance of this institution, he talked of the vacuum which the decline of this institution is causing. Expressing his deep sense of concern about *Morung* (youth dormitory), Alemchiba Ao (1972 : 482) writes that :

> "in the past the state of the Morung house in a village indicated the state of the village itself. A decaying Morung meant a decaying village and a well kept and a well used Morung a vigorous community. In it the unmarried men slept, strangers were entertained and all public affairs of the village or clan transacted. Apart from a watch house, it was a recreation club, a centre of education, art and discipline and had an important ceremonial purpose. The institution of Morung had made, through the ages, immense impact on the life of Nagas. It was here that the lives had been moulded to fall in line with the Naga way of life. The opinion of the contemporaries replaced here the disciplinary influence of the parents on young boys. Here they learnt the advantages of cooperation and responsibility. They became more self-reliant with commonsense and better discipline. It was here that their loyalty and sense of service to the community was developed. Till the recent past the Morung institution had been the most powerful influence in the Naga society. With the decline of this institution and in the absence of any other institution in its place the discipline and orderliness particularly among the young people became deteriorated and a vacuum was thus created in the village social organisation."

If the finer values in the tribal culture are to be preserved then the institutions like youth dormitories, which stand for the same, should not only be preserved but encouraged. And in the event of their fast decay this herculean task is to be achieved through combined efforts of the administration and the people concerned. The already hurt tribal psyche is to be revived which itself would need tremendous efforts. The youth dormitories have stood for some of the finest values which need to be preserved and cherished to project the special status of those simple folks whom we want to develop. Development for them should be a breakthrough keeping their cherished values intact. These tribal people should not be relegated to a secondary status to the so-called modernity oriented people who are, at least to the tribals, no better and distinguished. Without the traditionally prescribed finer cultural values the tribals feel uneasy and hence these are to be preserved and encouraged in the face of modernity and development challenges. And the youth dormitories need an encouragement to enhance this cause in larger interest of the tribals.

A ray of hope in the shape of cultural revivalism, in regard to certain items, is a healthy trend. Some of the tribal people are reviving their neglected heritage. They are again taking pride in symbols of the past. For instance log-drum is being attended carefully and Naga-shawls are finding market in the home state as well as outside. In this regard Ao rightly states that "though bachelors, dormitory on military principle has gone, it has reappeared in a new form. There are dormitories for the boys and girls of the village under control of the Church with facilities for educational and cultural pursuits. There is also revival of interest in some of the symbols of the past" (1966 : 102). In the wake of this revivalism the policy forwarded by Verrier Elwin, regarding tribes of N.E.F.A. (now Arunachal Pradesh), seems to be highly fruitful. He has suggested that the modern institution of formal education should work in cooperation, and not in competition and rivalry, with the youth dormitories to retain the best in tribal culture.

Some of the most important questions arise in respect of the change caused in social structure due to disuse of youth dormitories. A rugged individualism is taking the place of cooperation and corporate living in almost all the arenas of social relations. Youth dormitories, based on corporate ideology, cannot withstand individualism which canvasses for personal achievements only, neglecting the wider social obligations. Petty interests are overtaking the broader, liberal and wider welfare of the community. The strong sense of discipline which maintains the youth dormitory and the social organization at large cannot be achieved without the cooperation which is the chief characteristic of these institutions. In this regard Roy (1966 : 194) rightly states that "the Moshup or bachelors' dormitory for boys is very important institution in

Adi society. There are two underlying principles on which the institution is-built, namely, the creating of the habit of discipline among children at their formative stage of life and in the developing of a spirit of cooperation and collaboration so that the tribe can act as a unit, and fissiparous tendencies within the tribe may have very little room for growth. In addition, it develops among the young a spirit of responsibility, alertness and habit of taking risks in the face of danger". In the absence or disuse of youth dormitories the attitude of cooperation and discipline are bound to give way to rugged individualism and lack of discipline. It is specially evident in lack of interest in their own cultural themes and patterns and show of disrespect of the traditional value system. The tribal youth is more fascinated by modern cultural values as is clearly visible in their adoption of new dress-pattern, hobbies, religious-traits, music and dance etc. The new dress pattern has caused a great setback to the indigenous art of spinning and weaving and the cooperative feeling emanating therefrom. Today's tribal youth hardly required the services of the village elders for imbibing traditional cultural themes, in the youth dormitory style, as he finds alternate ways in formal schools. The youth seems to value the formal schools more because he dispises the old values on pretext of their being inferior to modern ones. This is why Elwin (1959) advocates the modern schools and hostels to work in assistance with youth dormitories and not in competition with the same.

An important function of youth dormitories has been the rendering of help to those who cannot manage work of their own, without outside help. The inmates of youth dormitory used to form a labour gang and work force to come handy in time of need. In the absence of modern machines and techniques of cultivation the simple tribal economy is dependent on cooperative venture of able-bodied persons who comprise the youth dormitory. The social relations are bound to take a drift from the normal course in the absence of cooperative attitude of people. Sick and old age care ; boarding and lodging of guest ; construction of anicuts and houses ; preparation of the *Jhum* (shifting cultivation) fields and the raising of a guard line virtually depend on the cooperation proposed by the system of youth dormitories. Almost a radical shift in the existence of youth dormitories has shown sign of structural change in the micro-level institutions in terms of interpersonal relations.

The youth dormitory, which is the training ground for many necessary activities, prepares the youth for later life. Besides martial arts the fine arts also grow in these institutions. The beautiful wood carving, showing the medals and trophies of heroic deeds, finds expression along the walls and wooden beams of the dormitories. But in the absence of the later this art is sure to decay and die, giving a large gap in rich cultural heritage. The disappointing situation, arising out of the disinterest of people in youth dormitory, is rightly discussed by Haimendorf who says that "the men's houses (morung) have all been maintained. Two of them, which were burnt in a recent fire, have been rebuilt according to the old pattern, but the carvings of men, animals and various symbols on posts and cross-beams are inferior to those which had perished. The same deterioration in the quality of wood-carvings is evident in other villages" (1973 : 3). The same holds true for the youth dormitories elsewhere in tribal areas of north-east India.

The function of entertainment, which the dormitory life catered, also deterred due to segregation of boys and girls in separate dormitories as the Church does not allow the boys visiting girls, dormitory on the plea of immorality. Such an attitude of Church functionaries led to the decline of dormitory and the life of entertainment and associated training thereof. Denial to such an entertainment sounds harsh under the condition of limited alternative means of entertainment. The suppressed emotions may take recourse to any other channel which may not be favourable to society.

There is a wave of cultural revivalism and people's urge to cherish the memory of few items like war-drum or hand-woven shawl which once were burnt and forgotten due to disuse. This revivalism shows the functional utility of these items which enhance the stability of social system. If functional prerequisite is the basis of any cultural item then the items like war-drum and shawl, which are a part of dormitory system, should be encouraged by all means and this is possible only through the revival of dying institution of youth dormitory.

The above review of dormitory system vis-a-vis later trends make the anthropologists and sociologists alert in terms of their concern to the tribals and their cultural heritage. Though some of them have already expressed their part concern on the growing decay of the institution of dormitory, not much of heed could be paid to their observations. As such the trend kept on adversely affecting certain elements of tribal culture. The issue assumes mounting importance, more so when preservation and promotion of tribal cultures is talked about all around.

On the basis of insights provided in the body of this paper, an alternative strategy has been devised to promote compatibility between the requirements of tradition and modernity in the interest of retention of dormitory system. To start with, one is required to react on two fronts, viz. ; (*a*) to arrest the decay of dormitory and (*b*) to revive and strengthen this institution. For this definite channels and processes needed to be identified keeping in view perception and mundane purviews of the natives as well as the outsiders. In the present review this could be best done through examining functional framework of the dormitory in respect of tribal life and culture. Broadly speaking, the functional importance of dormitory can be classified under following eight heads:

1. Maintenance of privacy in life.
2. Dormitory functioned as centre of socialization, training and understanding in diverse areas of culture including music, dances, songs, art of spinning, weaving, carving, painting etc., myths, archery, use of Dao, spears and weapons, sex mysteries and pre-marital sexual understanding.
3. It provided a mechanism for freedom in mate selection.
4. Dormitory generated community task force that assisted in: (*a*) guarding the village; (*b*) shifting cultivation operations, and (*c*) house construction etc.
5. The institution inculcated and imposed discipline among the youths.
6. The dormitory served as an important centre for entertainment.
7. It encouraged corporate and cooperative living and kept the inmates united in thought and action, promoting thereby sense of belongingness to the tribe.
8. The dormitory functioned as repository of cultural heritage, including material artifacts. At the same time it did provide channel for transmission of this cultural heritage.

It would be essential to mention that the functionaries of the dormitory never denounced the formal system of school education (including the schools run by the Christian missionaries), not even indirectly because the dormitory inmates were usually free in the day time. Their activities started in the evening and continued till late night. At the same time the system and its constituents did not pose any threat to the modernity-oriented trends. On the other hand the rise of formal schools, mission schools, churches and the trends of modernization and urbanization did give blows to the institution of dormitory, without realising the worth of this institution in the native social structure. Within this picture, and keeping in view the dormitory functions, one can identify the necessary elements of strategy meant to check the decay of dormitories, as also to promote their growth. To arrest the decay, the very perception of agents of change, connected to formal education, modernity, missionary activities etc., is to be re-oriented stressing on them that the dormitory system is an important ingredient of tribal social organisation and as such it is to be retained. They should not impose their own negative version of dormitory system. Once they are mentally convinced of the utility of dormitory vis-a-vis tribal life and culture, they should concentrate on upholding of some of the dormitory functions through school and mission activities. There should be no difficulty for them to promote functions as outlined from serial number five to eight. These can easily be taken care of at school level by forming them as part of school activities. What would, however, be needed is a little extra effort by the teachers and other functionaries. The latter may be given an orientation, if need be, by the experts on tribal life and culture. These efforts may help arrest the decay of dormitory system.

To provide further fillip to the continuation of dormitories, the remaining four functions, cited at serial number 1 to 4, are to be taken care of. And these can only be carried out after school hours and in a different environment than the one provided in school premises. Under such circumstances the best would be to provide for hostels on dormitory pattern. The functionaries of these may be the same as meant for the traditional dormitories, which may involve even some community members. A major part of the economic implications for this kind of infrastructure may be met by the concerned government departments—say tribal development, tribal welfare etc. However, the official functionaries are not to interfere in the native ways of such a hostel which will cater to certain functional requirements of the traditional dormitory system.

The best part of the above strategy is that it synthesizes the formal and traditional systems of socialization and learning, giving a balanced emphasis on tradition and modernity. It will integrate the native cultural values with those of the alien ones, as also the human elements who carry them forward. In other words the innovations, connected to formal education and modernity, will find feet in the continuity format of dormitory culture. These will work in compromise and conformity and not in conflict—which is the aim of planned tribal development and integration.

5

CHIEFTAINSHIP AND SERFDOM
Models of Tribal Stratification

Stratification, more so in Indian socio-cultural situation, has been a major characteristic of caste system. Theoretic concerns, regarding stratification, as proposed and propounded by social thinkers, philosophers and analysts have also varied widely-ranging from functional or integrationist theorists to conflict theorists. Mounting substantivism in their arguments imported facts chiefly from caste society of India. The hierarchical order of castes and their defined placement, alongwith all other attending requirements provided for in Hindu social, organization, do provide for an illuminating stratified social order. The scriptural and textual explanations, housed in ideological paradigm as suggested ideologies for caste system, are obviously experienced through interaction and behaviourism of persons belonging to different strata of caste social ladder.

Social scientists, the world over, have least bothered to search for, explain and interpret the nature of stratification in tribal societies. The reason and background could be obvious. By and large the tribal social order, which is obvious from the very definition of tribe, was taken as homogeneous in contrast to caste heterogeneity. Such an assumption was even supported by a predominantly reported homogeneous character of tribal communities, more so when such communities were marked by an acute form of isolationism. But the study of stratified social order, which could always be reported among some of the tribes and which has assumed more prominent form under added acculturative influence, remained largely unattended. Least researched and discussed in the anthropological and sociological literature is the topic of stratification in tribal society, though the latter is an integral part of larger humanity. Only of late a few attempts were made to search, explain and theories tribal stratification. Otherwise the sociologists and social anthropologists found caste-based social order as a richer and more fertile field for designing studies on different aspects of stratification. Under the present exercise are discussed, explained and interpreted the nature and extent of stratification among the tribes of north-east India.

The social analysts have, by and large, recognized the universality of stratification in human societies. They attribute it to diversity of functions which are required to be performed by diverse individuals for a smooth running of society and the connected ways of life thereof. Since different kinds of persons and their expertise are required to perform corresponding roles, they are accorded differing values, rights and privileges differentiating them from others. And when there is inequality of rights and perquisites, the society is bound to be stratified. In addition to roles, the stratification also reflects through prestige and esteem. Norms for each category are set involving ranking in terms of superiority and inferiority. In general, therefore, stratification may be taken as referring to ranking involving the elements of high and low among groups. According to Talcott Parsons (1964 : 9) social stratification refers to "the differential ranking of the human individuals who compose a given social system and their treatment as superior and inferior to one another in certain socially important respects". For ranking statuses a large number of factors are responsible. These may at times be common, as also differing from society to society. Taking these into account, as also of the social stratification characteristics of its inevitability and perpetuation, the theorists have come out with various theoretic concerns in respect of stratification.

While theorising on social stratification, two approaches have prominently been reported. One of these is popularly known as 'functional approach', or 'functional theory'. This theory was advanced by Davis and Moore. In the background of this theory it was assumed that functional differentiation is inevitable. And this has been true throughout the history irrespective of time and space. A major presupposition behind this thinking is that there are different functions to be performed in society. And one person cannot perform all these functions and rules. As such persons of different ability, intent, skill and understanding are required to perform different roles and duties. Some of these functions are rated higher than others, and so are the persons performing them. And they get better privileges, power, prestige and higher status than others. In other words the persons are rewarded as per the values attached to particular functions. This differential reward pattern in any society gives rise to stratification and inequality, making social stratification an inevitable social phenomenon.

For Davis and Moore, the concept of stratification simply refers to the unequal rewards that are attached to positions. They argue that in all societies varying levels and kinds of rewards are in some, unspecified, way, 'built into' positions. These rewards are the duties, rights, associated with a position and its privileges (perquisites). Davis and Moore further say that "if the rights and perquisites of different positions in a society must be unequal, then the society must be stratified, because that is precisely what stratification means". They seek "to explain", in functional terms, the universal necessity which calls forth stratification in any social system. An empirical-universal inequality, must have some purpose, must fulfil some need of society. Further, they attempt to explain this need using functional imagery. The functional necessity of stratification is "explained" by Davis and Moore in the following way:

> First, all societies have a division of labour, a set of interdependent positions that have to be filled. These positions can be seen as clustered in four functionally necessary areas; religious, political, technological and economic. Second, people must be motivated to fill positions and enact roles. Social inequality is, thus, necessary in order to motivate people to fill functionally important positions and enact roles. "Social inequality is, thus, unconsciously evolved device by which societies insure that the most important positions are conscientiously filled by the most qualified persons". Davis-Moore thesis is similar to other functionalist analyses of stratification, especially Talcott Parson's. Parsons (1954) argues that the fundamental reference point in studying stratification must be the values dominant in a society. These values reflect functional importance in that one societal subsystem (such as the economy) is seen as making the greatest contribution to valued ends in the society. Furthermore, within each subsystem, role differentiation occurs, with the result that prestige and power go to those positions functionally important to the subsystem (Bheghley, 1978 : 44-46, 52).

Davis and Moore supported inevitability and functionality of stratification. Inequality, in their terms, is general aspect of social structure, and a structural phenomenon which cannot be done away with. These stratification theorists considered stratification as natural or given, and hence something universal in societies assuming impossibility of unstratified society. But Tumin's thinking differs on this count while proposing for negative functionality of social inequality because of unequal rewards and unequal prestige. Because of its negative consequences, Tumin stated that society can be destratified. As a critic of Davis-Moore theory, Tumin refers to many dysfunctions of stratifications. Likewise, Buckley (1968) speaks of some weakness in the stratification model of Kingsley Davis. According to him, Davis confuses between specialised roles, *e.g.* differentiation and stratification. Social stratification, according to him, is a system of unequally privileged groups, whereas differentiation is a functional requirement without necessarily giving way to corresponding inequalities.

Another theory concerning stratification is popularly termed as 'conflict' theory. This is considered as an alternate approach with Karl Marx as its propounder. For Marx classes have been the basic features of social organization. And in his structural theory of society, Marx equated class stratification with all the other types of stratification systems. He takes power and status stratification as the products of class stratification. Classes, to Marx, are the product of productive system. For him the basis of stratification lies in economic structure, control over the means of production and human labour and services. Class is a social reality with consciousness regarding position and goal. In this dialectical approach to the study of social stratification, Marx considered economic system as the foundation structure for the superstructure of stratification system involving cultural, political, social dimensions etc. Keeping economic system at the forefront, Marxians identify two classes namely owners of the means of production (Bourgeoisie) and workers (Proletariat). These two classes are at a clash in terms of their interest, giving rise to class conflict. The surplus value, earned by the bourgeoisie, meets resistance of the proletariat, causing radical or revolutionary transformation of the stratification system of society. Marx, thus, established a correspondence between class as a social category, and as analytical tool to the laws of social motion, giving thereby a scientific theory of social change. Class struggle, which is motor to social change, is the result of changing dynamics of production which cause change in social formations themselves. According to Marxian concept of class, therefore, the class is inseparately linked to dialectical (*i.e.* one opposite in conflict with the other—the total situation yielding the picture of contradiction) theory of social change. To Marx, therefore, class is not primarily a category to describe a particular society at a given point of time, but is an analytical tool for extracting sources of structural change in the society, thereby identifying the direction in which the society is heading.

According to Marx's theory, "increases in the productive capacity of a society (in the quantity and variety of material goods desired by the populace) and in population sizes are associated with an increasing division of labour. The increasing complexity of the division of labour is associated with the rise of industrialization. Marx clearly suggests that the greater the industrialization, the greater the inequality. Industrialization is also associated with formation of a solidary and cohesive-subordinate class and with a great rate of conflict between dominant and subordinate classes. Further, the more both dominants and subordinates form classes, the more polarized they will be. And the greater the polarization in a society. The more likely is the conflict to be violent. The greater the inequality in a society, the more subordinates form a solidary and cohesive class and the greater the polarization in society, then the greater the rate of conflict and the more likely is revolution to occur" (Beghley, 1978 : 17-18).

Yet another theory propounded by Dahrendorf is termed as 'coercion' theory. The requirement of this theory is the presupposition of two classes in society. One represents the group which is coercive and the other which is coerced. For Dahrendorf no society is fully coercive or integrated. There are in simultaneous operation processes of change and resistance. The conformists and deviants subscribe to the element of inequality. However, key concept in Dahrendorf's model is coercion. And coercion of authority and power leads to clashes of role and interests. This leads to the organization of antagonistic groups in society.

Dahrendorf and C. Wright Mills tried to reorient social stratification theory by emphasizing the importance of coercion, conflict, power and constraint in shaping social relationships. Beghley (1978 : 57) mentions that "as a rationalist or conflict theorist, Dahrendorf argues that 'we shall have to revise over assumptions radically' and move away from the utopian image of society embodied in Parasonian functionalism. (The Utopian, another name for a Parasonian theorist, assumes society as a persisting, stable and well-integrated structure of elements. The element here can be individuals, groups or aggregates of various sorts. In such a society, each element has its unique function and each element shares a consensus of values with others). He, thus, makes a set of alternative assumptions; society is based upon the coercion of some elements by others; it is continuously subjected to disintegration, conflict and change. He has reiterated these assumptions in a number of places (1958, 1967). He argues that they present a more realistic picture of what societies are really like. Dahrendorf believes that the societies are not stable, but in continuous flux. He also believes that there is not consensus over values but rather coercion, conflict and change. Such assumptions, it is argued, are useful for scientific analyses generally, and for understanding stratification processes in particular (1959 : 161).

Weber suggested refinement over Marx's analysis while emphasizing the importance of non-economic factors of stratification. He brought in sources like prestige, religion, ethnicity, family background etc. Weber argued that "no one factor, be it technology or economy, can be ultimate or true cause of another. If we look at the causal lines, connecting the parts of a social structure, we see them run, at one time, from technical to economic and political matters, at another from political to religious and economic ones etc." (quoted in Roth, 1971 : 242).

Patterns of Stratification

The tribes of north-east India, comprising the states of Assam, Arunachal Pradesh, Nagaland, Meghalaya, Mizoram, Manipur and Tripura show a wide degree of variance in their social organization and cultural life, however certain predominantly common traits can not be ruled out. Since stratification, a specialised aspect of social structure is dealt herewith, we may not stress upon the formats of diverse cultural traits of the tribes in their totality. Even with various manifestations of stratification, as revealed through its patterns, a significant variation is apparent. These are borne of underlying reasons which vary from one situation to the other. The same holds true for connected norms.

I

One pattern of stratification, among certain tribes of north-east India, is exhibited through the system of chieftainship and the social categories which have been created as a consequence of this system. Social division, borne of chiefship custom, has led to the emergence of various social strata. Their interrelationship and interaction of various forms are also defined as per the customarily prescribed norms surviving on the strength of the system of chieftainship. One of the tribes where the chieftainship is prominently reported is the Nocte of Arunachal Pradesh. The Noctes present a distinctly stratified society. They have two distinct categories (though Majumdar, 1980 has also talked of an intermediate class) popularly differentiated as Lowangjat and Samajat. The former, which is socio-economically higher, is represented by the chiefs and their descendents and the latter by the commoners. With their social and economic superiority, the Noctes of Lowangjat social division have been ascribed with certain privileges and the people thereof enjoy the same in mundane life. A more elaborate account of this is given by Parul Dutta in his excellent monograph on the Nocte. According to Dutta (1978 : 211):

> "The Lowangjat are the administrators who extract work from Samajat. While the chief's class, called Lowangjat, may take wives from the commoner's class, the commoners may not do so from the

chief's class. In social gatherings, like community-feasts, the two classes take different seats. When a whole village goes for hunting and fishing the largest share of meat and fish go to the chief. The cultivation of the chief's fields are done by commoners. The chief's house is constructed by the village itself. The death of a chief is the concern for the entire village community. The villagers pay annual tribute to the chiefs in kind."

Representing Lowangjat social category of the Noctes the chiefs in villages control the mechanism of social control and thereby manage for law and order in society. The necessary powers for all this are vested in the chiefs who never hail from the Samajat social division of the tribe. The Lowangjat maintain their distinct identity of a higher order as the chiefship in hereditary and its succession goes by the rule of male primogeniture. For its further consolidation the office of chief has customarily been accorded a sanctity. The Noctes practise shifting (*Jhum*) cultivation. For this they require shifting, at defined intervals of time, from field to field. The Nocte chief are vested with the authority of distributing *Jhum* fields to the villagers. The Samajats have no say in the matter. Recognising the chiefs as supreme the commoners depend on them in various walks of life. They guide their political life, are expected to provide security in the moments of crisis and help resolve all forms of disputes. Customary laws have protected the interests of the social category of chiefs and their descendents which has perpetuated over the years. The traditional norms-framework has made the commoners so obliged to the administering chiefs that they have been liberally contributing to his granary, consisting such contribution as token of respect. The traditions pose for other requirements to be met by the members of subordinate group, that is, the Samajat. Dutta (1978 : 138, 212) writes that :

> "The death of a chief assumes a festival character as all the subordinate villagers also get enough to eat. A brief formal lament is followed by eating and drinking and dances that continue for several days. The villagers pay annual tribute to the chiefs in kind. Rice beer for any festival in the chief's house is prepared by the village. A chief is not supposed to do any manual work. There is a system of compulsory labour, called Pokat, by the subordinate villages. A chief enjoys precedence in all matters. Even in walking or marching he must lead, all others follow. No one may walk in front of him. A bamboo chair with a bamboo table infront has to be ready where the chief is offered rice beer, meat etc. While visiting other village, he stays in the house of local chief."

Quite akin to Noctes and the Semas are also characterized by the stratification of the nature of chiefly class and the one of commoners. Here again, every village has a chief and they multiplied as the villages themselves did. In this regard it would not be out of place to quote Ghosh when he stated that the Semas are still migratory in habits in the sense that they often set up new villages. The founder of the new village, some wealthy Sema, becomes the chief of the village and is known as 'father' of the villagers and the villagers are known as Mughemi, that is, orphan of the chief. The chief is the lord of the village and he is the government (1981 : 219). As in case of Nocte, the Sema chiefs are the administrators which are denied to the commoners or the dependents, popularly termed *Mangheni* or *Churl*. The latter are placed low in local social ladder. On the other hand the chiefs occupy a higher rung in social hierarchy and prefer to maintain marital alliance with the persons of the same status to maintain chiefly prestige. In case of stratified social system of the Semas, the *Kukamis* (rulers or chiefs) occupy the most privileged position followed by *Chochomi* (the ministers selected by the rulers) who advise the chiefs in decision-making. The Mangheni or Churl come in the last. The hierarchical order has its attending implications in social and material life of the tribe. There are categorically defined procedures meant to protect privileges and position of the people of chiefly class. These are well reflected by Hokishe Sema (1986 : 168) when he states that:

> "The land belongs to the chiefs and clans. The allotment of land for cultivation is done every year on a festival day called Tuluni. No money is paid for the land for cultivation. The land cultivated by the chief and his followers will belong to the chief. Similarly, the land cultivated by the Deputy and his followers will belong to the Deputy. This is the beginning of the system of land holdings among the Semas. The land for cultivation is distributed by the chief and his deputy to the families. This system still prevails in Sema society and thus the concentration of land is seen with the chief and his deputies in Sema area. The chiefs and deputies are entitled to some fixed days labour from their subjects, not more than twelve days in a year, in one village."

Like the Noctes and the Semas, the principle of social-stratification commonly marks the society of Konyak Nagas. In Konyak villages one finds well defined and distinguished social divisions or classes with differing social positions and rights and privileges associated thereof. In order of social hierarchy the top position in Konyak social structure is occupied by the Wangham class or division. The great Angs or major chiefs belong to this class. These Angs mark the hereditary chieftainship. Some great *Angs* (say of Mon and Chui) have smaller Angs under them as reported by Hokishe Sema (1986). As in case of Sema chieftainship, the Konyak Angs select ministers from various clans of the village. Among the Konyaks the class of commoners is termed as *Ben* or *Bin*. In between are the social categories of Wangsha and Wangshu. Their origin is attributed to particular forms of marital alliance. The Wangsha's origin is attributed to the union of men of Wangham class with the women of lower rank. Third in hierarchy, that is below the Wangham and Wangsha, is the Wangshu class. Though in certain sense included among the nobility, the Wangshu is just above Ben, the class of commoners. The great Angs from Wangham class seek their principle wives from clans and lineages of equivalent rank to produce sons to succeed them. For procuring secondary wives, sometimes referred to as concubines, the chiefs of Wangham class may approach commoner's clans, though it is not very frequently reported. But the men from Wangsha, a lower division of Ang class, often take their wives from commoners, that is, the Ben. The two categories, falling between the great Angs and the commoners, are not very conspicuously differentiated. Their status attribution and interaction are thinly defined. But the prerogatives and functions of great Angs of Wangham class are vastly differentiated, though the difference in working routine and living, in day-to-day life, of other Angs may not sound that conspicuous. In his micro study of Wakching village, Haimendorf (1946 : 98) states that :

> "You would scarcely think that there existed among them a difference of class, a difference between the high and the low, between aristocrats or Angs and commoners or Ben people. Their daily life does not seem in any way different, the aristocrats do not possess better houses or richer furniture, and except for the village chief himself, the people of Ang class are in no way outwardly conspicuous. The running of the village, however, lies mainly in their hands, the adult men of Ang clan forming the council of the chief, which decides all quarrels and settles disputes over field boundaries and the like. The position of the so-called 'Great Angs' is quite different. These powerful village chiefs have the sacred blood of the chiefs, pure and undiluted, in their veins. The great Angs take their wives from their own Great Ang clan, and it is only the children of such a union that acquire the father's rank".

The above kind of stratification based on classes created by the chiefs, nobles, sovereigns or aristocrats, on the one hand, and commoners on the other are also reported in case of certain other tribes. It may, however, not be as elaborate and complicated as reported for the Noctes and the Konyaks. For instance, there are well defined positions of chiefly class and the commoners among the Thadou. Rights and privileges attached with each social category are clearly defined. The equation of allegiance is also well established and kept up on relevant occasions. Here again the chief's position is hereditary. Writing on Thadou social classes, Pearson Hungyo (1985 : 6) asserts that "The Thadou chief has the absolute powers over the village land and he distributes the cultivable land to all the villagers at the beginning of every year. In doing so he has to consult his council of ministers called *Semang Pachang* nominated by him from different clans of the village. The villagers give tax to the chief for the cultivation of land. A basket ful of paddy (vaibeing) equivalent to five tins is given from each household as the tax called *Changsen* on a particular occasion fixed by the chief. On this occasion, the chief gives a feast to the villagers with plenty of meat and drink. *Changsen* is exempted from the widows and new settler of the village who has not established properly. An individual Thadou has no claim over any part of the land. He cannot sell or give it to others as the land belongs entirely to the chief. If he is not satisfied with the distribution of land or displeased in any manner, then he has to leave the village with his belongings leaving behind his house and other property'. More or less on the lines of chieftainship, described above in case of Nocte, Sema, Konyak, Thadou etc., the existence of social stratification is also reported in case of the Singphos. Like the Semas a Singpho becomes the chief of a village he has founded. The position of chief is hereditary. The chiefs exercise a variety of powers and authority. According to Baruah (1977 : 46-47): "The Singpho society may broadly be divided into three estates; the chiefs, the plebeians and the slaves. The first of these divisions is called *Ddufan* (represented by chiefs) and which is of highest status. The next lower division in hierarchy is called *Mreng-dong* (including the commoners). The lowest in social rank is the division called Mayam. The members of the last class are said to be the descendents of those men and women who used to be captured and kidnapped from Assam plains. In course of time they crystalized into separate social entity by adopting Singpho clan names, language and culture. A village chief is called Agi or Mirang in whom the social and political control of the village rest. Chieftainship is hereditary. He is not only a clan chief but also a territorial chief. So far his village is concerned, he is the dejure owner of the village land which he allows to his co-villagers to cultivate. Every Singpho village is an independent unit by itself and is ruled by a chief who holds the legal and administrative power. He directs all village activities concerning the welfare and well-being of the village community. He decides all cases excepting the inter-village disputes and punishes the offender with fine. In case a villager refuses to obey his order, he may even turn the offender out of the village. A Singpho chief normally possesses more than one wife as his social position necessitates him to entertain more guests with food and drink. Some instance of aristocracy has also been reported from amongst the Sherdukpens. In contrast to the commoners the aristocrats, among the Sherdukpens, represent a distinct class under a separate name of Thongs. No social mobility is permitted from other classes to the Thongs who are traditionally privileged with higher social status. Magnitude of social disparity is marked, among the Sherdukpens, by the fact that the inter-class marriages are usually restrained. Other parameters of social disparity are, however, not prominently reported. While discussing of the existence of pronounced status-distinctions and the ensuing social stratification among the Sherdukpens, Nair (1985 : 86) states that:

> "The Sherdukpens are divided into three classes, Thongs, Chhaos and Yanlos. The Thongs form the aristocracy and the Chhaos the middle class. The Yanlos are artisans. Except that there is no inter marriage amongst these classes, there is no other social disparity. Certain inter-service relationship exists among the classes."

In case of the Mizos the chieftainship was officially abolished long back. At one stage, just before Indian independence, the Mizos had the largest number of chiefs. Some repercussions of the old system form part of continuity. In perpetuation of the old system the classes of the rich and poor continue to be recognized as reported by the researchers. According to Dev and Lahiri (1983 : XII) "The abolition of chiefship was merely a post-independence phenomenon. But the fact remains that the families of ex-chiefs even today occupy a position of prominence having a status difference with the so-called commoners". Hinting at the rich and poor classes among the Mizos, Laitunga supports the argument of Dev and Lahiri. Laitunga states that "there is one important thing which cannot be minimized, that is, a gap between the rich and the poor in social status. Usually the members of rich families are honoured and respected by all whereas the members of the poor families are not" (1982 : 5).

The above kind of intra-tribe stratification based on chieftainship, commoners and the classes in-between continues, by and large, to mark the social systems of the concerned tribes. The chiefs, at times, may not receive the formal recognition from non-tribals but within their own system they continue to carry an image of higher social position and authority. Writing on the Noctes, Dutta (1984 : 373) explains that: "although winds of change is blowing among the Nocte yet the traditional institution of chieftainship is continuing without any change". Mention of a mild declining trend in chieftainship among the Sema and Konyak has been reported by Hokishe Sema. But in the next explanation he talks of the system's effectively and perpetuation. According to Hokishe Sema (1986 : 169), 'The system of Angship in Konyak area and rulership in Sema tribe is declining. But the influential Angs and Kukamis will still play an important role in the various councils because some of them are still popular and well-to-do in their societies. On a similar plane Hokishe Sema is joined by Haimendorf, more so in Konyak situation. Both think similar in terms of future projections. However, in respect of contemporary social situation the observation and reporting of both are alike. For Konyaks, Haimendorf asserts that:

> "The present generation of villagers still pays respect to the great Angs in recognition of their inherited status as the men of purest aristocratic blood, but the young educated boys are not likely to accept the supremacy of chiefs whose only claim to their position rests on the hereditary principle" (1973 : 12).

The above substantivism in case of the Nocte, Singpho, Sema, Konyak, Thadou, etc., leads one to certain issues of theoretic concern in respect of stratification. Firstly, these tribal societies are marked by the stratification chiefly borne of descent from noble, royal or aristocratic parentage. Secondly, people from such parentages want to keep up their distinct social division for high prestige and more privileges. Thirdly, they want to control the economic resource (their land which they are authorised to distribute for the purpose of shifting cultivation) which ultimately helps retain the authority of social control and the privileges of various forms already elaborated. Through this explanation it appears that the underlying cause of stratification is materialistic, which is protected through noble descent. However, the materialism, as reported among these tribals, is not of the nature and order reported among the non-tribal feudals. These people hardly accumulate wealth as the surplus is not bothered for. The disparity in terms of rich and poor is insignificant between the chiefs and the commoners, but the position of chief does provide psychic gratification in terms of certain amount of authority and privileges which are associated with this position. Since the economic disparity between different divisions is not of wide magnitude and since the chiefly classes have extended a variety of concessions, in terms of caring for people in general, the grievances against the system of chieftainship and chiefly classes are of rare occurrence. To some extent the economic egalitarianism is reported among these tribals inspite of the control over resources being concentrated in the hands of chiefly class. Among other reasons the prominent economic classes could not emerge among these tribals because of the nature of economy being that of subsistence in general. They being predominantly shifting cultivators could not afford to have more of surplus and savings. Profit motives and cash transactions remained, by and large, absent. Any meagre surplus grains, available in chief's granary, was shared with others in the hours of need or through feasts which chief would organise occasionally. From this point of view the traditional social stratification, reported among these people, sounds more of functional nature ; conflict being relegated to a very low level. It may be so because the economic exploitation, by and large, could not become a point of any serious concern to the commoners.

II

Another pattern of stratification, reported among the tribes of north-east India, is based on the criterion different from the one reported among the tribes having chieftainship. Such a stratification sounds intra as well as inter-tribe. It's origin is attributed to master-serf relationship. The system has been in existence for centuries as evident from certain myths explained by the people. Though legally banned since the fifties of the current century, the instances of the serfdom based relationship cannot be ruled out. Many studies speak in support of it. Writing on this aspect, Nair (1985 : 151, 158) states that "the Apatanis are the only people in the Subansiri region who have been practising terraced cultivation from time immemorial, whereas their neighbours the Daflas and Miris are votaries of slash and burn method. No wonder that the Daflas come and consign themselves voluntarily into slavery for they are assured of food, shelter, clothing and security. Thus, slavery, in the ultimate analysis, is in the logic of history. The economic condition of the people necessitated an uninterrupted flow of slaves". The Apatanis are stratified into two distinct classes known as the *Guth* (patricians) and the *Guchi* (commoners or slaves). The Guth is represented by the Apatanis of the village itself, as also by those who have joined the village through marital alliance. The Guchis are presented by the descendents or remnants of those who were captured, during wars, from the villages of Nisi and Hill Miri tribes. Over the years these people lost their original clan names and got largely assimilated with the Apatanis in terms of diverse ways of life including food, dress, shelter, behaviour etc. Though formerly treated as slaves (I would prefer to use the word serf which sounds more befitting to the situation) these people now live by the side of Guths and share many things in common. But still some inequality between the Guchis and Guths is maintained. Some areas of discrimination are also marked. The people of Guchi class are not allowed to join some religious festivals. The members of two classes, that is the Guth and Guchi or Mura, do not inter-marry and the commensality, specially on ceremonial occasions, is missing. A serf depends on his master for basic needs like food, clothing and shelter, and is even permitted to take his master's clan name. While in master's house a serf cannot possess any property. Even if a Guchi is rich, he cannot equate, in social scale, with Guth.

Numerous instances of inter-tribe stratifications are also prominently reported. The class of serfs is well identified in terms of local perception of high and low. The supraordination and subordination have their implications at operational level of the life-designs. The birth of this kind of stratification is attributed to inter-tribe contact and the ensuing relationship. The stratification on the pattern of master-serf relationship is more conspicuously reported from some tribes of Arunachal Pradesh. For instance, the *Bangnis* have been engaging, from the deep past, the Sulungs as their serfs. The *Bangnis*, recognising themselves as socially superior, belong to the class of Atto the masters. On the other hand the Sulungs, who are socially inferior and who serve the Bangnis, belong to the class of Bekrau, the serfs. Like the Bangnis, the Mijis also engage the Sulung serfs *(Bekrau)*. The Miji master's division is termed as *Tau*. Though not extensively, the serfdom is also reported among the *Akas* (Hrusso). Their two divisions of Kutsum and Kovatsum are higher than the one of serfs (of Sulung descent), known as *Khulo*. These instances reveal that the Sulungs have been serving a few neighbouring tribes as serfs for time immemorial. A few families of Sulung, forming a cluster, stay a little away from their master's village and serve them. Deori (1982: 54, 55) states that "the slave system continues among the Bangnis and Mijis of East Kameng District of Arunachal Pradesh. Each Sulung individual is inextricably bound up with a Bangni or Miji. The Bangnis also have slaves from their own community who are known as *Mera* (male slave) and *Paue* (female slave)". The latter explanation of Deori points out even the intra-tribe stratification among the Bangnis; the higher division is represented by the people of Tau category and the lower one by those belonging to Mera and Paue. The inter-tribe hierarchical order of the Akas is well explained by Majumdar (1980 : 28) who states that "the Akas who call themselves Hrusso, have two main divisions,

Kutsum and Kovatsum. These divisions are two political units under two chiefs. Among Akas the rich men occupy the highest status in the society and slaves occupy the lowest status. The slaves are known as Khulo and they usually belong to the Sulung tribe, a hunting and gathering tribe." How the hunting and gathering Sulungs became slaves to the Bangnis is well illustrated by a myth given by Deori. "The Sulung's relationship with the Bangnis is based on Mithun which is an indispensable item of bride-price. They do not have had mithuns of their own. As the myth goes, sons of Jago and Keya borrowed mithuns from the Bangnis and could not pay their values and since then they became age-old debtors to the Bangnis for mithuns. Thus the Bangnis brought the Sulungs under their full control and became master (Atto) over them. The system is still prevailing (Deori, 1982 : 52, 54). Though not very extensively studied and reported, the master and serf stratums are also reported the Mizos and the Reangs. According to Samant (1984 : 185), "The feeling of master and the slave that must have existed in the past between the tribes of Kuki-chin group and the Reangs is still evident today wherever these tribes have come in contact. In the Jampui Hills of Tripura the more numerous Reangs are nothing more than serfs of the Mizos a position which the Lushais claim as natural and the Reangs accept as their fate."

Though different levels, consisting of masters and their serfs or dependents, are identified, their interaction does not import rigidity of the nature usually prescribed for master-slave relationship. This specially holds true in case of tribes other than the Sulungs. The pattern of interaction and relationship between the socially superiors and inferiors sounds quite humane. The implications of relationship do not exactly fit in the usual right system of slavery. The arrangement is not based on racial or colour criteria. The treatment meted out to the inferior class is also comparatively relaxed, though the bondage in certain sense is almost permanent. For instance, the relationship between the members of Guth and Guchi among the Apatanis is not typical of slavery system. The master, among the Apatanis, is addressed as father, if he is elder, by a slave. And the master reciprocates by calling him a son. On similar lines Sinha, in case of Akas, writes that "the position of slaves is not extremely bad as we might anticipate under the system. The treatment meted out to them by their masters is not totally devoid of humanitarian considerations; it is on the other hand, often humane and sympathetic.

The masters generally do not maintain much difference with them so far as the sharing of field toil is concerned. The slaves may have to work hard, but nevertheless their masters do have to provide for their minimum requirements in turn for their services. The Khulo (slaves) are virtually the menial servants with the further imposition of that the services are compulsory. They are slaves in the sense that they do not have a right of liberation" (quoted by Nair, 1985 : 164). The position again seems to be little easier in case of the Nishi. Commenting on the slavery reported among the Nishi, Haimendorf states that "in Nishi society mobility has always been much greater, for a person born as slave could, if freed by his master, rise in the social scale and end up as a respected and wealthy man, whose slave origin was no handicap whatever, provided he was sufficiently energetic to acquire a reasonable amount of wealth" (1982 : 91). But then the Bangni and Mizi come rather hard on their Sulung slaves. In his monograph on Sulungs, Deori writes that "the Sulungs are not allowed by their masters to mix freely with outsiders as they might somehow loose their control over them. Though they do not work in their master's house all the time, they have to render their services whenever required. The female Sulungs are required to prepare yarn from the fibres of wild nettle shrubs, and to collect jungle roots and tubers for their masters. All major disputes of the Sulungs are decided by their masters in consultation with the elders of their respective villages. The Sulungs cannot take any decision by themselves in murder case as this is the business of their masters. For giving the upright judgment their masters are invited by the plaintiff and the decision is declared jointly by their masters in consultation with the elders of the village or effected villages and when a murder is committed then the master of the accused Sulung is to pay two mithuns, one cow and one bead, known as *Moje*, as a fine, and that fine goes to the master of the murdered Sulung" (1982: 7, 54-56, 70, 73).

Further implications of banning slavery by the government in early fifties have resulted in easing the master-slave relationship among the tribes. There has also been progress in the liberation of slaves. However, the least impact has been in the inaccessible areas. Writing on the Bangni-Sulung relationship, Deori (1982 : 55) states that " the Bangnis of today are more liberal upon the Sulungs than in the past". The Anti-Slavery Act has also curtailed the capturing of slaves. But in many cases the psychology of serfs, *vis-a-vis* their masters, is yet to be radically changed. Many intend keep up the relationship. Things are, to a large extent, left on the village elders who are, in majority of cases, pro-tradition. Viewing the situation after promulgation of the anti-slavery law, Haimendorf (1982 : 95-96) writes :

> "When in the 1960s the government decreed the freeing of slaves and undertook the compensation of slave-owners this measure brought about less change than one might have expected. Raiding for the sake of capturing prisoners and selling them as slaves had

> already largely come to an end, and many of the still existing slaves chose to stay with their owners because they considered themselves as member of the family and had nowhere else to go. Since the abolition of slavery people are no more captured with the intention of selling them as slaves, but in disputes arising from cases of adultery or fraud, offenders are sometimes still tied up and kept in stocks until the quarrel has been settled by negotiations. The administration wisely does not interfere with such coercive practices as long as the village elders (gaonbura) approve of them and involve themselves in the settlement of the dispute."

When Haimendorf and Deori seem to be optimistic in terms of abolition of relationship of slavery, as is evident in a few of the implications, Nair's explanation sounds the other way round. He has his own reservations on the issue. But a common point between him and Haimendorf relates to an attitude of unconcerned nature on the part of those who are meant to liberate the serfs. Specially stressing on Apatani slavery, Nair (1985 : 179) reports that "it is very difficult to abolish slavery as the owners fear that their ghosts will be unattended and without honour in the other world, if they give up their slaves. The eradication of slavery is further complicated by the fact that a number of tribal employees of the Administration such as Political Jamadars and village headmen who are recognised by the administration, themselves keep slaves, sometimes on a rather large scale."

III

Under the above pattern of stratification, which chiefly relates to inter-tribe situation, some academically interesting dimensions have emerged. In contrast to material base, already discussed under the first pattern of stratification, which chiefly reflected intra-tribe situation represented by the classes of chiefs, commoners and in-between, the underlying elements of second pattern of stratification are myth and supernatural ones. The served and the serving classes, that is the master and serfs, explain the origin of their stratified social order on the strength of their myth (reported among the Sulungs) and supernatural belief (reported among the Apatanis). But then the economic implications of such stratification pattern cannot be ruled out in mundane life. They are rather deeper under this social arrangement of inequality and hierarchy. More illuminating of these is the non-repayment of dues against mithuns which Sulungs take from the Bangnis and Mizis and pledge themselves to their masters. Being the poorest they go in for economic security under this arrangement.

The chiefly class controls the economic resource and distributes the same among the commoners. The masters, on the other hand, own the resource (say among the Apatanis, Bangnis and Mizis) and the serfs (say Sulungs) are usually the landless, or in a few cases the tenants at the mercy of masters. As such the gap in terms of rich and poor is far wider in case of stratified social order of master-slave kind. In case of the chief-commoner situation all are allotted Jhum land and the produce goes to the people themselves. Though the members of chiefly class enjoy certain extra privileges, specially in terms of petty materials benefits, the commoners do get a share in the major economic resource, that is, the land and the forest. As a common hypothesis it is assumed that the rich-poor gap should be wider in case of chief-commoner situation, but it is not the case among the majority of north-east Indian tribes (Mizos were exception at one time). On certain occasions, say one marking prestige of chief or in the event of some emergency, the granaries of the chiefs are also shared by the commoners. The element of economic exploitation, especially borne of stratification, too, is not that conspicuously reported in case of chief-commoner pattern. In fact the commoners only render some labour help on certain occasions, or at times donate a basket or two of the produce to the chief's granary or share portion of meat of the game killed in hunting in recognition of chief and his services to the community. Under the customary law the chief too is obliged to take care of the commoners. On the other hand the element of exploitation finds a prominent place in case of the stratified social order borne of master-serf relationship. The serving class of serfs suffers from a variety of complexes, denials and deprivations. They, and at times even their families, are bogged down under compulsions of various forms. Highhandedness is also reported in master-serf pattern of stratification, more so in case of Bangni-Sulung and Mizi-Sulung relationship. Most of them do not have right even over the land of their habitation, which usually belongs to the masters. However, they are looked after at the minimal level of human existence. People have been in bondage for generations. A great deal of voluntarism is reflected in case of chief-commoner relationship, each class responding in terms of reasonable reciprocity, a dimension largely missing in case of master-slave relationship.

The state of poverty is comparatively acute in case of the slave class. Worst, on this score, are the Sulungs, followed by the Miris and the Nishis or Daflas. Among the masters the well-off are the Apatanis, followed by the Bangnis and Mizis who are socio-economically far better than the Sulungs. The commoners (as against the chiefs), though at subsistence level of economy, cannot be equated with the abject poverty marking the class of serfs who attribute it to their poor fate. Master-serf pattern of stratification, thus, caters more to the requirement of conflict model of stratification, though its functional aspect cannot altogether be ignored.

In the sense of 'functional' the pattern of chief-commoner stratification sounds, more so at perception level, comparatively somewhat functional to all categories of stratums, but slightly more to the members of chiefly class who derive psychic gratification in terms of prestige and authority in addition to a few petty material benefits. Both in manifest as well as latent perspectives the master-serf or patrician-serf pattern of stratification appears more conflicting to the serving group of serfs. The material benefit, that they have been deriving, is of extremely a meagre nature. On the other hand the system proves beneficial, more in terms of material sense, to the masters.

As part of the structural analysis of the system of social stratification among the tribes of north-east India, a few models can be conceived as of interpretative relevance in terms of scientific analysis of the social system. The implications of these constructs cannot be ruled out in case of parallel social situations reported elsewhere too. One of these relates to the very creation or origin of stratification, of the chief-commoner kind, where it can be propounded that social arrangement is to be primarily and essentially attributed to the urge for acquisition of superiority, prestige, authority and power as elements of psychic gratification of humans, economic necessity could not have been the basis of this form of social system. The control over and distribution of economic resource, in this case land and forest, came up later as a consequence and intended follow up of the above given non-economic content of stratification base among the Nocte, Konyaks, Semas, Tangkhuls, Thadous etc. Even the rise of noble or aristocrat class, represented by the chiefs and their descendents, can be attributed to the subsequent stage through the process of seeking descent from the chiefs, recognizing them carrying pure noble blood. This could be further substantiated and consolidated in the interest of perpetuating the system, through the declaration of chief's position as hereditary. Indirectly, these steps made the commoner's class more differentiated and crystalized at social level than the economic one.

Quite contrary to the paradigm, given above in the context of chief-commoner pattern, is the one that can be conceived for the system of socially stratified divisions borne of master-serf relationship. In case of the latter it can be interpreted that it was basically the economic requirement that led to the rise of such social stratification. Such an explanation is of relevance to both the social divisions, that is, formed of the masters and the serfs. Hard pressing economic necessity led some to pledge themselves as serfs; and the requirement of additional working hands enthused comparatively big landholders to acquire serfs through various means. In former category come the Sulungs, Dafla, Nisi, Miri etc., and in the latter can be included the Apatanis, Bangni, Mizi etc. Under this model of conceiving the origin, rise and sustenance of social stratification, the craze for prestige, authority, superiority etc., grew at a subsequent stage, and that too not in any conspicuously illuminating form. Even in the contemporary social situation, economic requirement, in case of stratification of master-serf nature, forms an element of priority and prominence over the non-economic criteria. This is obvious from the perpetuating social situations too. The dominant group of the masters or patricians, representing higher order in stratification, has even provided minor concessions to the class of slave in the interest of relating the bondage system. Through these concessions the serfs feel obliged to serve the masters. The members of master's class occasionally extend what they call as human and sympathetic gestures. For instance, the serfs, in some cases, are allowed to call a master by the terms of father, and the master reciprocates it by the term of son. On some occasion the master may depute a serf, especially if the latter is intelligent, as his spokesman to represent on behalf of the master. At times the master may pay for the bride-price or fine penalty on behalf of the serf. Sometimes a piece of land may also be allotted to the serf family for cultivation. They use its produce for themselves though the ownership of land remains with the master. The Apatanis allow their serf class to even borrow their clan names so that they may mentally feel like the freeman. But they never marry with them and restrain their social participation in certain rituals and festivals. However, the motive behind all these concessions is to keep intact the serving class whose members help in meeting the economic requirement even if the process involves a deep underlying exploitation dimension.

Another model, characterized by a few ingredients, is of quite an importance in the context of social stratification reported in the tribal situation of north-east India. In case of chief-commoner pattern of stratification, a forceful element is that it is, in general intra-tribe. That means the people belonging to different social stratums are of the same tribe, and who share certain common characteristics, other than those barred by the stratification, at equal footing. This includes even their origin in terms of the tribe as a whole. It gives rise to the recognition of certain other common bonds based on obligations borne of common value system and 'in group' feelings. Background of this kind paves way to more humanitarian considerations. Among other factors, involving mutual obligations, the communal ownership of land strongly holds their fraternity and community feelings. Almost a fair distribution of this resource further strengthens the process. The force of communal ownership of land, in terms of many human and societal conditions and reciprocities, is almost as strong as the kinship ties borne of descent and alliance groupings. Belongingness to the same tribe, and as such sharing of many ideological and actual things in common, have correspondingly reflected in certain areas of stratification. Firstly, the stratum gap is not that wide in terms of social distance, rights and privileges. At the same time there are no rigidly ascribed deprivations and constraints, though the chiefly clans do enjoy an air of superiority. Then the exploitation of commoners is not of anv significant dimension. Petty favours given to the chiefs, who are their own tribesmen, do not exactly support the basis of exploitation as per native perception. The commoners, in general, take it lightly in the background of services rendered by the chiefs, more so in the arenas of social and economic control which they are authorised to exert. It appears that ethnic homogeneity at the level of tribe, and people's recognition of and adherence to the same have contained the stratification pattern only at mild level. The system sounds more voluntary rather than one involving serious elements of compulsion. Only a light expression of the latter is reported in rendering petty favour to chiefs who do not find time, because of other community engagements, to attend to some of their personal requirements.

But in case of stratification based upon master-serf tangle, and which is representative of inter-tribe situation, the picture is altogether different. Here the masters belong to one tribe and the serfs to the other. As such there is no affinity on the ground of belongingness to the same tribe when it comes to different social stratums placed in an hierarchical order. Each stratum is identified with a different tribe. In this background the nature of 'in-group' feeling and obligations differs widely. Against the communal ownership of land, reported in case of chief-commoner pattern of relationship, the ownership in case of master-serf situation is individual. The Apatanis and many others adhere to this form of resource ownership. The slaves are, by and large, landless. In this context, too, as the norms of the members belonging to two different tribes (one of masters and other of the serfs) differ, there is hardly any check on economic exploitation. The dominant masters, representing a common tribe, do come hard on the serving serfs who, in general, belong to another tribe. Under this arrangement the gap marking different rungs of social ladder sounds pretty wide. The wider gap derives its strength from ethnic heterogeneity and an extremely unequal distribution of resource. Since the tribes, under this situation, do seek different origin and descent, their feeling of fraternity lacks to a large extent. Because of differing ethnic background and other associated considerations, say unequal distribution of resource, there is no check on exploitation as the norms differ as per the tribe. Element of force and compulsion appear sharp, more so when we review them from the socio-economically superior to the inferior groups. And exploitation is more forceful under the purview of above explained conditions. This sometimes culminates into inhuman treatment at various fronts.

In the context of change in respect of two patterns (chief-commoner and master-serf) of stratification reported among the tribes of north-east India, two more systematized constructs can be delineated. In case of intra-tribe stratification, essentially borne of chief-commoner relationship, the trend of change is in terms of substitution of chiefs. The educated elites, more so of younger generation, sometime question the hereditary-based chieftainship. And they care to do so more because the fundamental of such customary system is non-economic, that is, prestige, authority and power etc., based. Many of these emerging elites also express their inclination to such elements of psychic gratification. The secondary base of resource control and its distribution, as managed by the traditional chief, is not difficult to mange even by these elites, as is evinced from their state of mind on the issue. However, in the interest of systemic arrangement, the change trend only suggests for alternative substitutes—say replacement of chiefs by the Gaonburas or by other educated and employed persons in the villages. As such the instance of total revolt against the ongoing traditional system is unheard of. But of late the people are keen to try alternatives challenging thereby the hereditary provision. Further, the total revolt against the chieftainship and their class is not likely to be resorted to as the distribution of economic resources is not usually unfair. Even the element of economic exploitation is not of any alarming form which could lead to any serious imbalance. As the commoners share and enjoy economic resource, though mainly at the discretion of chief and his assistants, they remain, by and large, quiet and contented. So, even if the hereditary chiefs are replaced, by the educated elites, in near future, the system as such would not collapse. Rather, it is likely to be restructured in the still larger interest of masses. But then the terms of privileges, attached with certain category of people, may not disappear. These would remain in the interest of running the system. As the system of chief-commoner nature has been quite accommodating, in terms of peoples interest, there has been no strong reaction against it from the insiders. Even the outside concerned administration has not cared to lay any hand on it.

On the other hand as the pattern of master-serf stratification always and essentially derived strength from the material or economic base, involving denial to fair resource distribution and more exploitation of serfs, some people have been keen to go for total revolt against the customary system. However, a majority of serf did not expose it or made explicit for reasons of economic oppression, obligation and lack of alternative, though it always remained at the back of their mind. Since people from within the system took this social order forced upon them, they waited for some opportunity to do away with the traditional socio-economic arrangement. Here the enthusing change base lies in economic deprivations. The serfs themselves being economically extremely weak could not organise any large scale movement against the tyranny of their masters. But feeling their pulse the government went for banning the slavery or serfdom. The depressed lot, in general, outrightly supported the move expressing solidarity for total abolition of the system. The change trend, in this case, goes for total abandoning of the traditional system by the new social and economic arrangement proposed by the outside agents of change in consonance with the affected insiders. The latter, in general, opted to support the new systemic arrangement as the customary one was felt as hard and forced upon.

The above structural principles framed in the context of social stratification, as reported among the north-east Indian tribes, may not remain limited only to this situation. In similar stratified social orders, tribal or non-tribal, elsewhere, this kind of structural analysis may hold valid. Further studies on similar lines, in the context of social stratification, are likely to support the structural ideologies as propounded and interpreted in this specific situation of tribal north-east India.

6

NATURE AND MAN
Instance of Cultural Ecology

In the academic discipline of social anthropology a debate regarding nature-man culture relationship has been going on for decades. Ideas of theorists, in this context, have ranged from the explanation of environmental determinism to ecological possibilism. Thus the culture-environment paradigm has been analysed in the cause-effect as well as adaptation perspectives. However, cultural ecology has of late emerged an important approach in the description and analysis of cultures and their variations. This has specially been the case in relevance to primitive cultures rather than those of complex societies. Cultural ecology got into sharp focus in 1955 when Julian Steward conceived this conceptual framework. Subsequent period was marked by many studies on these lines. Simultaneously followed the modifications and criticism that emanated from various corners. Marvin Harris (1969) mapped as a large arena when he perceived cultural structures within the background of ideology, social organisation and techno-economic and techno-environmental parameters. Avoiding determining or causal factor, Harris did talk of adaptive responses while propounding that the ideology and social organisation are adaptive responses to techno-economic and techno-environmental bases.

The development of ideas concerning eco-system involved elements of variance. Ellen (1982) and some others took eco-system as including general ecology taking behaviour and environment together. Andrew Wadya and Roy Rappaport proposed for biological ecology in the orbit of ecological studies of anthropological interest. They did stress on a single science of ecology covering cultural as well as biological dimensions. Cognitivists and other ethno-scientists did suggest of ethno-ecology. Fosbery (1963) included matter and energy while conceiving eco-system. Charles Frake and Harold Conklin have been the pioneers in proposing ethno-ecology as an approach to human ecology. Some others suggested for the inclusion of organic and inorganic and biome and habital in it

(Tanley, 1946).

Even under the climate of polemical arguments the cultural ecological approach in understanding and interpreting culture continued to grow. The humans could develop the mentifact and sociofact dimensions of culture through its artifact purview. Thus, according to Julian Steward cultural ecology involved :

(i) The inter-relationship between environment and exploitative or productive technology ;
(ii) the inter-relationship between behaviour pattern and exploitative technology; and
(iii) the extent to which those behaviour patterns affect other sectors of culture" (1955 : 40-41). Thus could be suggested the interactional analysis of environmental-culturė nexus. The origin and sustenance of many culture traits, customs and institutions could be attributed to and interpreted in respect of adaptive strategy of humans to their environment-physical as well as social. Among others Marshall Sahlins (1969) and James Anderson (1973) have theorised more illuminatingly on these lines. For Sahlins "The truism that cultures are ways of life, taken in a new light, is the ground premise-cultures are human adaptations. Culture, as a design for society's continuity, stipulates its environment" (1969 : 367-68).

The cultural ecologists also search for cultural variation in the adaptation of societies to specific environments. Among others Honigmann makes a very decisive .explanation in this regard, making thereby the formulation of cultural ecology further broad-based. His views contain that "for cultural ecologists the relationship between culture and environment is one of mutual interaction : as society's mode of ordering natural features, whether cognitively or through physical means, frequently leads to changes in the milieu, thereby confronting the society with new challenge to adaptation" (1976 : 287). A very elaborate paradigm of cultural ecology has been provided by James Anderson (1973), though certain part of it bears similarity to those of Honigmann (1976), Marshal Sahlins (1969) and Julian Steward (1955). This is in respect of culture heaving bearing in environment as part of adaptation strategy. The six point format of Anderson's cultural ecological approach encompasses the following :

(1) "Adaptation" is the major process of cultural change.
(2) The analysis of socio-cultural-environmental adaptation serves

to uncover variable that explain the origin of particular cultural features or structures in similar environmental conditions.

(3) The degree and kind of functional interdependence among the parts of culture are not equal; "core features", those closely interrelated with subsistence activities and economic arrangements, have casual priority over "secondary features". Thus similar subsistence problems (relevant environmental and techno-economic relationships) may require social adaptations which have far reaching consequences" (Steward, 1955 : 38). Both culture and environment are divided into relevant and essentially irrelevant parts.

(4) The functional relationship of relevant environmental factors causes certain organisational relationship, which in turn give rise to other relevant aspects of the culture, that is, causation is simple, linear and one-to-one. Analysis is confined to the investigation of the environment and subsistence concerns, that is, to the "relevant" or "effective" environment of the culture core.

(5) The creative cultural core-environmental nexus is usually conceived as intra-cultural and is little effected by historical factors and inter-societal relationships.

(6) The foci of study are the equilibrium plateaus of socio-cultural-environmental systems. Even in diachronic analysis stable adaptations are assumed to exist; the environment is seen for the most part as stable and the result of adaptation is a stable culture core.

In general the evolution status and variation of culture can be understood, perceived and interpreted in three perspectives. One of these pertains to the historicity, diffusion and invention. The second concerns the culture contact and consequent acculturation. And the third is the ecological adaptation. All these three, independently as well as in combination, are of significance in the understanding and explanation of cultural institutions and their continuity. In certain situations, more so where history and culture contact do not speak much, the ecological niches of the regions dominantly contribute in shaping socio-cultural network. The analysis of cultural matrix, as made in the following paragraphs, of the Ladakhis concerns the situation of ecological adaptation, as the chief mechanism in the origin and sustenance of various social and cultural institutions.

It may, however, be made clear that it is not always, and in all cases, that the natural phenomena alone have say in culture. But then the present analysis is an attempt to explore and explain the external environment in the context of certain elements of Ladakhi cultural milieu and with this end in view the following chain of hypothesis could be worked out validity.

1. That man's interaction with man is not always independent of environmental niche. Or, that man's relation with man, in certain situations, can be better understood when man's relation to environment is comprehended.
2. That the nature and arrangement of social groupings has relevance to the ecological framework.
3. That some social institutions seek support from physical conditions prevalent around.
4. That certain cultural elements or items support their origin, in typical forms, from the particular kind of non-human conditions around.
5. That man's adaptation to external ecology is a vital process even in shaping forms of certain designs of living accordingly.

Ladakh is the most north-westernly district of Jammu & Kashmir state of India. It is treated as high altitude or cold desert and human habitations are reported in heights ranging from 9000 to 14000 feet above sea level. Certain hill peaks are perpetually covered with snow. The terrain also marks the hills of loose and crumbling sand, absence of forest vegetation (trees are hardly seen except a few in some valleys), scarcity of rains (annual average rain fall hardly goes beyond inches), ratified, air and scorching sun rays causing dryness, fast winds and arid conditions, dry chill, very thin snowfall and that too on hill tops, scarcity of oxygen, extremely low temperature (going as low as-30° C at some places), narrow valleys with some rivers and tributaries, paucity of cultivable land, bridle paths, physical isolation, very low population density. The moment one crosses Zojila or Rohtang pass one enters into a different kind of ecological niches characteristic of cold high altitude areas. Zojila and other high hill ranges curtail the entry of monsoon into Ladakh. The region gives a desolated and barren look. Snow avalanches, frowning weather and freezing cold have fatal consequences. Bare mountains and forbidding climate helped retain the remoteness and isolation of the region. Blades of grass are few and far between and there are low thorny monotonous vegetation. The winter is long and severe. Life under such external conditions is mighty hard and difficult. However, people have been surviving there for centuries under remarkable adaptation of their life and culture. And this is well evident in man-society-culture-nature network of relationship.

Ladakh is predominantly a tribal district. More numerous of the tribes is popularly known as Ladakhi. The synonyms to this ethnic group are the Bhot, Bodh, Botpa, Bhautta etc. Among the earliest inhabitants of the region are the Mon and Dard ethnic groups. Gara and Beda tribals are also reported from almost all the large sized villages of Ladakh. The history of Ladakh supports that over the years there has been blending of various population groups. The so called Aryan stock, represented by the Dards and the Mons, mixed up with the people of Mongolian origin. It is explained that the present day Ladakhis, including Chanspas of Chang-Thang area, and the Baltis represent a mixed Aryan-Mongolian element. The Ladakhis are Buddhist and the Baltis profess Islam. Argon, another ethnic group in Ladakh, originated from Bhot mother and Muslim father. The latter came as traders. In spite of inter-mixing among various other ethnic groups, the Dards continue to represent as a different racial group. Those Dards who adopted Buddhism were termed as Dogpa or Brogpa and they now form a distinct ethnic group.

To avoid fast chilly winds, that blow in Ladakh, and for reasons of availability of pasture and cultivable land the villages in Ladakh are either in and along valleys or on the foot-hills. The valleys run parallel to river sides. The foot-hill village settlements are usually adjoining to those hills whose peaks perpetually remain covered with snow. The melting of this snow in summer months provides water for irrigation of agriculture fields. Because of the typical terrain and environmental conditions of Ladakh the people settle themselves in places where cultivable land, grazing ground, drinking water springs and irrigation resource are available. Simultaneously the settlement area is to be declared free of evil spirits. In the event of non-availability of such provision the proposed village site is rejected. This may be the reason that for miles together no human habitation is reported. What one confronts are the naked and crumbling hills posing for a desolated look. The above explanations speak of the pattern of village settlement in consideration of the environmental adaptation in the best interest of survival. Human adaptability is again reflected in house design. To escape from severe winter, by not going out, in the first floor of a Ladakhi house is kept an apartment used as latrine. It has a hole through which the human waste goes to the ground floor. The human excreta is covered with thin sand layer. To respond to the call of nature people do not venture to go out to escape from the severity of winter. The human waste keeps on piling up and in summer months it is transported to agriculture fields and used as a manure.

For mounting physical isolation of the region the Ladakhis try to meet out their needs of food, clothing, shelter etc., locally. Extreme cold and arid climatic conditions required special kind of food and clothing. To survive under arid conditions the Ladakhis drink butter tea. One may consume as many as twenty cups of this tea every day. In the high altitude desert of Ladakh a person suffers from breathlessness while walking fast or while carrying heavy load. To avoid this the donkeys and yaks are used as pack animals. The men and women carry only small weight and that too on their backs. Like the butter a large part of the Ladakhi clothing and shelter requirements are met by the material procured from the livestock which the Ladakhis domesticate. From yak's hair are made the ropes, knee long shoes and the tents. Wool from goat and sheep is used for making warm clothes. Goat and sheep skin is used as back wear by the women. Such a skin wear protects the garment worn by the ladies. The sole of the Ladakhi shoes are made out of the locally prepared woollen threads.

The songs and dances of Ladakhis are of extremely slow nature. They are never fast. Songs are normally duats; when one sings a line, the other relaxes by keeping quiet and *vice-versa*. In dancing the movement of body and legs are quite slow and smooth. Generally the Ladakhis avoid brisk physical movements. Arrangements are so made that they involve minimum of exertion. Any over-exertion in the height of Ladakh is risky to life. Because of high altitude and absence of vegetation, the oxygen content in the air is too less. Constant physical exertion makes one tired and exhausted at a faster rate. Breathlessness is often reported because one has to breathe faster to inhale the required quantity of oxygen. In order to overcome such difficulties, the Ladakhis have devised ways to avoid over exertions. Slow physical action, in various forms, help in the matter. People have adjusted their ways accordingly.

The force of gushing water in the hills is used to operate water mill meant for grinding grain. From Indus river and its tributaries the villagers divert water into small channels. In summer months this water flows with great force. The villagers have identified spots where the fall of water is more forceful. With this force of water move the stony wheels of flour mill. The movement of the wheels helps grind the grain. In winter months the water gets frozen and hence the flour mill does not work. As such the families manage for sufficient stock of flour in summer months for use in winter. The flour so stored does not spoil because of extremely cold climate of Ladakh.

Under the condition of extremely low rainfall, dryness and severe winter, when the water of rivers and springs get frozen for months together, the Ladakhis are very careful of the use of water. People use water carefully and miserly and worship water springs. The life, say fish, within water source is also protected. The Ladakhis neither catch fish nor consume the same. At the same time they recognise spring gods. People have devised means, as part of adaptation, to preserve the sources of water and to appease the gods responsible for the same. When a man dies, his wife is not allowed to cross the water channels flowing in the village settlement. The water of such channels is either lifted from the river or originates from the melting of snow on high hill tops. In the event of death of a wife the husband is also forbidden to cross such water channels. A common belief is that crossing of the channels would annoy the water gods. This may lead to drying up of the channels causing hardship to their economic survival. It may further be mentioned that the taboo against crossing water channels is also observed after the delivery of a woman. At the time of delivery of a woman and for seven subsequent days, her husband also stays with her inside the house. This custom is known as *Pakzam* or *Pankh*. Under this state the husband and wife are forbidden to cross water channels for a period of one month. If they ignore this taboo the wrath of *Lhu* (a water spirit) would affect the couple in particular and the village community in general. To cope up with the situation the concerned persons either stay back in the house for a period of one month or manage to live in the house of a *Phasphun* (a close social group member) whose house is so located that one need not cross any water channel while moving out. When no such arrangement is made the concerned person makes temporary tent shelter at a convenient place and manages to stay there for a month.

To adapt to the challenge of scarce resources and to meet the connected requirement of curbing sharp population rise the Ladakhis opted for sparing atleast one, if not more, son from each family to join the monastery. As a customary practice the youngest son has been the preferred choice for the purpose. He would invariably join *Lama* (monk) fraternity. While dedicating a son to such a cause of serving the religion, in adaptation to environmental pressure, certain prescriptions are to be observed. In addition to rituals, meant for the occasion, some life long taboos are to be observed. He has to devote to the religious learning and preaching. He takes the vow not to marry. Once initiated to Lamahood the boy has to leave his family of orientation and find an abode in the monastery premises. And the rest of his life is spent there. Because of special kind of relationship between man, nature and religion the Ladakhis remain obliged to the monastic organisation. The intricacy of such relationship reflects in the economic and political life of the Ladakhis. The Ladakhis make effort to enrich the *Gompa* (monastery) resource by making contributions in cash and kind. This is done directly or through the Lamas who perform various kinds of worship in the interest of common masses. For their religious services the Lamas are served meals in addition to nominal payment in cash and kind. The latter are usually deposited in the monastery. The Ladakhis are very submissive to monasteries and the religiousmen who guide their destiny. The people feel that even their economic life is sustained and grows under the blessings of Lamas and their ritual performances to contain some of the hard ecological elements. The more complicated disputes are resolved with the help of senior Lamas and their sacred literature. This is done in the campus of monastery. The composition of village council, especially the selection of its headman (the *Goba*), if finalised in consultation with senior Lamas.

In a Ladakhi family the interpersonal relations are predominantly free of inhibitions and constraints. Among the members of a family the discourse and expression are taboo free. Likewise the restraints are not reported at the level of talking, mixing, eating, drinking, singing, dancing etc. Factors like age, sex and kinship are not imposing in the sense of curtailment of liberty in behaviour. The women do not veil their face and are free to directly talk to any member of the family without any feeling of reservation. Element of privacy does not seem to carry much of a significance. As per the interpretation of Ladakhis themselves they cannot afford inhibitions in intra-family interaction. So much so that all members of a family share a common room for sleeping. This room has a fire place and in long winter the fire keeps burning inside this room. Fire in separate rooms cannot be afforded because of an extreme scarcity of fire-wood. The region is excessively devoid of forest and other vegetation. The family members have adjusted to sharing a common room without conceiving the concept of privacy. They all sleep around the common fire place. This is also the place where they indulge in sex. Such an adaptation to the environmental condition may have been one of the reasons why sex is not associated with the feeling of sanctity. Pre as well as extra marital sex relations are of frequent occurrence. They are not taken with much of seriousness. Consequently the social problems connected with sex are not of much concern.

As in case of intra-family relationship, the pattern of family structure also speaks of instance of adaptability to the difficult conditions in Ladakh. In native sense the family corresponds to household. The latter are of two major types which seek their origin in external ecology. In emic sense the major household is termed Khangchen and is composed of a man, his wife and unmarried children when they all live in the ancestral house. The second type of household is termed *Khaon* which comes into being after sometime of the marriage of one or more sons. Generally a Khaon originates when the married son begets a child. At such a stage the parents of the married son get separated and establish Khaon form of family unit. They are also joined by their unmarried sons and daughters who, too, leave the Khangchen. In the Khangchen are left only the married son/sons, their wife/wives and the unmarried children born of such union. Such kinds of family arrangements among the Ladakhis have deep roots in environmental milieu. To overcome hard external ecology of Ladakh, all able bodied persons have to work hard for their survival. Except the physically handicapped and the minor children the rest of the people are not permitted, within the customary framework, to live as dependents of others. As the married sons have to support their own children in Khangchen, the parents and their unmarried children, if any, have to earn their living through hard work. Dependence on others is largely discouraged as the other themselves remain hard pressed. The separated members constituting Khaon are given a part of agriculture land and the livestock. They chiefly sustain on the same, apart from what they earn otherwise, and thus avoid burdening their married sons. The latter are left to look after their own progeny. The system of Khaon demands even the aged parents to put in hard toil till they breathe last.

Other than the above structural arrangement is a feature that again has bearing to the family composition. Usually the family size, in most of the cases, differs in summer and winter months. This is not because of birth and death factors. It is observed that family size is comparatively large in winter. This is because most of its members then remain confined to the house and village. Extreme winter curtails their mobility. On the other hand many members move out of the village during the summer season. This is necessitated for reason of grazing the cattle. With the start of summer the new grazing ground are available at still higher altitude. And it is then that the able bodied youngmen move out with herds of cattle including goat and sheep which the Ladakhis rear in large number. With rising summer they keep on shifting to higher reaches. The approach of summer causes melting of snow at higher elevations providing thereof more grazing grounds. It is for about five months that the Ladakhis migrate to greater heights stage by stage alongwith their herds. Later on they gradually start returning with the start of winter season and ultimately join back their family members who were left behind. Such course of migration and the route thereof are well defined. And the Ladakhis have been following the same for centuries.

Environmental hardships also account for the existence of certain tribal customary laws. People have evolved and sustained the same as part of adaptation to locally prevalent geographical conditions. Experience of living in the heights of Ladakh led people to do the same. Otherwise the existence would have been difficult. The rule of male primogeniture in their inheritance pattern is a glaring example of adaptation. The terrain of Ladakh could provide only small cultivable landholdings. And for their economic viability they were to be kept intact and unfragmented. Any fragmentation would render them uneconomic. As the agriculture produce under the climatic conditions of Ladakh is already meagre (people can take only one crop a year) any fragmentation may further reduce it. Male primogeniture could be one protective legislation against the land fragmentation. And this is how the Ladakhis could make maximum use of the limited cultivable land resource. When the economic resource remained with the eldest brother the other brothers in the family cooperated with him.

The custom of fraternal polyandry has been an inseparable part of Ladakhi social organisation from very early time. The persistence of this custom could be attributed chiefly to economic constraint which found root in imposingly harsh physical conditions of Ladakh region. People realised that economic sustenance of a large population could not have been possible with very meagre agriculture produce. In Ladakh there is only one agriculture season which too is a short one. In rest of the months the region remains under minus temperature when nothing can be grown on the soil. Even otherwise the cultivable land is extremely limited because of high hills and undulating terrain. Because of insufficient rainfall the Ladakhi farmers chiefly make use of water produced by melting of snow on high peaks. As the river water flows at a lower level, most of them are unable to make use of it for irrigation of fields which are at slightly higher elevation. The water emanating from high peaks is diverted to the agriculture fields as required. Primitive agriculture tools and technology have their own drawback in the matter. Animal husbandry is a subsidiary occupation. For grazing of domesticated animals the Ladakhis move from place to place as the availability of pasturage is governed by weather conditions at different altitudes.

When others moved out with the herds one brother was left behind to look after the family. Even if the Ladakhis could explore and exploit such diverse economic resources they remained hard pressed. Whatever they produced was insufficient to support any fast population rise. And one of the ways of curtailing population rise could be the introduction of polyandrous system in their social structure. Under this pattern two to three brothers shared a common wife. The progeny from her would be certainly less than from what could be if all brothers kept separate wives, that is if they were monogamous. In the event of monogamous or even polygynous custom the number of children produced would have been much higher. The polyandrous pattern also suited to the requirement of looking after the common wife when other brothers had to leave the house with the herds of cattle to still higher reaches. To provide fillip to the sustenance of polyandrous system even the then royalty, consisting of *Gyalpo* (the King) and the *Kalhon* (Prime Minister), patronized it by according it a higher positive values. Simultaneously the survival and continuance of the system were further assured through the rule of male primogeniture inheritance which the Ladakhi society promulgated and retained. In the event of property inheritance by the eldest brother the other brothers, under the condition of isolation of the region, had no alternative but to join him in common wedlock. The common wife entitled them to survive on the property which the eldest brother inherited. Considering the impositions of hard ecology even the religion provided support and protection to the custom of polyandry. The monasteries kept provision for the absorption of females, who could not marry for reason for polyandry, into the fold of monastic organisation.

Such women were directed to dedicate themselves to the cause of religion. They were not to marry and took a vow of celibacy. They also shaved their head and wore particular kind of dress suggested by the monastery. The were then termed as *Chomos* (the nuns) and remained devoted to religious pursuits. If this cover, in the garb of Chomo formation, won't have been provided, these surplus unmarried women could be a problem in society. Even the formation of *Lamas* (the monks) helped curb the population rise as they also remained unmarried and devoted to learning and preaching of religion. They were also attached with the monasteries. Under the polyandrous pattern certain rituals have been there which provided social sanction to brothers to join a common wife. For instance the brother of the one who is actually getting married is to go, as a customary practice, to the bride's house to fetch her to the bridegroom's place, that is, of one's own elder brother. Such a practice guaranteed the brother's access, as an additional husband, to the female whom he escorted for his brother is whose name the marriage is being formally organised. In another ritual the brothers who are joining the common wife are made to wear a Khatak each on their head. A Khatak is a kind of scarf which carries religious significance.

It may be mentioned that in polyandrous as well as the monogamous patterns of marriage the age at marriage has been comparatively high among the Ladakhis. Generally the Ladakhi girls marry around the age of eighteen years and the boys around twenty four years. The child marriages are unheard of unless some cohusband could be of younger age. The higher age of marriage can be explained in tune with ecological adaptation. People explain that if a marriage is arranged at an early age the husband/s would not be able to support the family under hard environmental conditions. When they are grown up and matured enough the subsistence can be ensured. Then the late marriage could also be in the interest of restraining number of children in family.

Kinship relations and kin-based groups have an important place in societies. And they involve a variety of duties, rights, privileges, obligations, taboos, prescriptions etc. Implications of kinship organization are also defined in terms of reciprocities. Ladakhi society, for the matter, is no exception. It's analysis at family and *Gyut* (lineage) levels support the arguments. But in Ladakhi society if we go beyond *Gyut* the hold of kinship declines. It may be mentioned that the clan organisation does not exist among the Ladakhis. But then a social group, popularly referred to as Phasphun, is of very great significance among them. And the origin and sustenance of such a group derive their strength from the difficult environmental setting. While setting down at some place the Ladakhis search for favourable living conditions. And since such conditions are not reported at many places, the village settlements have come up at far off places from one another.

The Ladakhi villages are dispersed far apart from one another. In the event of any emergency the relatives living in far off villages cannot be easily contacted. It has been so because of difficult terrain and other weather limitations. In the past the means of communication have been extremely poor. At the same time one could not afford to wait for long for a relative to reach to help in the problem. To overcome this difficulty in the arena of human interaction people thought of alternative close group formation to keep up reciprocal dimension of human requirement. The idea of forming social group at local level, beyond kinship consideration, came to the forefront. One such social group among the Ladakhis is known as *Phasphun*. Under Phasphun organisation a few families, living in near vicinity, form their social groups irrespective of their being related or non-related through kinship ties. Members of the families in a Phasphun render mutual help and cooperation on all occasions, especially those connected to sad and festive situations. Such situations may arise on the occasions of birth, death, marriage etc. The families in a Phasphun worship common god and pledge support to one another. An annual worship of this god is resorted to. It may, however, be mentioned that of late the availability of help from various non-traditional agencies and institutions has already started adversely affecting the very spirit of Phasphun group. For a few problems, say those concerning disease, delivery etc., lately provided infrastructural facilities can be depended upon to some extent, more so if they exist in close proximity. But for many other requirements the Phasphun organisation is still depended upon. For clarity it would be better to state that the members of Phasphun are also mutually referred to as Phasphun. It is obligatory on their part to reciprocate for a healthy and happy living. Then the families are free to change their Phasphuns if they migrate to some other place. The Phasphun composition is flexible.

Phasphun group includes families from the same tribe. Such tribal groups are Ladakhis, Gara, Mon, Beda, Chanspa, Balti, etc. Phasphuns are, by and large, ethnic and religion specific. In emergency even the families from lower ethnic groups are rendered help. People consider avoiding low social status groups as Phasphun. However on many occasions people were found observing close relation forgetting their social gradation and religious diversity. For instance in *Nang Dung* (a birth ceremony), being observed in a Ladakhi family, even the Balti and Argon participate. In historical perspective the religion, say Buddhism, Islam or Christianity in Ladakh, never stood in the way of people being integrated in a social whole to achieve particular ends. One of the major reasons for this kind of integration has been their adaptation to the difficult natural conditions and the challenge they pose to human existence. People have been having no alternative but to stand together to meet the challenge of hazardous external environmental conditions for a smooth living. They could not afford to uphold rigidity in terms of ethnicity and religion. But of late the culture contact is giving way to parochial and narrow considerations at the cost of earlier integrated order of society in Ladakh in general.

Like many other culture traits a life-cycle ritual also poses as an instance of ecological adaptation. This is regarding disposal of dead. Ladakhis have two provisions of treating a dead body. According to one they cut the dead body into pieces and throw the same either on the hill tops, covered with snow, or in the running water of Indus and its tributary. The latter is done in summer months. It may be mentioned that even the river water gets frozen in winter months. The second method to which the Ladakhis resort involves cremation of dead. But in the face of shortage of firewood the cremation is done in a particular style. This speaks of adaptation to fuel wood shortage. The legs of the dead person are twisted to the extent that it assumes a sitting posture. Both the hand are brought closer. The body, in this posture, is then tied with the ropes and is inserted in a narrow round hole made in the centre of a square shaped stony platform. This platform has an opening underneath through which the Ladakhis insert fuel pieces to burn the dead body. Such a procedure is adopted by the Ladakhis to save the wastage of flames which could otherwise happen if the body was not placed in the hole of this platform. The severe winds that blow in Ladakh would disturb the flames from hitting at the target if it could be a cremation in open and thus more fuel consumption would be there. Under the growing new avenues of fuel availability the above procedure of disposal of dead is, in some cases, getting replaced by the procedure of normal cremation which many of the Ladakhis have otherwise seen in the event of death of non-Ladakhi Hindus serving in the region. However, their human habitation in higher reaches remain unaffected of their procedure of disposal of dead. The fuel wood or dry bushes is still a rare commodity in Ladakh and this has kept up the traditional practices to a large extent.

For the last three decades the region of Ladakh has experienced fast exposure to outsiders. Places of importance have been connected through roads. More communication has been established with other important trade centres of the country. As a consequence of such conditions, as also of some others like development of tourism, a large influx of people into Ladakh has occurred. Thousands of people have come to Ladakh in services, both civil and defence, and trade. The contact of local population with the non-Ladakhis has grown of an intimate nature. It was never so before. Over the years the contact has become more regular. Development of Ladakh region for various purposes has led to the creation of employment opportunities of various kinds. Now thousands of Ladakhis are in employment on regular or daily wage basis. The processes of the above kind have generated many non-traditional sources of earning and income. People do not now exclusively depend on traditional sources. Many alternatives have been thrown open. Supply of substitutes for many items of daily use in now better maintained. Formal education, especially at school level, has fast expanded. A comparatively good network of communication through road transport and air has been created. Things have gone beyond the imagination of Ladakhis. Advanced technology of outsiders has made the Ladakhis realise that certain things which could never happen, as per native conception, have really happened. Income of Ladakhis has largely increased, though with new aspirations.

Under the rise of new conditions the man-nature relationship of earlier kind has also shown signs of change. Such a trend has then correspondingly reflected on certain connected areas of Ladakhi life and culture. In some of the cultural items, already mentioned in the running matter under context, the past rigid adherence has been shakened. The difficulties posed by the hard natural conditions, that carried say in certain cultural elements, are not exactly realised in the traditional sense of their explanation alone. The relief to the same through man-made new opportunities brought from outside has had its place in the matter. Now with more money, better awareness, availability of things, emergence of alternative occupations and faster mobility, the Ladakhis do not look at certain cultural items in the old spirit and arrangement of man-nature-culture. People have got alternative ways of adaptation to new social and economic environments. Nature, in some sense, is no longer found that imposing because of viable alternatives to which the Ladakhis recourse to.

The earlier taboos connected to physical movements after birth and death in family are no longer observed by some people. They cannot afford to stay back in the house for one month in the event of birth and death. New economic opportunities created new outlook among them. The treatment with dead body has also undergone some change for reason of availability of fuel. But simultaneously the integrated nature of society has taken a new look. People do not feel as integrated as before. However, many parts of old cultural arrangements and adjustments still go strong and are yet to properly crystalise into new forms. But then the picture of transitional phase is not to be lost sight of for the purpose of cultural interpretations.

As referred to earlier the contact and interaction with outsiders led to the opening of new economic channels for the Ladakhis. The change started easing that situation when a Ladakhi had to look for his existence only on the meagre natural and inherited resource which, as the Ladakhis realised, could not sustain the large population. The alternative economies (based on labour wage, employment, internal trade etc.) provided after the opening of area to outsiders led to certain changes in life and culture of the people. Economic betterment and growing awareness led people to fast switch over to monogamous form of marriage. The can now economically afford to maintain exclusive wife and the children born of such monogamous union. However, the instance of polyandry continues though at a much less scale than what it used to be earlier when new economic means were not there. The hold of monastery, more so in economic life of a Ladakhi, has also undergone some change. The institution of nunnery, in its old form, has drastically changed. However, the formation of Chomo and Lama continues in Ladakhi society though at a less intensity. The Chomos now largely stay in their houses. But they do observe celibacy and devote to religious life. The inheritance pattern of male primogeniture has also been under attack in the light of changing conditions when polyandry is no longer the pressing requirement for adaptation to local environmental conditions. Likewise in the process of change there is marked some lack of commitment to obligation in respect of the monastery and its organisation, more so in terms of reinforcing its economic resources.

The above explanations support that persistence of and fixity to certain aspects of traditional Ladakhi culture are now reported alongwith some element of change. The strong reason for persistence can be traced to the continuity of typical environmental cosmos. The centuries old relationship of economic arrangements (that is the core features), religion and social organisation has not ceased to exist to any significant extent. However, the rise of certain new provisions in the ecological niche of Ladakh, as introduced through the wider network of communication, development agencies, deployment of military and paramilitary forces etc., have to some extent influenced the thinking, perception and attitude of some people in Ladakhi society. Cultural ecological studies will still be going a long way in this unique region where people have adapted to severest conditions of high altitude cold desert.

7

MAN AND SPIRIT

The Basis of Ritual Performance

'Holism' finds a very prominent place in the theoretic realm of the academic discipline of Social Anthropology. The focus remains on the inter-connectedness of major aspects of social organisation and culture. To what extent one aspect influences or is influenced by the other may not, in the event of diversity in human societies, be uniform. Such kind of variance is reported in time as well as space. But then the existence of certain common trends in respect of human interactions and inter-relationship are not ruled out. The portrait of a social structure may not be property sketched unless the major aspects of life are analysed in the entirely of social ways. A social anthropologist's approach, in this context, is well defined and the methodological tools are sharp enough to account for ongoing life designs at organisation and structural levels. Holistic approach, though time consuming, provides for exhaustiveness when one explores and unfolds ways of life systematically. The argument finds support in the explanation of Ladakhi life and culture with the help of monastery, its organisational and the religious tenets thereof. However, when one element is taken to explain other areas of social structure, it does not necessarily mean that this element alone is solely responsible for a particular happening or trend. In certain cases some other elements also have their say in the matter. The social-cultural analyst has to, then, define priorities in terms of viability of such elements. Those in closer relevance find prominent place in the explanations. It would then not be wrong to say that it depends on the social analyst how well he/she can highlight the role of single or multiple factors in the description and analysis of a social system keeping in view the interest of an exhaustive ethnography. But as part of clarity one has to justify the explanations while taking main and the subsidiary factors as contributing to the maintenance of particular aspects of culture.

The life and culture of the Ladakhis are strongly religion ridden. Religion, as a matter of fact, is a dominant force and its manifestations are revealed in many areas of Ladakhi culture. While studying Ladakhi society Bamzai (1962) and Bhandari (1970) have observed that religious contents, one or more, provide a great incentive to the people to keep up traditional cultural *status quo.* It is believed that religious attributes provide them a sense of security under the more difficult ecological conditions. The religion of Ladakhis can be better discussed in the context of their social organisation, economic structure and political arena (Mann, 1978). People seem to be highly obliged to religiousmen and they favourably respond to most of their calls. What Moorcraft (1937) observed in his time continues to largely hold true even today. According to Moorcraft Lamaism seems to be the dictator of their destinies and the words of a Lama (monk), however, inconsistent and unbelievable they may be to a man of common sense, are nevertheless law for them. People are under the sway of Lamas who act as their guides, advisors and liberators from sufferings. Anything concerning *Gompa* (monastery), *Kushak* (head of a monastery), *Lama* (monk), *Chomo* (nun) and other associated religious men in hierarchy is commonly and uniformly respected. Labha, Chanspa, Onpo, Amchi etc. are some other religiousmen among the Ladakhis.

In one form or the other religion and its organisation meet the socio-psychological and even economic needs and requirements of the people. There is a great deal of inter-dependence between the people and those belonging to sacred hierarchy. Of how much significance the religion is to a Ladakhi is well depicted by the abundance of religious institutions, rituals and places reported in the region. These exist at family, village and regional levels. For instance at family level are *Chot-kangs* (family worship room). There is either *Vihara* (mini monastery) or Gompa at village level and where higher order worship is arranged and which contain the force of religious persons. A group of villages, having Viharas, recognise one common Gompa for meeting out their requirements. It may be mentioned that in addition to a large number of Viharas there are nearly thirty-five Gompas in Ladakh. How much faith the Ladakhi have in religious attributes can also be assessed from Gompa festivals. While participating in Hemis Gompa fair I observed thousands of Ladakhi men, women, and children who had gathered to worship and to observe the display of their cultural heritage symbolised in various forms. The devil dances, so meaningful to the Ladakhis, were arranged on the occasion. More of the expressions reflected demonology and Lamaism which gave rise to certain definite philosophical arena to the people.

In addition to Chotkang, Vihara and Gompa there are Chortens and Manes which represent the other important religious structures. On some of the rocks are found carved gigantic figures of some gods and goddesses. Also reported are the prayer wheels of various sizes fitted at various points in the area inhabited by the Ladakhis.

The feeling that the Ladakhis thrive well under the blessings of religious men creates necessity of worship and rituals of various forms and contents. Blessings are believed to be showered by the Lamas through such performances. At the same time the religious men are believed to have power and influence connected to various walks of Ladakhi life. Over centuries the persistence of faith in spirits has greatly been maintained. What Featherstone (1926) stressed on the basis of his observations continues to hold true. He asserted that people have great faith in spirits and devils. Herein lies mostly the source of power of the Lamas, who alone are able to control these demons in terror of which the natives spend their lives. The people are ready to believe anything in Lamas tell and are always on the look out for omens, lucky and unlucky days.

Among a few other typical features characterising Ladakh (the most north-westernly district of Jammu & Kashmir state of India) is one of the existence of monasteries. The latter have existed over centuries with a close and intimate bearing on the life and culture of the people belonging to Buddhist religious faith. Many accounts on Ladakh refer to it as the land of monasteries, Viharas and Lamas. There is a well defined connection between a Gompa and the Viharas in its jurisdiction. Such a connection is expressed through links of various kinds including spiritual and the temporal ones. The common masses and the Lamas are well aware of such linkages and bonds. This equally applies to yellow and red sects of Buddhism that are reported in Ladakh. Such an arrangement speaks of wider network of monastic structure covering even the remotest settlements of Ladakhis. There are numerous other religious structures having linkages, in one form or the other, with the Gompas and Viharas. To a new entrant in Ladakh it sounds as if the religious attributes are over shadowing human life in this isolated and remote regions. And this holds true to a considerable extent. It is chiefly the Gompas and Viharas which have occupied the highest elevations of human settlements and have control over many walks of life. The organisational pattern of monastery is so scientifically designed that all activities, in and outside the monastery, run smooth. The social and religious/spiritual control in the monastery are strong and intact and the same is reflected when their extension to society is analysed.

Buddhism of Ladakh is a mixture of Bon, the old religion of Tibet, Tantrism and Mahayana. Some have also referred to Lamaism as the religion of the Ladakhis. Under the above religious canopy people worship various gods and goddesses and identify spirits of various forms. The concept of their divinity carries three dimensions *viz.* Gautama Buddha (*Sangyas)*, religious principles inculcated by *Buddha* (chhos kon chok) and the Lamas following these principles (Gendun Kon Chok). Demonology and idolatry are the other components of Ladakhi religion. Existence of certain primitive traits in the Ladakhi religion is believed to be the continuance of relics of Bon or Pon religion. The prevalence of mystic doctrines is still retained. Although Buddhism is now the prevailing faith people still worship and make offerings to some old divinities such as gods and spirits of hills, fields, tree, water etc. The accounts of evil spirits and traces of sacrifice are also reported among the Bhoto. There is a great deal of *Tantrism*. The activities and techniques under *Tantric Buddhism* are used for good and evil. It has been explained that a decadent form of Buddhism is Tantrism and it has been so owing more to ancient Bon religion, and also shamanism and animism. References reveal that before Lamaism two earlier religions flourished in Ladakh. These were Bonchos and Buddhism. Many features of both of these are embodied in the present day Lamaism. The Bon religion dates back to time immemorial in Tibet and the neighbouring territory and is described by Waddel as animistic, devil dancing or shamanist. It flourished in western Tibet from the earliest times down to A.D. 1300. when it's major form practically died out, though much of its ritual and demonology were absorbed by Buddhism and later by Lamaism. Lamaism itself is a big pantheon and includes diverse kinds of religious persons and the activities thereof. Broadly the Lamas are graded into three categories namely *Chung-Tung* (a beginner Lama or one who is just initiated to Lamahood). *Gheesul* (one who successfully completes his five to seven years of trial period as Chung-Tung) and *Gallong* (one who maintains Gheesul constraints and attains the age of about 25 years). He is then supposed to be expert in religious understanding. Seng-Nak is another category and it refers to a Gallong who devotes largely to meditations. Like the Lamas the Chomos have also been categorized. A beginner Chomo is known as Geyen Ma. In her next promotion she becomes Ghesul Ma and finally Gallong Ma. The Lamas in a monastery are also divided into spiritual and temporal sections. The components of the two are as below:

Spiritual Section

1. Kushok	—	An incarnation
2. Lobon	—	An abbot
3. Chos Timpa	—	Who controls religious meetings

4. Chhomspon — Who directs the religion.

Temporal Section

1. Chhag Jot — Treasurer
2. Nyerchhen — Steward
3. Nyerpa — Storekeeper
4. Phi-Nyer — Farm steward.

It may be mentioned that among the Lamas the level of attainment differs. As already mentioned the Gompa organization has two major dimensions : One represented by the purely religious persons and the other by civic ones. Those who perform the latter functions are also the Lamas. That way the number of Lamas is large but only a few are given the formally recognized civic position. The incumbents against such positions keep on changing, depending more on the will of *Kushok* (the chief of the monastery). However the positions achieved through religious attainment do not involve change on Kushok's will. The spiritual and temporal positions, in order, and as described by the informants include Kushok, Khonbo, Chhag-jot, Lobon, Nirpa, Gey-Kos, Umjey, Uchung, Chhamon, Chhabrel Chama and Kornniar.

The field explorations are revealing of the fact that monastic organisation in Ladakh has an important place in the social structure of the people. The wide spread feeling and belief among the Ladakhis is that they thrive well under the blessings of religiousmen occupying Gompa premises. And such a background demands for necessity of worship. The Lamas shower their blessings chiefly through worship which may be in various forms. The religiousmen of the monastery are generally believed to have power and influence in various walks of life. They are even said to have control over spirits and devils which the Ladakhis identify. In this state of affairs the people believe in whatever the Lamas say or suggest. Their directives are specially adhered to under the difficult environmental conditions of human existence. Under such conditions the religious attributes, provided, encouraged and propagated through monastic organisation, find lot of intervention in social organisation, economic structure and the arena of social control. People straightway admit that they are highly obliged to the religious order and to those who carry it forward. And the majority of Ladakhis respond favourably to the call of religiousmen. All events and matters concerning Gompa, Kushok and Lamas are almost uniformly respected without any fear of contradiction from any corner.

There is great deal of interdependence between people and the sacred order. Monastic order takes care of the community and the community looks after the interests of monastery and its occupants. Educative role of Gompa is of no less value. Even some professional specialists maintain links with Lamas and depend on Gompa in many instances. As an example Lharje or *Amchi* (A medicineman) and *Chanspa* (a spiritualist) do prescribe certain remedial measures against sufferings including disease. Such prescriptions are to be organised by some Lama of the monastic order. The Lamas are given first position in any function they are invited to. People have easy access to Lamas who are major links between the monastery and Ladakhi community.

Ladakh has been an area where people of diverse ethnic groups and races have been mixing in physical sense of the word. Dard and Mon Aryans got mixed up with those of Mongolian origin. In present population of Ladakh Chanspa of Chang Thang area and the Baltis represent the Mongolian element. The Baltis profess Islam and the Ladakhis are Buddhists. In addition to Dards and Mons the Bedas also represent the Aryan element. However, for reasons of inter-mixing the Mons and the Bedas do not seem to be categorically different from the Ladakhis. The Dards continue to represent as a different racial group. Those Dards who adopted Buddhist faith came to be known as Dogpa or Brogpa. The population composition of present Ladakh largely includes Ladakhi, Gara, Beda, Balti, Argon, Chanspa or Changpas, Dogpa, Brogpa, Dard, Tibetan etc.

The Mons and Dards are stated to be the earliest inhabitants of the region. Subsequently people came in from neighbouring Baltistan, Tibet and Central Asia. Now most of the bigger villages of Ladakhi have one or two families of Mon, Gara and Beda. The Ladakhi is not generic category. Rather it is a specific ethnic group with synonyms of Bhat, Bot, Botpa, Bhautta etc. It is also stated that Bhots are migrants from Tibet, who in due course of time, adopted Buddhism. But then some Ladakhis also point out that their ancestors came from Mongolia as well as Tibet between 500 to 600 A.D. Because of this background the Ladakhis living towards Kargil are termed as *Pot rik*, meaning Tibetan generation. Cunningham gave Mongolian origin of the Ladakhis and further stated that they now differ from the Mongolians because of the admixture of Hindu blood.

Because of being strong religion ridden the Ladakhis are always crazy for attaining religious merit and blessings. Many events in Ladakhi life are based on the achievement of religious merit. And the importance of religious merit is transmitted through the Lamas. Lamas have prescribed ways of imbibing religious merit which is believed to help in the present and future life. Along road, bridle paths and even on other spots one often comes across religious structures like 'Manes' and 'Chhortens'. While passing by their side the structures are kept to the right. Further a passerby would normally keep a stone on Mane structure thereby adding to its strength. Many stones used in Mane formation are having inscription of sacred hymn., *Om Mane Padma Hum*. The passerby would also repeat this hymn as many times as he/she likes. All this helps acquire personal religious merit. Similar to this is the practice of rotating the prayer wheel containing folded sacred literature prepared by the Lamas. One may rotate the wheel while sitting or even in course of walk when they carry smaller wheels. Some also indulge in rotating the bigger prayer wheels fixed at numerous places around. The old persons are often seen rotating the prayer wheels. They also indulge in counting the beads of a rosary. Such a counting goes on even when the Ladakhis indulge in talking. All the above actions help acquire religious merit. More they rotate the prayer wheels and more they resort to counting of beads of rosary, more religious merit they are believed to acquire.

In certain incidences the religious men also suggest to the fast repetition of these actions. The even suggest for installation of small sized flags and banners imprinted with the sacred hymn of *Om Mane Padma Hum*. Such installation is done on the top of the houses or on points at higher elevation where force of wind is more to wave the flags faster. The installation of flags is not for decoration but for the acquisition of religious merit. Higher would be the level of attainment of religious merit when the flags wave faster. The merit ensures of a happy and prosperous life for all inmates of the building where the flags are flying. The Lamas prepare these flags and suggest to the villagers for their installation. For general welfare of the masses such flags are hoisted on tree tops and the monasteries. Thus the monastic organisation has instilled the concept of religious merit. Objects of material culture, in their symbolic form, like the wooden and metallic prayer wheels and flags made of cloth carry religious value and help inculcate the same among the people.

Among Ladakhis the house construction commences only after the particular site is cleared by the Lamas. Such a clearance pertains to evil spirits and devils. After making religious calculations the Lamas approve or disapprove of the site. They may even help clear a site of evil spirits after organising the prescribed worship. The construction work would follow thereafter. Once a house is complete it is to be given a name. The family living there would continue to be identified by this name. While referring to any family the house name is always added to the name of head of the family. The pattern is used for the purpose of mailing also. The naming ritual of the newly constructed house is to be done only by a religious person of monastic order. Such family or house name goes with Khangchen, the ancestral house. This is because the family worship room remains attached with Khangchen. Against Lamas services, the members of Khangchen are obliged to spare a part of the agriculture produce for the monastery. The reciprocity of relationship between the Ladakhi families and the Lamas is also marked in certain other spheres where the Lamas are rewarded, in cash and kind, for their religious services. For the services rendered by the Lamas the village community is under an obligation to supply free manpower to monastery which is needed in various activities connected to it. Goba, the village headman, is responsible to depute people by rotation, from various families, to work for Gompa. On its turn if a family has no member to spare for the purpose, it would engage someone on payment basis and put him to work for Gompa. Such a deputation of manpower disturbs the pattern of division of labour in family. The same may happen in the event of a son becoming a Lama or a daughter becoming a Chomo. The novice Lama and Chomo, while they stay with their respective family, are not asked to do difficult job involving physical labour. Over and above, they are given more respect and care in comparison to other members of the family. For instance they are not put to agriculture activities or to grazing of cattle in normal course.

As mentioned earlier the people remain highly indebted to religious men and their tenets and verdicts. Among other reasons such an attitude is attributed to the harsh environmental conditions. As people could not find ways to conquer it they remained subjugated to religious explanations. This is reflected in all the three components of culture, that is, artifact or technology, socio-fact or behaviouristic perspective and mentifact or ideology. In continuation to what has been explained in the earlier paragraphs one can get into diverse areas of Ladakhi culture. While getting into social organisation pattern connected to sitting arrangement on a formal occasion one finds the say of religion. On the occasion of a marriage, birth, death or any other occasion involving people from diverse streams the sitting pattern is well defined and regulated. Such a social criterion is governed by religious considerations. Status recognition is the apparent reflection. In order of their hierarchy the Lamas occupy the first position which is an indication of maximum honour given to them. The *Kalhans* (the descendents of earlier nobles) and their close relations get the second position. The third place, in order of recognition, goes to *Goba* (village headman). Other elderly persons from Ladakhi tribe then follow. Gara, the tribe of iron-smith, follow the suit. People from Mon and Beda tribes (the flute and drum players) occupy the last two lower positions in order. Baltis and Argons sit separately if they are present on the occasion. And if there is a feast to be shared on a formal occasion the Ladakhi tables are also arranged on the pattern described above. In front of the religious persons are kept wooden tables of bigger size and height. The size and height of the tables gradually decreases as we go down on the rungs of status ladder. Mon and Beda are not provided any table. They even sit a little away from other people.

Almost a parallel situation in the context of social interaction is observed on certain other occasions. For instance in archery competitions, which are so frequently organised among the Ladakhis, the religious men again take a lead. In an archery competition in which the villagers and the religious men together participate the seniormost Lama (the Kushok) declares the competition open by shooting the first arrow at the target fixed for the purpose. And if he can remain present for long he initiates for every round and other competitors then follow as per their status in the community. After the competitors from the religious hierarchy have shot their arrows the Bhots take the chance. They are then followed by the Gara tribesmen. Mons and Bedas are not permitted to shoot arrows. They may otherwise participate at the level of providing music on the occasion. The event shows religious considerations as important factor in the social categorization and the connected constraint. In the religious dramas and dances, which are so common in Ladakh and which play an important role in cultural transmission, the participants are chiefly from the religious hierarchy. The participation in religious dramas and dances is again, though indirectly, the privilege of Ladakhis as they alone can become the Lamas. It may be mentioned that the Gara, Mon and Beda cannot become the Lamas.

The Lamas and other religiousmen are again important in the field of health and the connected area of disease and cure. The religiousmen can foretell about epidemic and calamities apart from curing a sick person. Through their art of worship they suggest the means helpful in the matter. As an instance *Chhasam* (a particular worship) is performed to get rid off the eye ailment. A single Lama can perform it in about an hour's time. Likewise the religious specialists prepare amulets which are believed to contain curing power as their wearing helps on protecting from the attack of harmful spirits. The latter cause sickness. The Ladakhis are commonly seen wearing Chantho, an amulet, in their necks. Sunha is another device which is believed to provide protection against the evil spirit and the sickness caused by them. Sunha resembles a thread and is worn in the neck. The divice is prepared by a Lama. It is believed to be quite effective in curing madness. Shonga is another type of amulet prepared by the Lamas. This to carried curing quality.

Onpo is another religious man. In the event of sickness, birth and death the Ladakhis contact him for relief and blessings. When some person is under the bad influence of stars he/she contacts an Onpo. The latter can forecast about the future, including one of a sick person. Among the measures suggested by him include organisation of worship and installation of Buddhist flags on the root or on some other important projection. He even suggests for the formation of religious paintings. An Amchi or Lharje, a medicineman of Ladakhis, does not necessarily belong to Lama hierarchy. But for treatment of a sick person he often takes help of sacred Pothis (books). Whenever needed he even banks upon Kushok and other senior Lamas for seeking clarification. If his particular process requires worshipping the Amchi himself sits in the Chhotkang of the patient's family and performs the same. People recognise the higher social and professional status of the Amchi. His appeal to the gods and goddesses and his prevailing over certain spirits is a sufficient support to Amchi being a religious man. Labha is another curer and religious man though not as popular as a Lama or Amchi. Such experts are very few in number. Usually a Labha serves two to three villages. He too occupies an important position. A Labha under the possession of a diety helps cure people from various ailments. With the help of diety a Labha is either himself effective or he suggests to organise a worship or to contact an Amchi. He himself does not perform any worship. A Labha is believed to be capable of removing poison from the body of a person. He is also expert in taking out iron object from the stomach of an animal if it gets stuck up there.

Yet another curer with spiritual attainment is Chanspa. He is usually from Lama fraternity and the one who lives in interior hill and chiefly devotes to meditation. His place of stay is known as *Homskang* (an isolated hutment in the hill). Long devotion to meditation helps develop spiritual knowledge and understanding in him. A Chanspa is capable of telling whether a sick person would recover or die. Those under severe attack of spirits are taken to Chanspa. Those who approach him are usually suggested to organise Lhuchas and Shilok worship which are arranged in respective Chotkang. A *Chanspa* is also believed to be helpful in begetting children. Issueless couple approach him for the purpose.

The paintings prepared on the suggestion of religious persons are also said to carry curative properties. They are also said to ensure general prosperity. Lhaskal painting as suggested by Onpo helps in having a better future. It is said to be helpful in removing hurdles from future life. In the same tone the Skistak painting ensures better rebirth. The belief in such painting is so strong that almost all the families are found having them.

The social culture, especially its social organisational part, has strong bearing to religious attributes. This is reflected through inter-human relations as well as through social groups which provide norms for particular kind of behaviour. Religious interventions are reported in intra-family and inter-personal relations as also in case of wider groups and institutions. Inter-personal relations at family level involve sacred considerations. As referred to earlier the Chang-Zung and Chomo stay with other members of family. At this stage of their initiation to religious life they do not join Gompa permanently. In the matter of treatment at family level they have a place of privilege because of their commitment to join religious life. They are accorded more respect by all the inmates of the household. They are better fed and clothed. Such a treatment is meted out so long as the Chang-Zung stays in the house. When the monastic organisation finds these novices fit to join Lamahood they shift to the monastery. And then they start getting preferential treatment by the entire village community. But the Chomos continue to largely stay in their respective households and keep on getting preferential treatment at family level. Whenever required they are spared for monastery service. Because the Chosmos and Chang-Zungs opt to devote to religious life they are shown more respect in comparison to other family members. No physically hard work is assigned to them. For instance they are never engaged for harvesting or for carrying compost from residence to the agriculture fields. They, however, participate in all kinds of worship. Daily worship in the *Chhotkang* (family worship room) is preferably done by them.

Like many other castes and tribes the Ladakhis also indulge in Ostracism or social boycott. Among others the religious ground is said to be the strongest factor for resorting to such a practice. Though there is a provision of social boycott in the social structure of Ladakhis the practice is of rare occurrence. A person or family can be ostracized more on matter religious in nature than on account of irregularities in social life. A person is liable for social boycott when he or she challenges or threats a Kushok or Lama. The same can happen when one involves oneself in politics against the religious heads. When one poses a threat to community or group life the community in general may decide for social boycott. When an individual or family is socially boycotted the Lamas are requested not to render any religious service to such a person or family. As a matter of fact they are deprived of all religious help. At the same time all the families are directed to shun their relations of all kind with the victim. All the deprivations and denials of the above kind render the person or family, affected by social boycott, totally shattered and helpless. The remoteness of Ladakh and its typical terrain add fuel to the fire.

Beyond the family the religious implications are also marked at the level of bigger social group termed as Phasphun. A Phasphun comprises of a few families not exactly connected on the principle of descent or alliance. The group is rather sustained by a common religious force. The members of all the families in a Phasphun worship a common god. Through such a binding the families reciprocate all kinds of help among themselves. They are specially committed to do so on festive as well as sad occasions. The common La (god) which is their binding force, is jointly worshipped at the time of *Losar* (Ladakhi new year day). Group apart the word Phasphun is also an expression of relationship. And it is in this context that a Ladakhi is often found remarking that so and so is his Phasphun. All Phasphuns remember the name of common god which they worship and are well familiar with its location. The image of Phasphun god may be kept in monastery or on some hill top. Sometimes it may also be kept in the house of one of the Phasphun families. The composition of Phasphun group is flexible. If found inconvenient, for some reason, a family can leave the Phasphun and join a new one. Such a joining is on the precondition that the new entrant has to recognise and worship the god of particular Phasphun. However the change of Phasphun is resorted to only under certain special circumstance, say migration of a family to some other place.

The Ladakhis do not recognise groups like the clans. Beyond Phasphun social formation is the village community. All families within the village community of Ladakhis recognise a common god. Other ethnic groups of the same religion may also join in the event of a village being multi-ethnic one. The common god of village community binds the people together for various purposes, commitments and reciprocities. Such a god is called *Yul-La*. The god is held responsible for prosperity and well being of all the villagers, their livestock and crops. People attribute to him most of the major events in the village. The expression of the image of this god is through a small stony structure which is usually decorated with animal horns, dry bushes, grass, wheat and barley plants. Such objects are replaced every year by the new ones. The replacement is done on the occasion of annual worship. Any ignorance shown to this schedule is likely to annoy the god and such anger may be expressed in various forms connected to mundane life of the people, Shamor-Ma-Gyamo is Yul-La of Sabu village. As per the villagers this is one god whose worship is done through the offering of a sacrifice. The Buddhist religion, however, has no provision for offering sacrifice. The above practice of sacrifice may be a relic of Bon religion. A white goat is sacrificed at the later of Shamor-Ma-Gyamo. Goba appoints a man for sacrificing the animal. This man should be unmarried. Some blood of the animal is sprinkled on Yul-La. The flesh is consumed by the participants. This particular god is believed to be a blood eater and hence to be offered a sacrifice to keep him in good humour.

The various stages of life cycle are connected to religious sphere in some form or the other. A variety of religious attributes intervene in human life. People keep on seeking religious favour from the time of birth to death. Accordingly the above situation has given rise to many religion based customs, practices and traditions. The general ideology of the people suggests that the religious elements help to live a healthy and happy life. The latter give way to contentment and satisfaction. If the couple go issueless for a few years after marriage they get worried. Like most other women the Ladakhi women too eagerly wait for pregnancy after marriage. In case of unusual delay the woman and her husband approach the Lama, Chanspa and even at times a Kushok for religious favour and blessing in the matter. The widely accepted belief is that these religiousmen with their supernatural attainment can help cause pregnancy. They make use of different techniques. At times they suggest that particular kind of *Thanka* (religious painting) should be arranged by the couple. The latter engage the Spon, the religious painter, to get the job done. In another technique the issueless couple are advised to arrange worship in certain Gompas. Dolma, a goddess for women, is also worshipped to beget children. Yet another way suggested to get favour in the matter is the formation of Shogpur. Such a formation is arranged by the Labha and Lama. They do so after performing worship in the house. The Shogpur figure is believed to provide energy to an impotent man to do the sex act properly. Such an act then leads to conception and birth. Shogpur resembles a human figure and is made from bamboo strips or some other dry stems. The figure is made to wear some clothes. Shogpur is accommodated in the Chhotkang, alongwith other gods and goddesses, and is worshipped. From all the techniques and ways, given above, one can infer that various components of religious order are involved. The religious specialists of various kinds take advantage of one another to get the things go. Thus the efforts culminate in reinforcing the importance of religion. The religious performances are also enthused. When a woman is in the carrying stage certain ceremonies follow. For instance during the seventh month of pregnancy the ceremony of Dhunuche is performed. This involves worship and reading of sacred literature which are managed by the Lamas. It is through the performance of Dhunuche that the child's future is read. In addition to this function of Dhunuche the ceremony also helps in prevailing upon the evil spirits, if any, in the child's future.

In case of pregnant woman faces some trouble at the time of her delivery a Lama is immediately called for. After making certain calculations the Lama mixes some butter with his sliva and directs the delivering woman to swallow it. Simultaneously he resorts to murmuring of some sacred words. This is believed to smoothen the birth of the child by keeping away the evil spirit. During the course of delivery the husband of woman stays with her. And he continues to be with her at least for seven days after the delivery. The husband's stay in the house in this post-delivery stage helps in looking after the mother and the new born. When the husband is bracketed with his delivered wife the stay of this kind is known as *Pakzam* or *Pankh*. Such a confinement of the husband alongwith the wife is done on religious grounds. It is feared that Lhato spirit would get annoyed if the husband moves out during this period. The husband's movement outside the house is okayed only after observing Laf-Tsang (the worship done on 7th day after delivery). The unclean period after delivery continues till Da-Tsang worship is observed after one month of delivery. With this worship the Khimla god of Ladakhis also gets appeased. Only a Lama can arrange for Da-Tsang. name giving to the new born is always the prerogative of religious persons. For this purpose the Ladakhis contact either of the Lama, Kushok and Labha. While consulting them the social status also comes in the way. The socially superior families do contact a Kushok or some senior Lama. Labha is one who serves all for the purpose. This process of operation is rather interesting. To start with he goes for the consultation of sacred book, then shivers a little and finally shouts the name to be given to the child. The Ladakhis believe that the name is suggested by the benevolent spirit through Labha.

Like most other societies the marriage among Ladakhis is an important occasion. And it is marked by many religious overtones. Religious rituals and ceremonies performed by the religious men mark the institution of marriage in its various aspects. Onpo, for instance, proposes an auspicious day on which the marriage is to be performed. The Ladakhis bank upon Onpo for such a fixation. When the members of a marriage party reach the bride's place the Lamas start Yangup worship. As part of this worship they read certain portions of sacred books prescribed for the purpose. The role of religion again comes forcefully when the bride leaves her parental house. At this juncture it is necessary for her to enter into family Chotkang and seek blessings from various gods and goddesses there in. The chain continues even when the bride reaches the bridegroom's house. When she just approaches the bridegroom's house Zabluk ceremony is observed. The Ladakhis opine that ill luck or misfortune may accompany the bride, being a stranger, if such a ceremony is not observed. And hence the ceremonial performance of this nature is essential to keep off such undesirable happening. The observance of Zabluk involves an interesting process. An earthen pot is first arranged. It is then filled with dirt residues and leftover of various kind. Then a Lama picks it up and whirls the pot over the head of the bride. While doing so he murmurs something as if he is scaring away the evil spirit of ill luck. Or he may be trying to trap the same in the pot. The pot is then forcefully thrown against a stone with the intention of breaking it into pieces. This part of the ritual helps keep away the misfortune, if any, accompanying the bride. There is yet another feeling behind the act of breaking the pot. The breaking of pot in the very first instance marks, as per the Ladakhis, a successful marriage.

A very common way of acquiring mate among the Ladakhis is popularly known as *Nama Khyon*. And the marriage arranged through this way is known as orthodox marriage. The label of orthodox is befitting because of the involvement of *Onpo* and Lama in such an affair. Both of these religious men in association with community members meet out certain requirements in the context of marriage. To start with the Onpo, a kind of oracle, approves of the feasibility of match. For this he makes his own calculations based on religious considerations. Once this clearance is obtained the Lamas are requisitioned to actually materialise the marriage. Once the bride and the bridegroom are declared married the community accords social recognition to the same.

The Ladakhis are now predominantly monogamous. But traditionally it has been a polyandrous society. Such unions are still reported though they are of a rare occurrence. One finds an answer to the custom of polyandry in hard environmental conditions prevalent in Ladakh. This is, however, not the issue here. What is of relevance at the moment concerns the place of religion in respect of polyandrous system. Such a condition, as per the Ladakhis, has been of a very intimate and reinforcing nature. In fact the religious institution of monastery helped sustain the custom of polyandry. The practice of adelphic polyandry has been there among the Ladakhis since time immemorial. Since the Ladakhi society accorded a positive value to fraternal polyandry the institution of monastery gave its own patronage though in an indirect manner. Under polyandrous system some females could not get married and had to remain single for the whole of life. The monastery absorbed them by diverting the females to the cause of religion. They could be channelised to the life of celibacy under the protection of religion. This was eagerly agreed upon by the Ladakhis. Otherwise such surplus females could be the cause of social problem in society. These females were made nuns and were subsequently diverted to nunneries attached to the monastery. Of late the nunneries have largely disappeared and the *Chomos* (nuns) stay on in their respective house. Otherwise they devote to celibacy and involve in religious learning and preaching. Thus, they remain in the religious fold within the wider Gompa canvass. This makes the female observe all restraints defined under religion. But then she also enjoys certain privileges being a religious person. Under such an arrangement one can infer that the monastery indirectly helped enthuse and sustain the social custom of polyandry. It's special contribution was in the absorption of unmarried girls who, without their patronage, could become a problems in society.

Sickness and disease among the Ladakhis are attributed to the effects of ghost, evil spirit and some other deities when they express their anger and annoyance. As such the death phase in rites-de-passage can indirectly be attributed to the wrath of supernaturals. People, in general, do identify various elements of superorganic world who cause harm to human life. One very prominent of these is *Shinde* (a malevolent spirit which is believed to have three forms termed as Chan, Gyao and Teemo) which can cause any kind of harm. As per the emic perception all the three forms roam about in the atmosphere. Symbolically they are identified through an expression as if they ride on horseback for their movements. During such a sojourn they adversely affect the human life. In terms of their conceptual framework regarding death some people have yet another explanation. They attribute life as well as death to *Sangyas* (Lord Buddha). Likewise many of the death rituals find their feet in religious overtones. While on death-bed a person is advised to concentrate on Chhotkang gods and the religious men. This is to divert the person from his worldly attraction which keep on mentally disturbing till he/she breathes last. Soon after a person dies someone is sent to call *Labon* (a superior Lama). Touching the dead body is tabooed till this Lama turns up and preaches his sermons. This ritual is locally termed *Phoi* or *Phoa*. The performance of this ritual helps channelise the dead through heavenly path. Not going for Phoa involves the risk of dead's going to hell. Another reason for favourable response to Phoa lies in the belief that its performance helps give a better rebirth.

Apart from advising the dying person to concentrate on the images of gods and goddesses, there is yet another religious ritual whose performance ensures delinking of the dead from worldly and material attraction. Such a ritual is known as *Yingshak*. It involves ceremonial offering or rice and wheat grain, butter, barley, mustard seeds, milk, *Chhang* (a Ladakhi beer) etc. to the dead. At the time of cremation these articles are thrown over the flames. No one else but a Lama can do this act. Such offerings are made in little quantity at certain interval of time.

The cycle goes on till the dead body is completely burnt to ashes. The functional importance of *Yingshak* is that the spirit of dead would not trouble the family members, and even others, for these items after the observance of Yingshak.

Under the banner of Lamaism and for the remoteness and isolation of Ladakh region, in association with the hardest possible condition of nature, there is great deal of fear and awe, in respect of the dead, among the Ladakhis. They are scared of the harm which can be inflicted by the spirit of the dead. That is the reason why the Ladakhis try to break away all the relations with the dead. They want to appease the dead and the form which it may take by offering these material objects. No belongings of the dead are retained in the house. Though the Ladakhis express that such items may be needed in the journey after death but such a consideration emanates out of the fear that the dead person's spirit may come hard on the surviving members of the family. And if someone suffers on this count the remedial measures are not very strong. The person may become chronic sufferer. Since supremacy of religion reigns, in the absence of alternative rationalities, more so for physical isolation of Ladakhis, the ceremonial and ritual performances of traditional nature continue to go very strong. It's basis remains the fear.

When the dead body is in flames accompanied by the worship performed by a group of Lamas on the spot, one of the dead person's Phasphun suddenly comes into action. He holds a metallic dish containing *Sattu* (barley flour) cakes and goes around the site where the body is being cremated. This Phasphun is then suddenly chased by a Lama who holds a small stick in his hand. The Lama's gesture communicates as if he wants to beat the Phasphun. After a little ceremonial chase the Phasphun, driven away by the Lama, keeps dish a little away from the cremation site. The philosophy behind this ritual again finds root in religious explanation though the element of fear is at the back of Ladakhi's mind. The dead's spirit is believed to be attracted by Sattu cakes, contained in the dish, and this spirit goes along with it. Driven away by the Lama, and being satisfied with eatable, the spirit of the dead will not, it is believed, trouble the family members left behind.

In the same context the role of religious men continues beyond. Personal belongings of the dead, which he was using prior to his death, are auctioned. Such articles generally include utensils, clothes and other personal material possession. During the post-cremation worship, which continues for a few days, the Lamas fix a day for auction. Everyone is free to buy these articles. The money raised through auction is either given to the Lamas or deposited with a monastery, preferably one which served the person prior to his death. The act helps augment the monastic resource. That means a person even after his death does not sever his equation of obligation to Gompa. This ritual of auctioning personal belongings of the dead is locally termed as *Bulba.* In its non-economic content the organisation of Bulba is functional in severing all connections of the dead's spirit from his surviving family members. A commonly accepted belief is that if Bulba is not organised, the spirit of the dead might visit the family for its personal belongings and thereby cause trouble to family members. Further to debar the entry of such spirit inside the house the Ladakhis go for the formation of Samgo-Namgo. It resembles a human figure and is made out of clay paste and long thin reeds or grass. The skull of a goat or sheep is fixed on top of it and this gives it an impression of a human like figure. The Samgo-Namgo is carved on the outer portion of front wall of the house. The symbolic expression of this kind is either above the main entrance to the house or just adjoining to it. This is to guard the entrance and to forbid the entry of evil spirit. As referred to earlier the upper portion of the Samgo-Namgo is represented by the skull which is surrounded by dry grass. The body portion is made of clay. The lower portion is made of clay paste and dry grass. The Lamas advice regarding Samgo-Namgo carries lot of weight in reference to people's imagination and belief system. And this strength gives them a feeling of protection against the fears of supernaturals. The Ladakhis do regard Samgo-Namgo as competent enough to drive away the evil spirit. Every main household of Ladakhi, popularly called *Khangchen*, must have this figure.

To contain evil spirits and ghosts which originate, as per the emic view, when the dead person's soul fails to find a suitable abode the Ladakhis have evolved certain other mechanism in addition to what has been stated in the preceding paragraphs. The combination of Lama and Onpo religiousmen works in this mechanism. This is all the more a reason for strong belief of a common Ladakhi in after death cosmos which emanates strong sense of fear for living beings. Every Ladakhi family keeps cloth paintings inside their Chotkang. A painting, known as Skistak, is specially got made soon after the death of a person. A Lama suggests for the formation of this painting with religious significance. The *Onpo* prescribes for its design and the painting is finally made by the Spon who is an expert painter. The Ladakhi's provide long explanation in support of the background of Skistak formation. People opine that all individuals commit some in their life time. It is further believed that those who commit more sins would fail to get rebirth. And the souls of such persons would roam around, without finding any abode, and ultimately assume the form of evil spirit. The Lamas have the expertise of determining the degree of sin a person has committed. In order that the soul of a sinner may not roam about, and may get a suitable abode the Lamas suggest for Skistak formation.

Most difficult in Ladakh is the economic existence of the people. Scarce resource and imposingly difficult terrain and environmental conditions limit the economic production to very great extent. Whatever the Ladakhis can manage is attributed to the cover of religious blessings. Else, as the people express, even this would not have been possible. The external ecological conditions make the people helpless. Monastic organisations, economy and society are intimately connected. At economic level there has been a great deal of reciprocity and exchange between monastery and society. The two reinforce each other. Means of production are also activated under the blessings of religiousmen. The latter even ensure crop protection as per the native conception. Why religion is taken such a force is relegated to man's inability to largely conquer the environment. And he seeks for help elsewhere in the interest of survival. Relations of production are also intervened at the level of religious attributes. Depending upon the nature of requirement and situation religiousmen influence economic life of the Ladakhis.

The economic position of major Gompas is generally sound. This has been so all along. In case of need the monastery loans out wheat, *grim* (a kind of barley), butter, *Sattu* etc., to the needy villagers under its religious jurisdiction. These articles are spared from the surplus stock in Gompa. The villagers may also borrow in cash from monastery fund. Such a borrowing is not interest free. While returning it back to the monastery the villagers do make some addition to the borrowed quantity or cash. It would be of interest to mention that when an issueless couple take some loan from Gompa, and if they fail to return it in their life time, their land is permanently attached to Gompa. Even otherwise if the loans taken by any Ladakhi from Gompa are not returned foı long, the Gompa management decides to take possession of some of the land belonging to the borrower. Such a land is acquired in the name of Gompa and is cultivated on its behalf. In case the loans are not returned even after this the land in question is permanently retained by the Gompa. For the purpose of borrowing the village Gompa is preferably approached. In case there is no such Gompa at village level, the one to which the family belongs, from sect point of view, is approached. Within the framework of Gompa-village relationship it is almost obligatory on the part of Gompa to spare loan for villagers in the event of difficulty. Since the Gompa resource is rich they do not mind sparing the commodities of daily use. In normal course people keep on strengthening Gompa store and fund by raising crops on Gompa land (and giving the produce to Gompa) and by making offerings and contributions. Sometimes the personal agriculture work suffers when people have to meet out the labour demand of the monastery. Again as part of Gompa-village relationship the required number of men and women from the village are to be spared to work for Gompa. They work on agriculture fields belonging to Gompa and do other odd jobs requiring physical labour. No remuneration is given to them for their services. People are supposed to carry it out in the name of religion whose experts provide them protection against evil.

Ladakhi religion and agriculture economy are intimately connected. Some of the activities connected to agriculture economy are linked to religion in one way or the other. There is only one agriculture season in an year as nothing grows in winter months in this high altitude desert. The first ploughing of the season is preferably started on the advice and clearance of Kushok. For this purpose he suggests an auspicious time and day. This may be different for different people because some fields are ready for ploughing early than the other. This is because of the location of fields at different levels for reasons of typical terrain. Altitude variations have their own place in the matter. Likewise the day to start harvesting of crops is also fixed in consultation with head Lama. In case of standing crops the plants in question sometime start getting pale in premature stage. If not checked the process would culminate in poor yields as per the cultivators view. At this stage the farmers requisition the services of Lamas to help them out of the difficulty. The Lamas who are familiar with the situation organise Chha-Chhush worship to eradicate such a crop disease. Soon after the worship the Lamas carry, in turn, a ball like leather container to the affected agriculture fields. They are accompanied by the noisy sound of bells and gongs. After covering all the fields with such a procession the container is finally thrown into the river or in some other running water source. The commonly accepted belief is that the crop disease goes off with the leather container. The latter moves in the direction of water flow. If by chance the container is collected by someone on the way and opened for curiosity the crop disease is then believed to pass on to the fields of the village to which the person who opened the container belongs.

For the protection of crops against pests the Lamas again come into the picture. The worship which Lamas perform is believed to not only control the pest but also proves as resistant to the same. So, the villagers get it organised in normal course and request the Lamas for their service for the purpose. *Sarak Doldol* is the name of worship which Lamas organise to prevent and protect the crops from various pests. This is an annual worship performed at the time when ear heads shoots up and are in the process of ripening. The worship involves the reading of concerned sacred literature. Prior to the start of reading a heavy mass of clay is collected from the bank of some water source. This clay is then kept in front of the images of gods and goddesses installed in the Chotkang. Just after the reading the Lamas blow air towards the heap of clay. Finally these clay pieces are thrown over the crops in all the fields. Such a performances acts as anti-pest.

In order to be on the safer side the Ladakhis always try to appease the spirits. Certain spirits are believed to preside over agriculture pursuits. For their propitiation the Ladakhis go for a ritual performance. They tie a bundle of full sized plants, including the earheads, on the central wooden pillar of the house. On the occasion of every harvest the old bundle is replaced by a new one. The arrangement is believed to appease the spirits. The bundle serves as an offering to them.

Like some other mechanisms Boamskar is a worship done for the prosperity of crops. It is performed on a grand scale at the time when earheads shoot up. The performance ensures protection to crops against any kind of damage. Through Boamskar the two gods, that is Chhok Tum Gyamo and Shamur Ma Gyamo, are especially revered. The Boamskar performance is rather interesting. On the day this worship is to be performed the adult male members of the village community report at Gompa. Many *Pothis* (books of sacred literature) are then taken out from the stock room of Gompa. This is done by the junior Lamas under the supervision of a senior one. These religious books are then distributed among the villagers. Each one is given two to three Pothis. duly wrapped in cloth these Pothis are then carried on the back. Sometimes the photographs or portraits of Chongapa and Kushok are also carried by one or two villagers. The Lamas then worship Gyamos by chanting religious hymns. Then the villagers and Lamas come out of Gompa and shout the praises of gods and goddesses who can, it is believed, neutralise the evil effects of malevolent spirits. Then they get into a procession which is headed by the local musicians and followed by the Lamas and villagers in order. The procession goes round the agriculture fields. The other villagers who do not join the procession greet the processionists at different spots and give offerings, including cash, to them. The processionists also stop for est after certain intervals of time. At such moment all the Pothis are kept at one place. This is subsequently followed by taking of food and local tea offered by the sectional heads of the village. In the meantime the Lamas perform some worship. Then the processionists move further and repeat the same operation till all the sections of the village and their fields are covered. Finally, they return back to Gompa and deposit all the Pothis. The village participants then disperse being assured that their crops would not be damaged by the wrath of supernaturals.

Water for irrigation of agriculture fields is necessary for having good crops. Since the Ladakh terrain is hilly and undulating only the fields at lower elevation can be irrigated with river water. Those on higher elevation depend upon the snow water which runs down the hills and passes by the side of such fields. Rainfall is otherwise extremely scanty. To ensure water supply to irrigate the fields the Ladakhis request the Lamas to perform Chharben or Chharbip worship. This worship helps to have more rain, snow and more supply of water in springs as the spirit responsible for such sources is appeased. When snow melts at higher peaks of hills the Ladakhis get water for irrigation. Such a worship becomes all the more necessary under the condition of water scarcity. The spirits of water and snow are Lhu, Magzur and Sadak. These get appeased through Chharbip worship. Water scarcity is faced when such a worship is not organised. As part of this worship the Lamas throw certain substances in spring water. In addition to worship the villagers observe certain taboos to keep the water spirits happy.

Quite in tune with economic structure the mechanism of social control is also largely influenced by the religious men. The selection of *Goba* (village headman) and other members of Village Council is directed by the senior Lamas. This specially happens in case of villages having Gompas. Generally the villagers approach the Kushok and request him to nominate the Goba and member of village council. Such a nomination is never challenged. A Kushok's decision in the matter reigns supreme. Even if there is a difference of opinion people digest it. Likewise decision making, more so in complicated cases, is left to the religiousmen, especially the senior Lamas. In major conflicts and other issues of wider interest the meeting of village council is organised in Gompa premises. All the villagers consider such a venue as neutral and bias-free because of the religious climate around. The religious sanctity attached with the place influences the participants to go for a fair deal in the matter concerned. Even those involved in the dispute are believed to present the facts of the matter for fear of religious implication. But for petty conflicts the villagers do not approach the head Lama. They may resolve such cases at their level. Head Lama's intervention is rarely required. The officials of the village council approach for Lama's intervention when it becomes difficult to identify the offender under strong arguments from both the parties involved. In the event of such complications the village council decides to approach the senior religious persons who readily extend their help. While in Gompa campus the persons involved in the dispute are asked to swear in the name of Lord Buddha before they explain their respective view point.

According to the religious ideology the Ladakhis cannot tell lies after taking oath in the name of Lord Buddha. A common feeling is that if the wrong statements are made the supreme god would get annoyed and then any kind of harm can be inflicted on the person. For such an implication the Ladakhis do not try to hide the facts. Such an atmosphere helps identify the offender. And if this does not happen and when the matter is not resolved the members of the Village Council request the head Lama of the village to keep a sacred book on the head of the person who then is asked to make a statement in respect of his position. The same procedure is repeated for the other person, if any, in conflict. The Ladakhi belief system explains that no one can afford to speak lies once the sacred book is kept on his or her head. And if the matter is still not resolved for lack of clarity in statements the persons involved are taken to the main worship room of the Gompa. They are then again asked to make statement on the issue. The belief is that people cannot afford to tell lies in this sacred room. False and distorted statement would, it is believed, invite the anger and wrath of gods and spirits. The people of Sabu village told of yet another method of detecting crime and offender. This also involves fear of supernaturals. The concerned persons are asked to eat little sand collected from the cremation ground. One who can afford to do so is believed to speak the truth. And the guilty, it is believed, would not do it. If he does so he would be harmed by the spirit of the dead. It is generally stated that Ladakhis cannot afford to be damaged by the spirits by merely concealing the facts related to some matter. Like the Lamas the others who are consulted in certain matters include Chanspa and Onpo. Since the latter are also believed to control the spirits their leadership is formally recognised. Since their opinion is sought in various matters their social and ritual superiority is accepted.

The relationship of Village Council and monastic organisation at the level of socio-political life can be extended to wider political linkages. Such an arrangement can be traced upto the level of national political parties. Some of the Lamas are not only reported having a place in village council (say Lama Lob-Zang in case of Spituk village council at the time) but they also find place in national level politics. The wider politics has also influenced the traditional pattern of socio-political control. The monastery seems to have one foot in village politics and the other in political activities at regional as well as national levels. The induction of wider political parties in Ladakh can be traced to 1947 but its force could be felt only after 1962, more so after the active involvement of *Kushok Bakula* (the then head of Spituk monastery) in national politics. It may be mentioned that the superior-most religious position of Kushok Bakula did help him in political life not only in Ladakh but also beyond. The big force of Lamas under him could prevail upon the village communities to mobilise their support for the Kushok. They helped in his election campaign for the Lok Sabha (Parliament) seat. The village councils, so obliged to the monastic organisation, in the constituency impressed upon the people to support the Kushok. Those not responding to such a call could be deprived of the services of Lamas was also a slogan during the course of election campaign. Religion and politics could be forcefully mixed. The campaign could be reported intervening even at the level of interpersonal and inter-family relations. The opponents in election widened the disparities at inter-human level. In fact there was hardly any opposition in the initial phase of Kushok Bakula's political career. He continued to enjoy his spiritual as well as political positions. In subsequent phase of political rise the inter-play of religion, society and politics continued unabated. Such state of affairs was in prominence when Kushok Thikse and Sonam Wangyal contested in the election of State Assembly. Gradually more religious heads showed their interest in wider politics, so much so that there appeared in 1969 serious rift in National Congress. Then the National Congress of Ladakh was divided into Congress 'A' and Congress 'B'. The two divisions were headed by two Kushoks belonging to different monasteries. One of these was headed by Kushok Bakula and the other by Kushok Thikse. This correspondingly reflected on religious structure and the common masses paving way to certain adverse feelings. Things trickled down to the mental level of Lamas and the community whom they serve. This gave a new colour to mutual attitude of the people. The Ladakhi Buddhist Association, an old organisation of Ladakhi region, also got a jolt in those hot moments. However, the techno-economic backwardness of Ladakh, a common issue for all, kept the Ladakhi Buddhist Association going strong. Of late there were some ethnic disturbances in Ladakh where this Association was actively involved. But the tension gradually subsided after certain assurances were given at political level.

Fixity to and persistence of traditional cultural life-designs of Ladakhis is still the picture at grassroots level. Change is rather insignificant in comparison to continuity. Religious intervention in diverse walks of life persists unabated. In the difficult environment, of remoteness and isolation, so prominently and mountingly featuring in Ladakh, the supernatural cover is perceived as the best protection against many odds and eventualities connected to life and culture. Lately introduced means of communication, economic opportunities and social provision have affected only the selected aspects. The areas of Ladakhi life and culture dealt in this account have hardly been influenced in terms of innovations. These continue to be predominantly governed by the monastic organisation. Great deal of persistence and intactness, both at the level of cognition and reality, continue to mark the scenario.

Monastic organisation, as a repository of religion and its dissemination, keeps going many rituals, practices, beliefs, ceremonies etc. Lamas continue to hold the community with their religious baggage and people's reliance on them has not been adversely affected, retaining many rituals and customary practices intact. Though a few of the Ladakhis make use of modern medicines their concept regarding disease still finds root in supernatural elements, especially the spirits.

Quite parallel to the trend in social organisation the economic life of the Ladakhis too is little affected barring the inhabitants of some village around Leh, the district headquarters. The loaning system of Gompa continues to function effectively. Economically needy ones still bank upon the monastery as they are yet to be mentally convinced of the new economic system. As per the natives the Gompa is still preferred for securing loans of various kinds. Likewise the villagers continue to supply manpower and labour to the monastery on the traditionally defined pattern. The role of Lamas in the agriculture sphere has not at all been discontinued. They interact in various activities wherever and whenever required to do so. Pest control measures provided by the Lamas are in use. However impact of certain approved and improved agriculture practices has been felt in villages around Leh. In this respect the Mutse Agriculture Farm has helped diffuse some innovations, especially connected to vegetable cultivation. In total context the new seeds, chemical fertilizers and pesticides are marginally used. With all this the traditional practices are not denounced. The irrigation potential of a new order is being exploited by the experts. But this is in addition to, and not in contravention of, what the Lamas suggest to increase water supply. The customarily prescribed taboos and impositions at the hands of Lamas are well within the respectability framework of the people. The status and role paradigm of social control mechanism have experienced the least change. The place of Kushok in respect of positions of Goba and Members is not at all adversely affected. The processes of decision-making remain the same. The value of senior Lama's say stands as before. Even at mundane level they are not ignored. Rather the Lamas have further intervened at wider level beyond village and district. But such an involvement has not adversely reflected on social control arrangement at village and inter-village levels. Senior Lamas and the main worship room of the monastery maintain the same stature not only at the level of cognitive mapping but also in day to day activities with traditional bearing on them.

The force of traditional belief system is at times so strong that it overrides certain elements of modernity. While doing field work among the Ladakhis I entered into a Ladakhi house on the attraction of going music being played there. The then Cultural Officer of Leh was also accompanying me. The owner of the house was one Tsang, a Ladakhi of socially superior category. One of his sons was a Medical Officer, an M.B.B.S. who happened to be then present in the house. I was well received and entertained by the officer. After talking to him for some time I requested the doctor to take me to his Chhotkang where Lamas were worshipping and operating on gongs. After expressing my reverence to the images of gods and goddesses in Chhotkang, I enquired of the purpose of worship. The doctor explained that it helped cure, in native belief system, the sick person who was for long suffering from some chronic disease. This would happen after the concerned spirit would get satisfied through the worship. Under the influence of elderly lot the doctor was sitting quiet as if he is a party to the worship, though technically he carried a different opinion of the disease and cure.

According to the common perception of Ladakhis the abode of gods and spirits is in hillocks, trees, water springs etc. And as such the latter are shown respect in diverse ways. The religious spots so identified are protected against all kinds of damage. It is also believed that the supernaturals may even change their abode. In the above context and in reference to a modern technological innovation an interesting case has been cited by the Ladakhis of Spituk village. How a sudden technological addition could be related to native belief system is depicted in the case. While constructing the Leh airfield close to the Spituk Gompa, some of the rocks, Chhortens and Manes were damaged and they were razed to the ground while leveling for runway. Also, some of these religious structures, as abodes of supernaturals, were to be removed to make the take off and landing of aircraft safe. The Spituk people explained that these rocks and other religious structures were destroyed even when these were the abode of supernaturals. The latter got terribly upset and subsequently showered their wrath and anger on a Packet aeroplane which crashed there in the initial stage of runway's operation. There would have certainly been a technical reason for the crash but the Ladakhis attributed the incident to the wrath of spirits who were disturbed in the making of airport.

The villagers further added that after the disturbance of these supernaturals the more fierce and faster winds have started blowing around the place. These not only pose hindrance in the safe take off and landing of aircrafts but are also causing damage to the crops in near vicinity. The latter implication perturbed the Ladakhis who showed immediate concern. They managed to organise the Hustor worship through the Lamas. As part of this worship the supernaturals were ritationally and honourably shifted to other safer places. Such a performance is believed to have pacified the supernaturals and the things are stated to have calmed down to some extent.

Yet another instance explaining the intervention of religious belief in the development venture could be reported by the people. The development department of the state government once planned to deepen and also to widen the existing water springs so that more water could be made available to the inhabitants of village Spituk. Accordingly the work started on one of the water springs. But within the few days of the start of this work some of the workers on the site developed skin disease involving severe itching and rashing. When *Amchi* (the local medicinemen) was contacted for relief, he expressed his inability in the matter. Subsequently the Chanspa was consulted who supplied amulets to the victims and some of them got relief. But simultaneously the Chanspa announced that the skin disease was caused by Lhu, the spirit living in the water source. And then the talk in general was that whosoever would work on the spring site will suffer the same way. The work on the spring came to an end and the patients gradually recovered. On the ground of religious belief the work for development of the spring stoped.

The mounting persistence in certain spheres of socio-political and socio-economic life of the Ladakhis, as discussed in detail in this paper, is an expression of typical mental make up of the people. Within this background the pattern for and pattern of living seem to be closely coterminous. As such social organisation purview and the social structure network are easy to understand. The intimate relationship between some religious attributes and many elements of social structure seeks support from the belief system which the people have been holding. And such an equation speaks for the background of functionality and purposiveness. The strength of belief system pertaining to supernaturals lies in people's sense of insecurity which itself is emanating from fear regarding their survival in the most difficult environmental condition prevalent in the region. Certain elements of environment are far beyond the control of Ladakhis. And they mostly remain scared of the adverse consequences of such imposing elements. Though people have lived under such hostile geographical conditions for centuries but always keeping their fingers crossed regarding the question of survival. More it has been true for physical isolation and remoteness of their settlements. In all historical times the barriers could not be broken to the extent where the Ladakhis could feel secured economically and socially. Even of late not many alternatives could be made available in terms of relief mechanism where sense of fear of the people could be removed to any reasonable extent. Some job opportunity is of more relevance in the matter under context wherever the communication is through.

The remedy to the anticipated fear in terms of human survival under harsh environmental conditions could be provided by the religious men and the same is so elaborately explained in the text. Lamaism and its implications in life and culture were, in emic sense, taken as protection against many odds. Such a background of functionality, more prominently at the level of mind of natives of Ladakh, has been keeping the interrelationship of man and spirit so intimate. The Lamas and village community seem to be inseparable not only in day to day life but also at the level of people's cognition. Only some hilarious economic revolution, if at all it is feasible in the lifeless heights of Ladakh, may interrupt in nature-man-spirit complex. And if it is not sustained the interruption would vanish thereby reverting people to traditional ideology. The instance of a little change in activities of social organization seem to be economy based, and this too has to go a long way in assuming the form of a new pattern.

8

SIMPLER SOCIETIES AND ETHNICITY-BASED GENERALIZATIONS

Of late the social scientists have given an increased focus on ethnic studies. Among others, one major reason support has been the unprecedented growth of new ethnic problems and issues of mounting concern. Under the stormy social-cultural dynamics, caused under planned as well as unplanned forces and sources of change, in societies at large, there are exerting varieties of pull and push on ethnicities. Various social processes are in simultaneous operation. Some people from within the ethnic groups over-assert for retention of traditional ethnic identity. There are others who search for new ones by developing fresh affiliations and affinities under some new garb. There are still others who want to remain in-between, adhering thereby partly to the traditional system and partly to those of the outsiders beyond their traditional ethnic identity. In other words some are keen to uphold ethnic exclusiveness or isolation; some want to break away from it, resuming thereby to almost assimilation, and there are others who seem to have chosen a path of integration with larger groups, oscillating thereby between two systems. Other than the insiders themselves, the policy/s from outside, in respect of treatment meted out to various ethnic groups, have also, in many cases, added to the problem complexity. This has specially happened wherever the perspectives and perceptions of insiders and outsiders expressed more of incompatibility. The massive transitional phase has created a climate of dilemma regarding ethnicity issue and its wider ramification. And so has been true in respect of problem complex born of such dilemma, opening thereby new vistas for the attention of experts of ethnic studies.

In the near past the trend on ethnic studies spoke more of a static perspective of such groups. Stress on dimensions of constancy and consistency remained at the forefront. And this seemed more feasible and effective approach under the conditions when the ethnic groups, by and large, cultivated physical isolation and cultural boundary maintenance. In their micro setting, even if there were minor problems, these were taken care of at local level in the interest of smooth running of the concerned social-cultural system. But since the rise of intense culture contact situations with others, and the ensuing imposing acculturative influences, the dynamic perspective in ethnic studies found a prominent place. This desired the experts to switch over to studies on social-cultural dynamics and ethnic mobility both at process as well as manifestation levels. Interactionism of various forms beyond specific ethnic group level reflected on internal social organisational paradigm, generating thereby social currents of desired as well as undesired nature, depending on the context in which these were generated. These demanded further attention of social scientists to explore, explain and interpret the flux in social scenario in micro as well as macro setting.

Ethnic group or ethnicity has been conceived in a number of ways. The scholars have tried to conceptualize ethnic group in micro perspective, differentiating it thereby from national societies and nationalities wherein membership is volition-based and not acquired by birth as is the general rule in case of an ethnic group. For national societies and nationalities the identity symbol, state power and control over definite territory are also the requisites. Glazer and Moynihan (1975) held the view that people used the word ethnic to denote minority and marginal subgroup. But it does not provide very categorical framework as some larger groups have also been studied as part of ethnic studies. Some brought in the idea of tribal groups as belonging to ethnic fold. A general consensus has been on the explanation that a tribe has many featural similarities with an ethnic group. But then all ethnic groups are not tribes (Burman, 1984). Since the focus of this venture is elsewhere it is not appropriate to get into controversies and commonalities of ethnic group, caste and tribe. This has all along been a debatable issue.

To Shibutani and Kian (1965), a common ancestry, real or fictitious, and the emanating alikeness therefrom determine an ethnic group which is so recognised by the people. Being alike people get united through moral bindings and emotional bounds and they express concern for their preservation. The emotional ties seek support from collective perception of its members. Normatively internalized value system reflects on their common type of behaviour patterns. For Frederick Barth (1969) ethnic identity is associated with culture-specific value standards.

Cliford Geertz (1963) seeks conception of ethnicity in primordial consciousness. Such fundamental structure strengthens behavioural and relation superstructure, more so through collective consciousness of being alike. As such ethnicity and its wider linkages to nationality are to be understood in reference to actors world-view and the meanings (Dilthey and Witgenstein, 1978) they attach to it as part of their social structural framework.

From what has been said above, while conceptualizing ethnicity, it is to be accepted that an ethnic group carries great force in terms of cultural moorings, thought processes and overt expressions. And as such its identity is not to be underrated, more so in terms of its relationship to nationality. Promoting the cause of national chauvinism without considering the ethnic perspective in the matter may not be a rewarding experience in terms of progress. Primordial consciousness of an ethnicity can neither be easily eroded through coercion and struggle nor through increased education and industrialization. Primordial consciousness of ethnic groups has survived well in most of the places including U.S.A (Epstein, 1978) and U.S.S.R. (Bromley, 1976). It may continue to remain so as ethnicities have solid footing characterized by social-cultural modes and value standards, deep-rooted structures of human organisation and human mind, people oriented world views and meanings, and corporate relational network.

The best under the circumstances seems integration of ethnic groups without adversely hitting at, or encroaching upon their respective primordial consciousness reflected through collective perceptions and world view. The task is herculean as channels other than the planned or intended ones also operate simultaneously, and to which the ethnic groups respond, many a times, in one way or the other. Within the background of a complex ethnic plurality in India, the task seems to be of more concern and challenge. In this context I would explain the ongoing processes in two situations, that is, of western India (focusing on Bhil, Mina and Garasia tribes of Rajasthan, Gujarat and Western Madhya Pradesh) and of north-west India (focusing on Ladakhis of Ladakh), Jammu and Kashmir state). In spite of great deal of intended integration on move, a few issues, inherent in native ethnic structures, invite increasing concern.

The Bhil is the largest scheduled tribe of western India and one of the biggest in the country. They are recognised as the oldest inhabitants of southern Rajasthan and adjoining parts of Gujarat and Madhya Pradesh. In Rajasthan the Bhil are concentrated in Dungarpur, Banswara, Udaipur and Chittorgarh districts. They have had a very long history of culture contact with caste Hindus.

An important element of Bhil social organisation is attributed to their contact with the non-Bhils. This concerns the stratification perspective. From amongst the Bhils, some isolated themselves, as socially superior group, because of their claim of being descendant from Rajput father and Bhil mother. The Bhils who did not mix with others continued to belong to the original stock. In course of time these groups got so much separated that they declared, and practically observed, their respective endogamy. But still the groups continued to share many elements of culture in common with the larger ethnic group. The Pal-dwellers or *Palia Bhils* have continued to largely protect their original culture traits. Others, who started living with the non-Bhils and submitted, for various purposes, to them are referred as *Kalia Bhils*. Observance of traditionality is comparatively less in their case. Some explain that Palia Bhils are original or 'Ujle', clean or pure, whereas the Kalia Bhils are polluted or Mele. But regarding this point, the Bhils have involved themselves in controversy. Those open to acculturation claim that they are more advanced, civilized and progressive, and so are *Ujle* or clean or pure. And the Palias, who are in less contact with outsiders and maintain primitive ways, are 'Male' or dirty. The groups, referred above, prefer to be respectively endogamous. Those who have been highly differentiated, at times even as separate tribes, and who socially consider themselves as above Bhils, and who maintain endogamy, are Bhilala, Bhil Garasia, Tadvi, Dholi Bhil, Rawal Bhil etc. Some of these are recognised as sub-tribes of the Bhils. Ranked order or social stratification is, at times, a feature reported among the sub-tribes and even in case of some clans of the Bhils. The latter specially holds true where the higher caste clan names have, somehow, come to the Bhils. This might have happened through miscegenation and borrowing. At times, the social differentiation is of such a magnitude that the members of two groups express it at the plane of 'we' and 'they'.

The break of former complete isolation of the Bhils is not merely a phenomenon of the very recent times but had occurred even as early as the immigration of Aryans. The Nishadas, at one time or the other, and for short or for long, developed contact in one form or the other with the Aryan people. But nothing definite and much can be said about the nature of that contact and so it will not be correct to enumerate what might have happened then. In later years when the Bhils came in contact with Marathas, Rajputs and Britishers, the contact situation involved flow of culture traits. The relationship of Bhils with the Rajputs was more or less cordial, as also lenient. But the treatment of Marathas was merciless and cruel. The ways through which some Britishers made attempts for the pacification and ramification of Bhils were such that most of it led to adverse consequences in Bhil social organization and economic system. The impact of new political agencies, land tenure and administration, during the course of contact with Britishers gave rise to new situations.

Another contact of Bhils, which has been comparatively more intimate, has been with the caste Hindus and the Christians.

The impact of Muslim ways has not been effective and long lasting. Wherever they exist, the Christian agencies of culture contact have a long past and have strongly influenced Bhil families. The impact of Hindus and their social system has been most vital and long lasting. In mixing villages, the Bhils and the caste Hindus have lived together for centuries. The transmission of cultural traits of caste Hindus is more identifiable. Acculturation has, however, not been uniform. As a result of the contact with Christian and Hindu ways of life, there have emerged new segments in the Bhil society. The formation of such social divisions has not merely given way to the feeling of social superiority and inferiority but has also adversely affected the behavioural and interactional patterns between the members of the same tribe.

Because of the impact of Christianity the Bhils are divided into two groups—the converts and the non-converts. The approach of Christian missionaries involved extension of material benefits which the convert lot could get. This attraction encouraged and gave way to the process of proselytization. The conversion to Christianity has also involved changes in the social life of the Bhils. Certain old taboos and sanctions had to be perceptionally redefined under the influence of Christianity. The converts form almost a separate social identity with distinct ways. Except the economic pursuits, which more or less have remained common for the converts and the non-converts, many other social and religious ceremonies and practices now widely differ. The converts are bent upon declaring themselves as an endogamous group and at times deny their tribal identity. On the other hand the non-converts consider themselves socially superior to the converts. Many of them equate the Christian Bhils with the untouchables and neither prefer to eat and drink with them nor marry. The Bhils with Christian influence have come out as 'Isolate' and their social relations with their non-converts brethren have been largely severed. The traditional structure of the Bhil ethnicity is more towards disruption, especially with the formation of this new endogamous unit within a tribe.

A similar form of stratification, in the once homogeneous Bhil society, has taken place under the influence of *Bhagat* (devotee) movement, a product of the influence of caste Hindus and their social organisation. The oldest Bhagat movement among the Bhils of Rajasthan is one of Mavji. It is nearly three centuries old. This Vaishnavite movement continued with interruptions. The *Bhagats* (devotees) of this sect are also referred to as Baneswar Dhamis or Baneswar Dham Panthis. The Mavji, considered as the tenth incarnation of Vishnu, has had a very large number of Bhil followers in Banswara and Dungarpur districts of Rajasthan. The sect is carried forward by the *Gurus* (chief disciple) one after another. Another sect, popular among the Bhils, is known as Lasodia. It was carried forward by Govindgiri and is more popular in Dungarpur, Banswara, Udaipur and the adjoining areas of Gujarat. This sect originated among Bhils around 1910. Another category of Bhagats is of those who have embraced Kamdia/Ram Dev Panth. This sect, among the Bhils, has a history of about 40 years. Shambhu Dal or Nathji sect provides another popular process encouraging Sanskritization among the Bhils. This is of recent origin and the number of followers is comparatively less.

The principles of Bhagat movement have a great equity with the traits of higher Hindu castes, especially the Brahmnic ones. Some Bhils have developed an understanding of the caste hierarchy in Hindu social system. The pattern of orderly placement of various castes in the social ladder is also not much hidden to them. With this background and with the adoption of the principles of Bhagat movement a new social stratification in Bhil society has emerged. This has, to some extent, disorganized the old ethnicity pattern and has provided a new relationship pattern. The Bhils who have discarded non-vegetarian food, who have stopped taking liquor, who wear Hindu sacred thread and saffron clothes, who do prayers, who take bath regularly, who have given up criminal habits and who speak truth, now associated themselves with a religious sect, known as the 'Bhagat'. Others who keep up their traditional habits and practices continue to be categorized as the non-Bhagat Bhils. Basically, the Bhagats and the non-Bhagats are from the same ethnic stock, have been considering themselves as the descendants of the same ancestor and had been maintaining the same type of socio-cultural and the value system. But a great gulf has now been created between the members of two divisions because one has lately switched on to a different way of life and value system. The *Bhagat Bhils* express that their social position got elevated because of the adaptation of new culture traits (as these are nearer to the higher caste Hindus). They now socially consider the non-Bhagat Bhils as their inferior. As a result of the feeling of this superiority, the Bhagats have already started breaking their social relations with non-Bhagat Bhils. As far as possible they do not arrange marriages of their children in the families of the non-Bhagats. They do not accept food from them and do not participate with them in any functions. If somehow a marriage between a Bhagat Bhil boy and non-Bhagat Bhil girl takes place, the latter has to undergo a great hardship for sometime. After marriage, when she goes to her in-laws, she has to maintain a separate set of utensils for herself; she will also not cook for any other member of the family of Bhagats. This is so because the Bhagats do not accept food prepared by a non-Bhagat, and also do not share the same utensil. After a few months when the daughter-in-law is turned into a Bhagat, her free and full participation in the household activities is allowed. After this, when she happens to visit her parents house, her participation is again restricted. She being a Bhagat prepares her own food separately and does not join her parent's common kitchen as the latter are non-Bhagats. The restrictions have thus been imposed even on the already existing free interaction in interpersonal relations. The Bhagat group of Bhils has further subdivisions. The Bhagats, specially in parts of Mewar, divide themselves into two distinct sections *viz.*, the *Kabirpanthi* and *Shambhu Dal*. The former is regarded socially superior to the latter. This is because the 'Shambhu Dal' Bhils or *Dhuniwalas* are comparatively less strict in the observance of the principles of Bhagat movement. They, at times, become more considerate in the matter of their relationship with the non-Bhagat Bhils. Unlike the Kabirpanthis, they are not strictly endogamous and many of them marry with the non-Bhagats, and also at times eat with them. Because of this consideration, the Kabirpanthis do not give an equal status to the Bhagats of Shambhu Dal. Under these conditions, ordinary Bhils and the Bhagats of Kabirpanth form the two extreme ends in the social hierarchy. The position, in between, is occupied by the Shambhu Dal Bhils who are in transition phase.

With the segmentation of Bhil society into diverse groups, socially inferior and superior, and with the prolonged and increasing contact with the caste Hindus, the Bhils could acquire knowledge in respect of the practices of the pollution and untouchability. They even observed that in the matter of social relations, privileges were enjoyed by certain caste members, while the same were denied to others. The Bhils also observed that in the matter of eating, drinking, smoking, house entry, sitting, use of well and the cremation grounds, participation in some public function etc., certain limitations were traditionally defined and marked in Hindu social system. It was further noted that even the touch of certain categories of people could not be tolerated by others. Under the contact situation, the Bhils too started considering certain category of people as untouchables. The idea of caste-based social inequality, which is reported among them, are mainly of Hindu origin. A sense of untouchability has also developed. In many areas, the Bhils, like the clean and the artisan castes, do not accept food from the *Bhangis* (scavengers) and *Chamars* (leather workers) considering them as untouchables. The Bhagat Bhils, who consider themselves more Hinduised, are comparatively more strict and they even sense pollution in respect of many tribals as well as the non-tribals. Traditionally, the Bhil society had never cultivated untouchability and inequality. The contact with caste Hindus, however, gave direction to the same.

The contact of caste Hindus and the Christians with the Bhils has also led to some breakdown in Bhil culture, and hence of the ethnicity supporting values. The detribalization was further strengthened by some workers who condemned certain native customs and practices, considering the latter as evils in Bhil society. Such people actually failed to take care of certain integral and related aspects which were part and parcel of Bhil life and kept them happy. For instance, the Bhil art of oral literature including folk songs, folk tales, folk lores, local proverbs and sayings rapidly declined in the absence of a right approach. Likewise, their folk dances and music, having great rhythm and movement, are under a setback.

The Mina, a scheduled tribe, is considered one among the earliest aborigines of Rajasthan and forms the largest tribe in the state. Maximum concentration of Minas is in Jaipur, Alwar, Bharatpur, Sawai Madhopur, Tonk and Bundi districts. Otherwise the Mina settlements are also found in other adjoining districts of Haryana.

Social divisions/segments among the Minas are many. The *Zamindar* (agriculturists and animal husbandry men) Mina is a major division. The people of this group are also known as *Badagaon Mina*. In fact the Zamindar Minas are believed to be those who surrendered and submitted to the more powerful Rajput invaders. The rulers then gave them land, with other help, and made them properly settled. They are comparatively well-off and docile in comparison to Chowkidar, another division, Minas who belong to denotified category, and once were labelled as the ex-criminal tribe. The Chowkidar Minas have been indulging in anti-social activities like the robbery, dacoity, theft, violence etc. They are said to be the descendants of those Minas who did not surrender, for long, to the mighty rulers and kept on waging guerilla warfare against them. They resorted to violent activities to express their resentment. Over the years the two divisions became more differentiated, so much so that many severed the connubial relationship with the Chowkidar Minas. This happened because of their socially low gradation. Another version, however, is that the Chowkidar Minas did not prove themselves cowardly, by not submitting themselves to the Rajputs, and they uphold their originality and hence higher status. Within this background they do not like to give their daughters, for marriage, to Zamindar Minas. But the version of Zamindar Minas is that they do not prefer to marry one from the Chowkidar group. As a means of pacifying the Chowkidar Minas, the Rajput rulers, Jagirdars and other villagers started engaging them as watchmen. And in case of any theft or dacoity, the Chowkidar Mina himself would be held responsible. Many of them continued in this job. But still in terms of their activities and habits, the Chowkidar Minas are well identified and differentiated from the Zamindar ones. The Chowkidar Minas are also called as Naya Basi, that is, the latter settlers. In course of time, the Chowkidar Minas, too, gradually started settling down. And Naya Bans, a place near Neem Ka Thana, is a settlement of Chowkidar Minas. Since the Zamindar Minas are the older or early settlers, they are also called as *Purana Basi*. Since the *Naya Basi* and *Purana Basi Minas* are originally the same, and the divisions crystalized only after the Rajput rule, they continue to share common Gotra names, say Chhapola and Bagri.

On the basis of descent and some eating habits, the origin of groups, known as *Ujla* and *Mela,* are reported. The *Ujla* stock explains its descent from Rajput father and Mina mother. They also refrain from eating beef. The Mela ones go in for beef (flesh of he-buffalo). Some also refer to them as Dhedia Mina. The concentration of Ujla is around Jaipur, including parts of Alwar and Tonk districts. It does not, however, mean that the Mela ones are not staying there. Those who ate he-buffalo flesh could be grouped as *Padihar* (Pads means he-buffalo) Mina. There is, however, yet another group called *Parihar* Mina. They are supposed to be the descendants of Parihar Rajputs of Mandor. Another division which grew on the basis of occupation is termed Chamaria Mina; the term referred to the Minas who resorted to leather work. Occupational specializations also led to the rise of certain other groups, say *Luhar Mina* (blacksmith Mina) *Khati Mina* (carpenter Mina), *Teli Mina* (oil presser Mina) etc. Another group which originated as a result of physical mixing of Mina and Bhil came to be known as Bhil-Mina. The Bhil-Minas are specially reported from Ajmer, Udaipur and Bagar, that is Dungarpur and Banswara. (Likewise the progeny of Mina man and Mali woman were named as Suretwal Mina. The descendants of marital alliances with other parallel castes of Mali were also included in the same category.) In this sense, the Minas who did not mix with any other ethnic group, in terms of physical mixing, were identified as Adu or Asli Mina. The other important divisions, based on the criteria other than those already mentioned, are referred to as Dassa and Bissa. The supporting structure to these divisions is provided by the practice of burial and the degree of criminality. The Dassa Minas resort to more criminal habits and cremate a dead body. The Bissa Minas, on the other hand, claim to have dropped most of such criminal habits. At the same time they have resorted to the practice of burying their dead. In other words the pattern of such divisions has religious roots. The fear of latter was affected the social life of the people, especially through the emergence of new principles.

The interaction of various divisions of Minas, already referred to, is well regularised in terms of concessions and limitations. By and large each proposes for its endogamous nature in terms of marital links. But on occasions the rigidity is not kept up. The same applies to the commensal relationships. However, there are certain groups specially those of Mela, Padihar, Dhedia and Chamaria where strictness is strongly observed, and the relationship with them is normally avoided by others. Since they are rated socially inferior, because of their eating and occupational pursuits, others like Zamindar, Ujle, Asli, Luhar and Khati Minas avoid them for occasion of dining and marrying. Whatever laxity, in terms of relationship, is observed remains confined to diverse groups falling almost in the same scale or very close to one another. Otherwise the people prefer not to cross their social boundaries, and limit their activities to the members of their own group. Another interesting phenomenon of sociological and anthropological importance is the fact that the divisions, as found among the Minas, are the creations of their contact with the non-tribals, especially the caste Hindus. For instance the Zamindar or Purana Basi and the *Chowkidar* or *Naya Basi* divisions or Minas were made only after their contact with the Rajputs. That the formation of divisions was initiated under the situation of culture contact is again clear from the groups like Suretwal, Luhar, Khati, Teli etc. Out of all the divisions, mentioned, only Bhil Mina is such which came into existence after the contact of Minas with another tribal group, that is, the Bhil. The ideology that eating of a particular food, say beef here, or the following of a particular occupation, say leather work, are degrading and make one impure or untouchable are again of Hindu origin. The Minas, thus, could differentiatic their own men, as separate social category, when they found them occupied with impure activities, say eating of beef or to work in leather. Thus were isolated, as outcastes, the Chamaria, Mela and Padihar. Further on, the understanding of concepts of purity and pollution kept on getting momentom because of the growing contact with caste society around. This strengthened the trend of divisiveness within the once homogeneous situation of the Minas.

Unlike the Bhils and Garasia, the Minas do not seem to be relegated to a socially low position by the caste Hindus. The Minas claim that their position in the hierarchical caste order is pretty high. They accept the socio-ritual superiority of Brahmin alone, and equate themselves with the Rajputs, Jats, Thakurs, Mahajans and Gujars of the area. The Minas higher social position is also reflected through their interaction with various caste groups. For instance, the Brahmin serves them on all relevant occasions. He does not mind accepting cooked food from them.

But still the raw and fried food is more acceptable to Brahmins. Thakurs, Jats, Mahajans and Gujars also accept food from Minas. The Minas themselves recognize *Khati* (carpenter), *Chhipi* (tailor), *Kumhar* (potter) and *Nai* (barber) as clean castes; the Rana, Fakir and Khangar as unclean, and Balai and Bhangi as untouchables.

Among the Scheduled Tribes of Rajasthan, Garasia stands third in terms of its numerical strength. Some, among Garasias, call themselves as Garaya. Chiefly concentrated in Udaipur, Sirohi and Pali districts of Rajasthan, the Garasias occupy the hilly and forest tract of Aravali hills. Some population of Garasias is also reported from the adjoining districts of Gujarat, specially from Banaskantha and Sabarkantha. In fact, a contiguous region bordering Sirohi, Udaipur, Pali, Banaskantha and Sabarkantha, is the present home of Garasia tribesmen. The are numerically dominant in this region, though a minority of other ethnic groups is also reported in the area.

The contemporary social organization of Garasias does not propose for a complete homogeneity. There are numerous divisions and groups based on definite criteria. Superior and inferior groups do exit and their differentiation is reflected in the network of actions and activities. Among the Garasias there are three broad social divisions. Because of these divisions the Garasia society presents heterogeneity—there is regular social stratification on the basis of descent and ensuing superiority or inferiority. The social stratification of Garasias is represented through (1) Rajput Garasia/Solanki Garasias/Palla Garasia (pure Garasias), (2) Garasia/Dungri Garasia and (3) Bhil Garasia. The lowest in social status are the Bhil Garasia, and the highest the Rajput Garasia. But some Garasias, specially of Abu Road Tehsil and those of the adjoining areas of Gujarat report of another division. They term it as Baba Rajput Garasia, and this stock represents the descendents of Rajput father and a Brahmin or Lohar mother. In other words there is no tribal blood in them. But they seem to have been differentiated as Baba Rajput Garasia because no other group accepted them. It may be mentioned that the Baba Garasias are accorded the superior-most social position; the Rajput Garasias follow. Obviously the Rajput Garasias are the descendants of Rajput man and Bhil woman. Likewise the origin of Bhil Garasia is sought from Garasia man and Bhil woman. The hierarchical ladder, socially speaking, is a complex one. Each of the divisions, mentioned above, is endogamous. It is not only the inter-marrying is forbidden, but some of the Baba and Rajput Garasias even prefer to avoid eating with Bhil Garasia. However, it is not a hard and fast rule. The Garasia hierarchy, thus, goes in tune with the nature of groups mixed. Since the Brahmins and Rajputs occupy higher position in caste stratification, their mixing with the aboriginals has reflected accordingly. In other words the reference group of Garasias is again the higher caste people. But as different from Bhils, the division among other Garasias are not really borrowing-based but involve kinship element in terms of descent. Bhil groupings, on the other hand, are totally devoid of kinship base. With pure tribal origin the Bhils are rated socially low than the Garasias. Such an hierarchy of Garasia and Bhil is socially accepted by both the groups. In addition to intra-Garasia hierarchy and Garasia-Bhil hierarchy, the Garasias also recognize their specific placement in social ladder in respect of certain caste groups of the region. But then such castes do not necessarily agree to what is explained by the Garasias themselves. At such a juncture certain inter-ethnic relations may be more revealing. Castes of the upper segment, that is the twice-born ones, are considered socially superior by the Garasias. The untouchable castes of the region, including Chamar, Dhed and Bhangi are taken as socially inferior by the Garasias. This is in tune with what the caste Hindus do. Also considered low by the Garasias are the Sargara and Bajania. In their relationship to other neighbouring tribes, the Garasias have a definite view-point. Bhils and Minas are considered socially inferior. The Bhils too accept their inferiority. But such a social placement is unacceptable to the Minas. And this sounds reasonable in the light of Mina's social position, already explained. Except the twice-born ones, the Minas express their inferiority to none.

The Garasias do not accept food and water from the untouchable castes. This kind of relationship is maintained with the clean caste people. Rated at the top of local social hierarchy is the Brahmin. Since the Garasias have not been assigned any specific placement in caste hierarchy their assumption of a social position involves contradiction. For their being numerically dominant in the area, the Garasias are reluctant to accept their inferiority to the serving castes. But then they maintain commensal relationship with some of them. Drinks, for instance, are acceptable to Garasias from *Nai* (barber) and *Kumhar* (potter). Many express their hesitance in accepting food from them. No commensal relationship is maintained with Bhil, *Bhangi* (sweeper) and *Meghwal* (leather worker). On the occasion of marriage of a Garasia, the Kumhar supplies earthen pots, Bhil provides music through the beating of a drum, and the sweeping is taken care of by the Bhangi. For specialised services rendered to the Garasias there is a provision of occasional as well as annual remuneration. The latter may be in cash or kind. The Brahmins do not serve all the Garasias. The affluent ones, among the Rajput Garasias, do invite and consult Brahmin for various auspicious occasions, including marriage. The Brahmin, too, does attend them. Such an interaction remains marginal.

With whatever has been said above one may safely derive that the stratification element in Garasia society is now more complex than ever before. The differentiation, in terms of superiority and inferiority, is not only limited to Garasias themselves but also extends to other caste groups in respect of whom the Garasias assess themselves. In other words these tribals have, of late, entered into a larger arena of inequality posed by the caste society around. In certain terms they are copying the caste Hindus.

Ladakh is the north-western part of India falling in the state of Jammu and Kashmir. Earlier boundaries of Ladakh district included Leh, Kargil and *Zanskar* (Padam) tehsils. Lately, however, Kargil has been carved out as a separate district. The word Ladakhi does not refer to every inhabitant of Ladakh. It does signify a specific ethnic group. Ladakhi apart, the other synonyms of this ethnic group are Bhot, Bod, Bodh, Botpa, Bhautta or Bota. In Ladakh, the Ladakhis form the predominant group and are all Buddhists. However, there are no exclusively Ladakhi villages; among others living with them are the Gara, Mon, Beda, Balti and Argon. Though the religious philosophy of Buddhism speaks for egalitarianism, there is reported a categorical stratification among the Buddhists. (The Balti and Argons being Muslims present a separate order.)

The Ladakhis occupy the highest rung of social hierarchy and are categorized as Mangric. They are predominantly agriculturists and animal husbandry men. Next lower category to Mangric is that of Dolba which includes Gara, Mon and Beda. The Garas have been practising blacksmithy and occupy a position immediately lower to the Ladakhis. They are followed by the Mon and the Beda respectively. Both of the latter groups are musicians; the Mons play on drum and the Bedas on flute.

A Ladakhi, being socially superiormost in Buddhist order of village community, describes the position of Gara, Mon and Beda through an analogy with arrow. A Gara's position is comparable to iron-head of an arrow ; a Mon's to the thread work, in-between iron-head and the shaft, and the Beda's position as equivalent to the shaft, the lower portion of the arrow.

A feature, more like the caste characteristic, is that the Ladakhi's social superiority is explained on the basis of occupation. The Ladakhis, who are basically agriculturists and animal husbandry men, regard blacksmith as a low profession. The Garas, who are blacksmiths, have thus, been given a lower social status. Likewise those who play music are underrated. Except in case of a few, the traditional professional set-up continues to be intact. Lately some artisan families have switched on to agriculture and labour. Many of them now work as civilian labourers in army organizations. This kind of job is also done by the Ladakhis. But even under new set-up a Mon plays on drum whenever the finds time. Likewise the Beda acts as flute player and Gara as blacksmith. The Ladakhis still treat Gara, Mon and Beda as serving class who serve them whenever required. On certain occasions it is obligatory for Gara, Mon and Beda to serve the Ladakhis, a system more akin to caste Hindus. For the service rendered they get the prescribed remuneration in cash or kind. The instance of professional change, marked in recent years, has neither affected the social position of various groups nor their role-system. The Ladakhis are of the opinion that the affiliation with a particular group is determined by birth and not by his change of occupation.

In the village layout no definite places have been marked for the members of different ethnic groups. It is not that the Ladakhis, being socially higher in position, would occupy particular section where none other would be accommodated. One can observe Mon's house near to that of a Ladakhi. Also the house of a Gara can be centrally located and surrounded by those of the Ladakhis. The position is, thus, not like a multicaste village of plain India where, in most of the cases, various sections are typically marked by the specific caste groups. However, a common pattern, which symbolises the social superiority of the Ladakhis over others, is that the houses of the Bhotos are nearer to the *Gompa* (monastery). In general the houses, belonging to others than the Ladakhis, are built little away from Gompa.

There is no customarily proposed taboo for entry into houses belonging to any group. But in actual practice many people express reluctance. Those owning better houses were also reluctant, largely out of their inferior social status. Further, the Gara, Mon and Beda would always wish a Ladakhi first by uttering *Zu-Zu* (style of wishing).

On the occasion of a worship or feast, organised by a Ladakhi family, invitees are made to sit according to a fixed pattern. This order is traditionally fixed in the light of the positions assigned to the individuals and the groups to which they belong. For instance the positions, marked as superior in the order of arrangement, would be occupied by the Ladakhis alone. Next, in order, would come Gara who would then be followed by the Mon and Beda respectively. Even the serving of food is regulated in the same process. The Ladakhi tables kept in front of the invitees are of different sizes. The biggest, in size, is kept in front of the Ladakhi, if *Lamas* (monks) are not there in the feast. The size of the tables then gradually decreases while coming to Gara. The Mons and the Bedas are not served on the tables. Generally they receive food either in the hands or on some leaf, or in their personal utensils which they carry.

In regard to commensal relations the avoidance of inferiors is not that sharply defined within the traditional framework. A Ladakhi can dine in the house of a Gara, Mon and Beda. There are no customary norms to prevent him in taking food in the houses of socially inferior people. But in actual practice the Ladakhis avoid to eat, with one or the other pretence, in a Mon or Beda house. But they easily join a Gara. The restriction is not for food but for the container in which it is served. A common container cannot be used by the members of all the groups. They have to be served in separate utensils. Some of Ladakhis have stated that they can eat in the houses of Mon and Beda if the food served to them is cooked by the Ladakhis. The Gara, Mon and Beda join in all the feasts arranged by the Ladakhis. On such occasions, the Mon and Beda either bring their own containers, or manage otherwise. Normally, a Ladakhi family does not provide them containers. The rules governing eating reflect on smoking too. The number of smokers is, however, less in Buddhist society of Ladakh. Smoking, under the religious cover, is regarded as a vice. A Ladakhi smoker does not circulate the same cigarette to a Gara, Mon or Beda. He rather restricts it among the Ladakhis. The same form of restriction is imposed in the matter of drinking *Chang* (a local hard drink) and *Gur Gur* (tea). The Gara, Mon and Beda can share a drink with Ladakhi, but not in the same cup. The application of rule is more severe for Mon and Beda. While sharing a drink they do sit together but with their respective cups. Members from all the groups make use of the common drinking water source. Neither anyone is denied the use of this source, nor they have different springs for different groups. So much so that anybody reaching the spring first is given the first chance. It is not that a Ladakhi gets priority over others.

In the formation of *Phasphun* (it refers to a group of families whose members help each other in the event of a birth, marriage and death) the social inequality is taken note of. The Ladakhis will have a Phasphun represented by their families alone. A Gara can never join a Ladakhi as his Phasphun member. Even if there is only one family of Mon in the village his Phasphun would consist of the families of Mons belonging to other villages. He is never allowed to have a Ladakhi or Gara or Beda Phasphun.

In the sphere of connubial relations the custom demands of each group to be endogamous. No regular marriage can be contracted between the members of two different groups. It is exactly akin to the characteristic of caste. Customarily the marital alliances are not appreciated outside one's own group.

Anyone, irrespective of his group affiliation, can express sorrow over the death of a person. A dead body is cremated by the Ladakhi as well as by the Mon, Gara and Beda. Usually the Phasphuns share a common crematorium. At the time of death, families from all the groups utilize the services of Lamas. The latter are not meant for Ladakhis alone. But then the social position again counts in the matter of carrying the dead body. The Ladakhis do not help carrying the dead body of a person belonging to any group lower than them. Thus, a Bhoto never carry the dead body of a Gara, Mon and Beda. According to the principle followed, the dead body of a person can be carried to the cremation ground only by the men of the dead man's group, or by those who occupy a socially lower position than the one of dead. In the absence of members from the same group the Ladakhi may, however, help to carry the dead body even if it belongs to lower social group. This is, however, rare and unusual.

The entire Buddhist population, including Ladakhi, Gara, Mon and Beda have access to Gompa. All can worship the gods and goddesses housed therein. In tune with the Ladakhis, the Mon and the Beda do make offerings and are free to consult Lamas and Kushok as and when required. The Lamas visit their houses to perform worship. The religious protection is equally shared. With all this the religion has again denied one privilege, enjoyed by the Ladakhis, to the socially inferior groups of Gara, Mon and Beda. The Ladakhis and others meet differential treatment in the selection of *Kushok* (head of monastery) as well as in the formation of *Lamas* (monks) and the *Chomos* (nuns). The Ladakhi children can become Lamas and Chomos. But the Mon, Gara and Beda, of the same village, are not allowed this concession. Kushok from the socially inferior group has never been heard of. Even if a Mon is willing to make his son Lama he is not allowed to do so. Inspite of their sharing a common Gompa and a common religious faith, the members of the socially inferior groups have been deprived of the concession. In almost every house there is a worship room and anyone, from any of the groups, can enter into it. For this purpose the entry into the house of a Ladakhi is not blocked for Gara, Mon and Beda. That a Ladakhi alone can become a Lama or Chomo is itself a point of superiority for him.

Gara, Mon and Beda inferiority is again reflected in the celebration of festive occasions at village or inter-village level. Only the Ladakhis dominate the scene in respect of participation. The people from the socially inferior groups do come but chiefly as observers. The archery competition is quite a popular festive occasion. Most of the villagers gather to participate. But the Mon, Gara and Beda are not permitted to shoot an arrow. Nobody would prefer to join their team. In certain other functions if all the members from other groups, than the Ladakhis, are allowed to participate they are given the roles rated as inferior and which the Ladakhis themselves would not be keen to perform. For instance, the performance of music, symbolised with inferiority, is always assigned to the Mon and Beda. Sitting in one corner, slightly far off, they play on their instruments as and when required. The right of full participation is denied even to the Garas who are rated as next to the Bhoto. In sacred dramas and dances which pave way to cultural transmission and provide entertainment only the Lamas participate. Indirectly, this is again the privilege of Ladakhis because it is only they who can become of Lamas.

In spite of the fact that the Gara, Mon and Beda form integral part of village community they are not given any position in leadership hierarchy. Their say in matters connected to socio-political control of the village is minimum. The Ladakhis provide social control mechanism and the rest adhere to the same. In all the villages the leadership continues to be in the hands of Ladakhis. The *Goba* (village headman) and the Members (sectional heads) are the agencies controlling life in the village. These positions, filled through selection, have always been denied to Gara, Mon and Beda. The latter, being in minority, are not in a position to assert for any position. A support to Ladakhi, in the context of village leadership, is the Gompa with which the village is attached. The Gompa organization, especially the Kushok and *Chang-zot* (the treasurer) have a say in the selection of Goba. As the Gompa hierarchy is always represented by the Ladakhis, they prefer to have a Ladakhi headman of the village.

In spite of the social stratification, of the kind explained in earlier paragraphs, there is tremendous amount of interdependence among the Ladakhis, Gara, Mon and Beda. This speaks of their high degree of organic solidarity. The Ladakhis being agriculturists and animal husbandry men provide various kinds of food stuffs generated through these occupations. The Gara, Mon and Beda get most of these produce in return of their services to the Ladakhi. There is great deal of reciprocity in terms of services and rewards. And such a relationship keeps, in general, the cohesiveness of the village community.

The Garas have been doing blacksmithy. They continue to prepare and provide all kinds of iron implements and tools to the needy villagers. Some of them also own land and do agriculture as a subsidiary occupation. The Ladakhis consider Gara as socially low because of the blacksmith profession. Between Gara and other ethnic groups in the village there is a specific kind of relationship involving rendering of service and returns. It does, to some extent, resemble the *Jajmani* (patron-client) system of caste society of plain India. For any iron tool or implement, to be made from Gara, the needy ones supply the iron. The workmanship is provided by the Gara and for which he gets the traditionally prescribed remuneration in cash as well as kind. Under the system, as prevalent in Spituk, a Gara makes and repairs various iron implements throughout the year for the families whom he serve. He also provides locks and keys. In return, he gets seven to fifteen Seers of wheat from each family he serves. More of it is given after the harvesting is over, and the rest before the start of sowing. At times the Gara is also given butter. In addition a Gara also receives *Bojha* (headload of fodder) from every family for whom he makes and repairs iron implements. On the occasion of a worship organized in a Ladakhi house, the Gara, Mon and Beda do attend. They are served meals over there, and while returning each of them is given a bag of *sattu* (flour of baked wheat and barley). One bag weighs about a kilogram. On the day of Losar, a Ladakhis festival, the Gara supplies iron needles to each family he serves and gets food in return, as also about a kilogram of Sattu. When a child is born in a family the Gara is given two seers of Sattu. In marriage he gets food and *Sattu.*

The Mons and Bedas are professional musicians. They have been, for centuries, playing on drums and flutes. Musical performance is a prerequisite to certain celebrations connected to Ladakhi life and culture. By and large the Mons and Bedas are landless and work as labourers whenever they find themselves free from giving musical performance. A few of the Mons own small acreage of cultivable land. Some are also engaged in carpentry. A few of the Bedas, specially the landless ones, depend on begging. As beggars they move from village to village. Such beggars are mostly the Buddhist Bedas who move with their tents and stop at a place convenient to their requirements. They keep dogs and pack animals, usually the donkeys. The Mons are permanently settled and thinly scattered, having one or two families in each village. The land-owning Mons do not cultivate it themselves. Rather, they get it cultivated by a Bhoto who is in possession of resource for the purpose. On most of the occasions the musicians, in attendance, are served Gur Gut, Chang, and food. Money is given only on the occasions of marriage and birth. A main source of income to a Mon musician is the annual gift which he receives from the Ladakhi families after the harvesting of crops is over. Depending upon the economic status each peasant family spares two to three Seers of wheat, gram or barley for the Mon family. This act is more of less obligatory for the Ladakhis, and is done in recognition of the services of Mon. On the occasion of Losar Mon offers an arrow to the male and a spinner to the female of all the families he serves. These articles are offered only to the senior members who reciprocate through the offering of food and *Sattu.* During the course of *Gyud,* a dance performed at the time of marriage, the Mon and Beda musicians get rupees two to three after every round. At the start of sowing of crops the Goru songs are sung by the Mons and Bedas. These songs are sung in praise of the cultivators, livestock and the crops. In return they get two kilogrammes of grain from each family. After harvesting the Mon and Beda visit all Ladakhi families and provide Larango music. They are given grain and salt on the occasion. After a death the Mon and Beda are offered two kilogrammes of *Sattu* each.

Relevant Issues

Model - 1, Western Indian Situation

1. Traditional elements of ethnicity supported mechanical solidarity. However, historical events and incidents, physical mixing plus intense culture contact with the non-tribals (chiefly caste Hindus and mildly the Muslims and Christians) have impaired this solidarity. This is supported by the growth of stratified order within the tribe.
2. The impaired traditional ethnicity has remained oscillating between its original form and those of the dominating surrounding groups, paving way to ethnic uncertainty and dilemma.
3. With the rise of new divisions, even the instance of organic solidarity could not be supported (some exception being the Minas) as the social segments or divisions, within the tribe, under this new order of stratification do not support much of functional inter-connectedness among various groups. And this is because these groups are not largely based on division of labour. Rather, they are mainly born of physical mixing and new religious tenets which the tribals are imbibing in search of new social status and identity.
4. Even the current inter-tribe and tribe-caste stratification indicates of no element of organic or mechanical solidarity among them. Structurally speaking the tribes have not been admitted into the caste order. Though they aspire, the tribals have not been able to find a place in the social ladder of caste hierarchy. And if at all it happens, the turn would involve more of assimilation which may gradually get them away from original ethnic identity.
5. And even if the tribals get a place in caste system, their problems would remain; they may even increase because the castes and the caste system have their own problems to add. But this is not being realised by the tribals as they strongly continue to consider higher castes and the caste system

thereof as their positive reference models. As the requirements of caste system are not in tune with those of a tribal organisation, the trend might pave way to their identity crisis in due course.

6. Though the current tendency of tribals to get into the wider nexus of caste based inequality and stratification has already started impairing their ethnicity, this trend is an indication of their getting closer, because of sharing of certain culture traits, to larger society and the nationalism thereof. But since the adoption of alien culture traits is haphazard, some of these may ultimately go contrary to the interest of tribals in general and nation in particular. (The trend might catch up in the form of religion-based fundamentalism, untouchability, caste-based feuds, dowry, *Purdah* etc.)
7. Since the stratified order, grown of late among the ones homogeneous tribes, has its roots in social and cultural parameters, and not in economic ones, it has failed to involve their elites to any significant order to carry forward serious kinds of agitations (exception being those mobilised for entry into caste Hindu temples). Comparatively more actively planned economic and social integration is containing them at this front, except the snow for sporadic and minor protests. In terms of ethnic mobility, their religious considerations seem to have over-shadowed economic hardship.

Model-II, North-Western Indian Situation

1. Traditional element of Ladakhi ethnicity remains intact in the absence of intense culture contact and for their being physically isolated due to ecological conditions. Dominant force of Buddhism and hard ecological conditions have helped retain organic solidarity of Buddhist groups.
2. No dominant positive reference group is available to the Ladakhis in near vicinity. They have the least contact with caste Hindus and their social-cultural system. This has also been helpful in the retention of traditional ethnicity. The Ladakhis association at macro level is rather slow and weak. Such trends did not provide scope for oscillation of ethnic identity and the connected crisis of ethnicity.
3. Under the conditions of isolation, there has been less scope of planned economic and social integration. This helped perpetuate economic hardship and alienation. Economic

discontent and deprivation have given them a feeling of beingunderprivileged. This hasprovided fillip to solidification of local ethnicities.

4. Under such circumstances the local elites have, time and again, tried to mobilise ethnic ethnocentrism for economic and power gains. Group consciousness, as also ethnicity-based violence seem to be promoting to fight against alien exploitation, more so in economic sense.

Issues and Questions

1. Ethnicities head towards loosing their primordial consciousness, traditional culture-based value patterns and solidarity in the event of intense culture contact with others. The process is speeded up under the condition of adoption of newer positive reference group/s. Should it happen, more in the interest of locals ?
2. Even in the event of birth of new stratified divisions, during eroding ethnicity, in them and even when the new ethnicity does not crystalise nor recognized (as the people are not accepted at a definite rung of social ladder under new system), people come closer to the nexus of larger society and macro nationalism in terms of sharing of wider perceptions, value system and other ways. Should it be encouraged ?
3. Rigidity of ethnicities persists in the event of their physical isolations and under absence of cultural communication with people at macro level. Their solidarity and homogeneity also remain intact. In that case the element of affiliation with wider society is either weakly developed, or is absent. People, by and large, then remain handicapped of macro nationalistic considerations. Should it be tolerated ?
4. Fxcessive solidification of tradition-based ethnicity makes people more ethnocentric in terms of in-group feelings and collective consciousness. This happens all the more when people feel that they acutely suffer from various kinds of economic deprivations, in diverse forms, at the hands of outsiders. Should this trend be allowed to grow when nature and degree of economic deprivation lead to corresponding level of unrest and violence among the ethnicities ?
5. To fight for the cause of their ethnics, the elites react faster in case of comparatively more isolated ethnicities, culminating, many a times, into upsurge and violence of

strong form, more so against those outsiders whom they find oppressing and exploiting them. Others blow off their stream through minor and short-range protests. How should such trends be reacted upon ?

Suggestions

1. Ethnicity should be contained to that extent only where it does not pose hindrance to larger national interest and integration. It should not be, otherwise, sacrificed at the alter of national society.
2. To regulate and achieve the above, the development of guided culture contact and awareness, as also the economic protection to the ethnicities should form prerequisites of intended integration.
3. To retain best in ethnic cultures, as part of broad policy of integration, the necessary and effective framework needs to be provided by the social scientists in general and integrationists and culture specialists in particular. This continues to remain an incomplete exercise, and hence the issues and problems of ethnic groups and their integration.

9

CULTURE CONTACT, ACCULTURATION AND INTEGRATION ISSUE

The tradition of studying changing context of tribal milieu mountingly emerged alongwith the baggage of improvement suggest over structure-functional orientation, an arena of grand-range thinking in the academic discipline of socio-cultural anthropology. The change paradigm, then, was chiefly measured within the framework of native-European contact (say Max Gluckman's study on Zulus) and the consequent acculturative influence. But when gradually the concept of acculturation crystalized (refer to conceptual framework of acculturation as propounded by M J Herskovits, Ralph Linton and Robert Redfield), the focus of studies within this format started extending even to culture contact without the element of European.

The idea concerning constancies and consistencies of enduring relationships started getting shaky with the switch over to change studies. In theoretic realm of social-cultural analysis, the ego or actor oriented approach was added to the continuing institutional approach. And this paved way to midrange ideas of 'network' analysis and the connected transactionalism (popularly known as theory of exchange on the lines suggested by G. C. Homans and Peter Blau). Believing in extensional nature of relational network, J. A. Barnes (in his study of Norwegian island parish) thought of 'network' approach which so well was made use of in social-cultural analysis of Indian tribal as well as non-tribal people by F.G. Bailey in Orissa and by Edward Jay and Adrian Mayer in Madhya Pradesh.

Studies of the above kind were suggestive of the processual explanations rather than surface touching in terms of network of relations or groupings based on enduring groups borne of descent or alliance formulations.

At one stage of our concern about Indian tribals the results of acculturation were more pronounced in negative sense when the anthropologists did talk of harmful effects of culture contact. Among others, this band was joined by S C Roy, J H Hutton, Verrier Elwin and partly Furer Haimendorf. Their ideas culminated in the policy of 'isolation' (including concepts of exclusion and partial exclusion of the tribals). However, some of them changed their vision over the years subscribing thereby to 'Integration' approach within the background of planned acculturation. But even then the difficulties remained and the clarifications still need to be sought on the issue of acculturation. Rethinking on its consequences is required.

Under the canopy of acculturation studies, more so in the light of ego-centred approach of cultural analysis in combination with processual analysis of social-cultural dynamics, the Rajasthan tribal situation poses for certain trends of growing concern. And I find that many of these are equally valid for some other tribal-nontribal situations in India, and hence all the more important for discussion.

With intermittent break, my anthropological research operation in tribal Rajasthan extend over a period little short of two decades (precisely from 1964 to 1983). My intensive studies and publications in the form of books and articles, have sustained my interest among the major Rajasthan tribes including Bhil, Mina Garasia, Bhil-Mina and Damor. Over the years, some of their villages were studied by me more than once, using extended case method (Victor Turner and Max Gluckman) and the technique of situational analysis (Van Velson). These helped understand the ongoing processes with better interpretive strategy. Otherwise the usual focus of studies has been on organizational aspects of mundane tribal life and culture.

Rajasthan finds place within the first five states of the country in terms of numerical strength of tribal population. Barring Bhil, which is so extensively studied by the scholars, the rest of tribes, more so the Seharia, Damor, Garasia, Bhil-Mina and even Mina, need to be explored more and more not only in respect of continuity of *status quo* but also in respect of culture contact, interaction and consequent pattern of change. In my focus I have tried to provide an overview of tribal Rajasthan in the sense mentioned above. Though my interpretations are specifically based on the study of seven villages, they derive strength from villagers interaction and contact with the neighbouring tribal and non-tribal populations in villages and urban centres. The pattern on interaction of little traditions (in the sense of Redfield), carried forward by the tribal folks, with those of great traditions (in the sense of Milton Singer), carried forward by educated literati belonging to higher caste segments, provided further avenues to explanations.

While talking of culture in the context of culture contact and acculturation, one should not, as a procedure, take it in an ordinary sense of those who associate culture only to various forms of art, aesthetics, dramatics or theatrical performances. Nor one should associate oneself with those who cultivate rigidity in terms of treating culture as mere part of a whole, adding thereby to multiple definitions of culture. It is desired to carry forward an inclusive concept of culture. This inclusiveness is at two levels ; firstly, when culture is seen as an abstract as well as substantive or reality, and secondly when culture is conceived with its all the three components, that is, sociological ideological and technological. These components, put together, present the totality of cultural milieu. And ingredients of each of them are to be explored when we account for acculturative influences and culture change. This makes the paradigm of culture broad-based. But for the purpose of a paper presentation, it becomes unmanageable to analyse all the traits/elements and complexes of any culture. I would, therefore, limit myself to certain sociological components of culture while explaining my view point concerning the issue of tribal integration.

The approach to, and policy regarding the Indian tribals, in general, have been changing from time to time. Under British colonial yoke the policy was one of 'isolation'. Under this were declared the 'Excluded' and 'Partially Excluded' tribal areas to provide protection to the inhabitants against non-tribals and their culture contact. The common thinking imbibed was that by keeping the tribals in isolation, they will be protected from all sorts of exploitation and will, thus, have a healthy and happy life. Those who thought of disadvantages of isolation policy, and those who realised that the tribals cannot be kept in isolation under the growing interaction in society proposed for the policy of 'assimilation'. The inherent idea in this approach was to assimilate the tribals with the non-tribals, specially the caste Hindus. They realised that it would help the tribals grow socially and economically, which was not possible under the condition of isolation. The social workers, social reformers and the religious missionaries largely subscribed to this policy. So much so that a few religious movements were also initiated, which holds true even for the tribals of Rajasthan, to gear up the process of assimilation. In fact the policies of isolation, an official one, and assimilation, largely a non-official one, continued simultaneously. It was after we took over from British rulers that both these policies were reviewed and found harmful in the larger interest of the tribals. It was realised that no iron bar could be put between the tribals and the non-tribals under the growing situation of culture contact. Nor the intended constitutional provision of developing the tribals, socially and economically, could be achieved by isolating or assimilating them. Against assimilation, it was agreed upon that such an exercise will make the tribals only a second rate copy of caste Hindus, or even of others who involve in such a venture. They would become poor converts from poor tribals, and would get confronted with more problems than getting relief. Analysing all these pros and cons, it was generally agreed upon that the policy of 'integration' of tribals should be adopted. As its prerequisite the tribals were to be integrated into the Indian mainstream (though this stream could not be clearly defined) without uprooting them from the best qualities of their life and culture. Any trend which would hurt their value system and sentiments was to be avoided. The tribals were to be helped to develop along the line of their own genius, without adopting any element of imposition on them. This was to be attempted through the directed programmes of tribal development as part of planned or induced programme of change. One of the requirements of the integration policy was to break the isolation. As such the tribals were exposed more and more to alien social-cultural situation. Indirectly, though beyond the official intentions, it enthused even assimilation as its operation found no curb from any corner.

Under the changing conditions and new requirements, and for various other reasons, the issue of tribal integration got more prominence. But in case of tribal situation the process of indiscriminate assimilation also got a fillip. Because of the planned programmes of change, some tribals were definitely benefitted in their material culture. But what really happened to their social integration is a point of concern to both, the social scientists and the integrationists. My observations, in this regard, are presently limited only to the Rajasthan tribal situation.

The network of village communities in Rajasthan is of a composite nature. This is born of the fact that the majority of the villages are multi-ethnic. In addition to multi-caste villages, there are mixed ones where inhabit people belonging to different religious faiths. However, the existence of some uni-ethnic villages cannot be ruled out ; these are specially reported from tribal areas and interior desert settlements. The causes of such diverse nature of human social network are varied. Apart from typical social organisations, where human interaction and kinship occupy an important place, there are the historical and ecological reasons. The history and ecology of Rajasthan have been so vast and varied.

The people of Rajasthan can be broadly classified under two categories, that is, the castes and the tribes. They have lived together for centuries as supported by the depths of historically. The culture contact between the members of castes and tribes is of a very deep past. The mode of contact and nature of interaction and relationship, however, speak of diversities of various kinds, involving healthy as well as unhealthy situations. In many a sense the influence of acculturation, more so on the recipient tribal aborigines, proved rather of an unwanted nature. This is well supported from certain aspects of life-designs where acculturative influences have affected the tribals adversely. This is mainly treated as an outcome of non-directed culture contact. Certain attributes of advantage, in a few ways of life, are also reported simultaneously as a consequence of culture contact situation. This is mainly the contribution of planned efforts of social change, which is essentially a phenomenon of post-Indian independence era.

There is a substantial tribal population in the State of Rajasthan. The major tribes reported are Bhil, Mina, Garasia, Sehariya, Damor etc. The concentration of Bhil is chiefly in south Rajasthan comprising the districts of Udaipur, Banswara, Dungarpur, Bhilwara, etc. The Garasias are largely found in Sirohi and Udaipur districts. The Sehariya are the inhabitants of Kota district. The major concentration of Minas is in Jaipur, Alwar, Saway Madhopur etc. The Bhil and Mina, who form the large bulk of tribal population, are said to be the earliest inhabitants of Rajputana and bear the longest history of culture contact and acculturation. Some of them had been even the rulers in certain parts till the Rajputs took over from them. Nature of contact with the non-tribals have been of various forms. For the present issue of discussing the tribal integration, I would analyse it in the arena of social organisation, and the ensuing segmentation thereof.

Observations on Bhils chiefly pertain to three villages, *viz. Masoron Ki Obri*, Alsigarh and Undri of Udaipur district. There usual network, in terms of relationship widens to Kherwara, Kesaryaji, Nai, Jhadol and Udaipur. The latter house the caste Hindus whom the Bhils consider as their positive reference groups and evaluate their own value system *vis-a-vis* others who are considered as the repository of great Hindu traditions. The members from the latter have carried forward many religious movements among the *Bhils* (both Vaishnavites and Shaivites). With their variety of implications, these have gone deep into Bhil socio-religious structure. Some of these are fairly old. These centres near Bhil villages have also exposed the tribals to new social order based on caste system and its inherent implications concerning social superiority/inferiority, touchability/untouchability, social segments etc. Feelings of high and low, clean and impure, inequality were let loose among the Bhil egalitarian order. With the rise of new segments (say Kalia, Palia, Bhagat etc.) the traditional patterns of commensal and connubial relations have also been disturbed causing distance and rigidity among the people and their interaction. The economically affluent ones, from such centres, penetrated into Bhil villages for money lending business. Over generations they have been maintaining creditor-debtor relationship on festivals like Holi and Diwali by distributing sweets and some piece of dress to their client Bhil families.

For quite sometime a movement, known as 'Bhagat movement', has grown popular among Bhils. A *Bhagat* is a devotee belonging to any Hindu religious sect introduced among the Bhils from outside. The religious reformists, who carry on the Bhagat movement from within and outside, have posed for a variety of conditions, as part of their principles, to be regulated in case of those Bhils who opt to get into the fold of Bhagatism. The oldest Bhagat movement among the Bhils of Rajasthan is one of Mavji. It is nearly three centuries old. This Vaishnavite movement continued with interruptions. The Bhagats of this sect are also referred to as Baneswar Dhamis or Baneswar Dham Panthis. Mavji, considered as the tenth incarnation of *Vishnu*, has had a very large number of Bhil followers in Banswara and Dungarpur districts of Rajasthan. The sect is carried forward by the *Gurus* (chief disciple) one after another.

Another sect, popular among the Bhils, is known as Lasodia. It was carried forward by Govindgiri and is more popular in Dungarpur, Banswara, Udaipur and in the adjoining tribal areas of Gujarat. This sect originated among Bhils around 1910.

Yet another category of Bhagats are of those who have embraced Ram Dev Panth. This sect is about forty years old. Shambhu Dal or Nathji sect provides another popular process encouraging Sanskritization among the Bhils. This is of recent origin and the number of followers is comparatively less. Because of the increasing culture contact with caste Hindus, and the subsequent growing consciousness about the hierarchical order of castes, involvements of Bhils in Bhagat movements has rapidly increased. The trend continues to get impetus under the impression that the Bhils social status would enhance through such a process of Sanskritization.

The Bhil society is being disintegrated by the creation of divisions formed of Bhagats and non-Bhagats ; the two groups of the same tribe are now falling apart even in terms of connubial and commensal relations. And their position in caste hierarchy is still not fixed ; the caste Hindus of upper and middle caste segment continue to treat the Bhils as socially low.

The acculturative influence of the above kind is more intensively reported in case of the Bhil-Mina of Barapal, a village between Udaipur and Kherwara. This village is comparatively more exposed to alien influence being situated on the national highway. Considering themselves as the descendants of Mina father and Bhil mother, the Bhil-Mina profess of their superiority to Bhils but inferiority to the Minas. Being Pal dwellers they also assume superiority over their non-Pal dweller brethren. However, the others do not agree to it. In terms of economic exploitation and social divisiveness, they sail in the same boat as the Bhils. But the age at marriage has fast been reduced in their case in comparison to the Bhils. This trend, among the Bhils, is reported more in case of families more exposed to alien influence. In Barapal, there is more rigidity about *Purdah system* (veiling of face by the woman), a typical culture trait of the caste society around. Child marriage and Purdah system are restraining women emancipation and curtailing their involvement in various programmes of change. Regarding the use of forest they share common problems with the Bhils of Alsigarh and Undri. Though Alsigarh had been having a Van Sramik Sahkari Samiti, the ignorance of its Bhil inhabitants paved way for outsiders' exploitation.

The Garasias of Tulwaron-Ka-Naka, a village in Abu Road Tehsil and the Damors of Sadri village in Simbalwara block of Dungarpur district share many features in common with the Bhils and Bhil-Mina, though they socially place themselves at a higher level. Both consider themselves as the descendants of Rajput father and Bhil mother and enjoy social superiority over the Bhils as well as the Bhil-Minas. They have imbibed more culture traits of higher caste Hindus and hence more rigidities in terms of Purdah system, child marriage, untouchability etc. Their regular and intensive contact with the neighbouring urban centres has strengthened such trends. Whereas the Garasias of Tulwaron-Ka-Naka are more in the clutches of *Sawkars* (money-lenders), the problem in case of Damors is not that acute. But then the Damors marry comparatively at a younger age. The impact of religious movements is equally strong in case of the Garasias and the Damors. When some of the rituals and ceremonies speak of the great tradition influence, there is also the continuity of folk gods, goddesses and deities. The Rajput and Baba Garasias crystalized themselves as higher social groups than the Bhil Garasia. In case of the former the acquisition of alien culture traits is more and prominent. Though not in alarming form, the instances of land alienation could be reported from Garasias, but not from the Damors. The Bhils too share the problem of land alienation. Unlike the Garasias, the Bhils are involved in the system of bondage (Sagri), though the system is said to be officially abolished. The practice of bride price, an in-thing in traditional tribal social structure is getting a jolt, more among the Damors, Garasia and Bhil-Mina. Though it is still predominantly reported, there is growing inclination to dowry, again a feature of higher caste Hindus in the area of their habitation. The Bhils are largely free of this menace. While the Bhils continue to provide more freedom (in terms of mate selection, movement, speech etc.) to their females, the Damors have fast curtailed it. The Garasias are less considerate in the matter than what they used to be at one time. They are now putting restraints on various activities which did speak of woman's freedom sometime ago. Pre-marital sex relations and freedom of mate selection are now curtailed. However, the Bhils continue to respect the traditional provisions in their social structure regarding conduct of females in pre- and post-marital stages. Even the age at marriage is comparatively high among them, exception being those Bhils who have been more influenced by the non-tribals.

The acculturation, intended or non-purposed, has also influenced certain spheres of tribal customary laws. For instance, among the Bhils and Garasias marriage by elopement has been a socially sanctioned mode of acquiring mate. But then the social system of caste Hindus, as also the provision of formal legal system do not approve of the same. Likewise, the alien social criticism has affected pre-marital sex freedom, *bride-price* (dapa) etc. *Natras* (frequent remarriages) of the old form are denounced under new social situation. *Nukta* (a customary death feast) among the Minas has been occasionally interfered with. Customs, practices and rituals of the above kind have been having functional importance in the native social system as per peoples cognitive mapping.

The Minas of Mainpura, a village in Sawai Madhopur district, pose for many characteristics distinct from the Bhil, Garasia, Damor and Bhil-Mina. Though the history of culture contact among the Bhils is of very deep past, the acculturation instance among them is of a far lower frequency than the one reported in case of the Minas. Unlike the Bhils, Garasias, Bhil-Minas and Damors, the social system of Minas has come too close to the caste social order. Baring a few instances, they practise what other higher caste Hindus of the area do. That may be the reason that the Mina equate themselves with the Jats, Gujars, Rajputs, Ahirs in the local caste hierarchy. They very well understand of the social rungs and their placement in various caste segments. They maintain patron-client relationship with other caste people and observe reciprocities of various forms. These are not frequently reported in case of Bhil, Garasia, Bhil-Mina etc. But like the Bhils and Garasias, the Minas also got divided in different segment marking social inequality. For instance, they have Zamindar, Chowkidar, Chamaria, Khati Mina etc. Unlike other tribals, they have imbibed great traditions to a very large extent and created a place in local caste hierarchy. Their mechanism of social control differs from rest of the Rajasthan tribals. Their Panch Patel, Samaj and Pargana Panchayats are still very strong and represent an elaborate regional political system. Economically, they are far better than the other tribals. Problems of exploitation, land alienation, indebtedness etc., are minimum in comparison to Bhil, Garasia, Damor, Bhil Mina etc. Being more influenced under culture contact, the Minas have an acute problem of child marriage. The practice of dowry has gone deep into their system. Both of these customs do not yet seem as big problems in rest of Rajasthan tribals, though some have fallen in the process. When the women seem to be enjoying a better status among the Bhil, Garasia and Bhil-Mina tribes, the Mina women are too suppressed. They have no say in mate selection, their mobility is curtailed and they hardly enjoy the kind of freedom as the Bhil or Garasia women do.

The once homogeneous social organization of Minas started getting impaired mainly after the development of their contact with the wider caste-based social order of plural society. Over the years a large number of social segments have emerged among them. The major division is termed as *Zamindar* (agriculturists and animal husbandry men) Mina. The people of this group are also referred to as Badagaon Mina. The Zamindar Minas are believed to be the descendents of those who surrendered and submitted, in the historical past, to the more powerful Rajput inductees in the region. The powerful intruders gave, in due course, land and other help, to make the then revolting Minas properly settled. This group of Minas is economically well off and docile in comparison to those who carried forward the label of denotified category and once were labelled as ex-criminals. The Chowkidar Minas, another group reported among these people, carried forward a history of rather anti-social activities including robbery, decoity, theft, violence etc. Those belonging to this group are believed to be the descendents of those who did not surrender, for long, to the mighty non-tribal rulers and kept on waging guerilla warfare against them. And to express their resentment, their fraternity resorted to violence. Over the years these two groups of Zamindar and Chowkidar Minas got conspicuously differentiated, so much so that many severed the connubial relationship with each other. This happened on account of ascription of socially low position to the Chowkidar Minas. The Chowkidar Minas are also called as *Naya Basi*, that is, later settlers. The Zamindar Minas, being early settlers, are also referred as *Purana Basi*. There is yet another group called Parihar Mina. They are supposed to be the descendents of Parihar Rajputs of Mandor. The group Chamaria Mina includes those Minas who resorted to leather work like the Chamars among the caste Hindus. Occupational specialisation, on caste model, led to the rise of certain other groups, say Luhar Mina (blacksmith), Khati Mina (carpenter), Teli Mina (oil presser) etc. Suretwal Mina, another social group, are believed to have originated out of Minas physical mixing with certain members of castes belonging to the middle segment of caste hierarchy.

The above referred divisions, born of culture contact and acculturative influences, have devised set rules of interaction. In terms of marital alliances, each group proposed for endogamy. However, this has not proved as a very rigid constraint. Likewise some relaxation is also granted at the level of commensality. But with certain groups, say Dhedia and Chamaria, strictness is cultivated in terms of connubial and commensal relationship. The Zamindar, Luhar and Khati Minas would never approve of such relationship. Except in case of groups, more close in terms of social status, people duly observe the limitations imposed by the members of their respective groups. The Mina ideology that eating of a particular food, say beef, or the adoption of a particular occupation, say leather work, are socially degrading, making one impure or untouchable again has its root in Hindu social system. And because of the practical implications of such an ideology, many of the above-referred categories crystalized. The familiarity with the concepts of purity, pollution and untouchability, again emanating from caste Hindu way of life, added to the divisive tendency in the once homogeneous situation of Minas.

Expressing their affiliation to caste system, the Minas claim that they occupy a fairly high position in the local caste hierarchy. Accepting social-ritual superiority of Brahmins alone, the Minas almost equate themselves with the Rajputs, Jats, Thakur, Mahajan and Gujars of the region. Even the nature of Mina interaction and relationship with the members of various castes speaks of their socially high placement as far as caste order is concerned. Brahmin, Thakur, Jat, Mahajan, Gujjar etc., accept Mina food. At the same time the Minas recognise Khati, Chhipi, Kumhar and Nai as clean castes; the Rana Fakir and Khangar as unclean, and Balai and Bhangi as untouchable.

That the Minas have been largely integrated into caste hierarchical order is again supported from the patron-client relationship they have entered into with certain caste groups. For instance the Ranas entertain the Minas ; the Nais serve them as they do to other castes ; Balai works as their Panchayat messenger ; the Dhadhi and Dhom act as bards or ministerels of Minas and Joga records their marriage and death feasts. The Brahmin serves Minas as he does in case of other castes. Certain other practices also speak of their nearness with upper caste Hindus.

The above empirical exercise supports that Rajasthan tribes bear a long history of culture contact and consequent acculturative influence. These seven villages and their surrounding social network are also on intimate contact map. All fall within a radius of, say, twenty kilometres from the urban/religious centres or the big multicaste villages. At least for the last few decades the communication network connecting these villages to non-tribal social-cultural situation has fast developed. Most of them are connected by road communication. The villages have, thus, remained more open to planned or directed contact on the one hand and unplanned or non-directed contact on the other. The former is chiefly an outcome of programmes of community and tribal development launched after Indian independence, and the latter bears centuries old history.

Whereas the tribals have gained from the agents of planned programmes of change and development, especially in the field of education, health and partly agriculture, the process of suffering under unplanned culture contact situation has caught further momentum. This maintains continuity of many socio-economic problems and the connected background processes thereof. The processual network analysis, given in the body of this paper, supports the existence and continuity of many issues of concern to social scientists in general and anthropologists in particular. And as part of future projection, it may be said that these may continue unless controlled and regulated by scientifically designed strategy. The fixity to such processes may be maintained in years to come as no iron curtain can be put in-between the tribals and unplanned or haphazard culture contact and the agencies and social categories thereof.

The major areas of concern involve the following :

(1) There is growing divisiveness and incoherence in tribal social organisation—an oscillating form not finding feet neither in the traditional milieu nor in the one they got familiar with under the situation of culture contact. On the one hand the mechanical solidarity has been impaired and on the other the organic one is by and large not grown (exception being the Minas). Instances of intra as well as inter-tribe stratification have come on the surface. Now the Bhils, Mina, Garasia, Damor, etc., can be placed in a definite social hierarchy. Inequality also marks different social divisions within the tribe. These are attended by certain traits of social distance and cultural disparity marking growing signs of disintegration. The emic conceptions and etic expressions (through a variety of symbols) speak of such processes and inclinations.

(2) The culture contact and widening network of relationships have given a wrong and misleading impression on the tribals in terms of gain in exchange through interaction. In the process of simply copying, the tribals are not clear in their goals. A usual explanation is that since others are having a

particular web of social institutions and cultural values, they also need to have them. What gain they will derive is not clear. Rather they are loosing in certain sense.

(3) In addition to social disorganisation in the native designs of living, the tribals (except the Minas) have since long fallen in the outsider's channel of their exploitation. In spite of relevant protective legislations and direct measures of development, the majority of the tribals continue to face acute economic hardships. Poverty, indebtedness, bondage etc., perpetuate unabated through various forms of exploitation.

(4) Within the brittle 'thought of order', born of acculturative influence, certain other areas of their 'matter of fact' social world are also in the process of transformation in wrong channel. Two of these, that is, changing trend from bride-price to dowry and the rising trend of curtailment of the freedom to tribal women, are more prominent. These are heading to the induction of new social problems. The ongoing process has already started adversely affecting the status of tribal women. The new constraints on women are of high magnitude among the Minas than the Bhils and Garasias, though the latter are also in the process of toeing the line of Minas.

(5) Certain customary laws, in the best interest of native socio-cultural system, are also in the way of threat from external forces—formal as well as informal. Considering the tribal customs and practices as exotic or archaic, the outsiders pose hindrance through unpalatable criticism and derogatory remarks along with other form of intervention.

Most of the trends of the above form are also reported from other tribes of central India, though the same is of lesser magnitude among the tribes of south India and still less among the north-east Indian tribes. And the tribes in the thick of such trends have reached a point wherefrom it is not easy to think of revivalism of traditional homogeneous tribal identity in the broad sense of the word. Such movements have, however, been frequently reported from the smaller tribes particularly of north-east India.

Anyway, the pressing demand is to resolve and reformulate the conflicting views among the existential and the academic social scientists regarding the issue of introducing change and transformation, or even for regulating the same. The professional ethics and methodological requirements come in-between the two categories among sociologists and social anthropologists while discussing whether we should commit ourselves to bringing about change or interfere in the change process. The academic sociologists or social anthropologists stress on research and research findings, and suggest not to go beyond that within the framework of their professional ethics. On the other hand the category of existential ones demands that we should suggest for change and involve ourselves in suggesting, causing as well as directing change processes.

The scholars and intellectuals need to intervene on such fronts concerning society and culture. They are required to devise alternative strategies for trends going contrary to human interests in general by recreating philosophy and ideology keeping in view new requirements of society caught in the storm of multiple form of dynamism born of induced and haphazard change. If scholars continue to put up with undesirable trends at the level of grass root empirical reality thenthey would be charged for lack of commitment to society. New ideologies are to be provided, in tune with the emerging trends, befitting to larger interest of society and its integrated social order. Curbing of disintegration and divisiveness is the demand of the day.

Within the above background I have made a modest culture-based attempt which, as I understand, can provide incentive for further debate.

Taking stock of the implicit and explicit tribal culture contours, born of social organisation vis-a-vis change, I need to stress on two fronts. Firstly, we have to assess the correct state of mind of the tribals in respect of the growing social tendencies. Understanding of such mentalism is essential to grasp the situation. Secondly, we need to explore as to what have the tribals apparently gained, in terms of concrete, out of new social formations and how do they account for it. Putting these two perspectives together, the social scientists need to streamline and consolidate the approach to curb the divisive tendency in the interest of integration, both at micro and macro levels. To make the proposed approach effective one would need to initiate revivalism of relevant tribal traits ; in this case the age-old tribal consciousness is to be revitalised in respect of this particular area of social organisation.

Those who can readily be engaged to do the above job are the change agents involved in the massive programme of planned tribal development. Some like-minded social workers may also be involved in the task, especially those who do not subscribe to assimilation. However, both these categories of workers would need specified orientation for the purpose. The efforts through individual and mass contact, as also through various other modes of propaganda and publicity can help revive positive perspective of native tribal world-view which usually remained wedded to integrated and united living. Once it is generated to a sufficient extent, the tribals would not even subscribe to the deadly caste system, which itself is an evil and barrier to integration. The agents of planned change, both official and non-official, would need to convince the tribals that their socio-economic development is possible without their cultivation of pro-caste tendencies and the attendant evils. And that the segmentation on caste lines will not only destroy their better value system but would ultimately be deterrent to their socio-economic growth. Simultaneously are to be checked the unwanted penetrates in tribal settlements who carry forward a variety of messages, in various religious garbs, which go, directly or indirectly, contrary to the interest of integration. This may be tried through protective legislation. However, more is to come from within the tribal milieu for which they need to be mobilised and oriented in the best interest of integration—a crying need of the day.

BIBLIOGRAPHY

Aiyappan, A., 1935, "Fraternal Polyandry in Malabar" *Man in India*. Vol. XV, No. 11, Ranchi.

Anderson James N., 1973, "Ecological Anthropology and Anthropological Ecology", in *Handbook of Social and Cultural Anthropology*, ed., John J. Honigmann. Rand McNally and Company, Chicago.

Ao, Alemchiba, 1972, "The Problem of Readjustment to a new situation (with special reference to Naga Tribes)", in *Tribal Situation in India*, ed., K.S. Singh, Motilal Banarsidas, Delhi.

Asosoyonon, 1974, *The Rising Nagas*, Vivek Publishing House, Delhi.

Bamzai, P.N.K., 1962, *History of Kashmir*, Metropolitan Book Co., Delhi.

Bareh, H., 1970, *Gazetteer of India*, Nagaland Kohima District, Saraswati Press, Calcutta.

Barth, Frederick, 1969, Ethnic groups and boundaries in the social organisation of culture differences. Quoted in Multiethnicity and problems of national integration by S.K. Gupta, G.B. Pant Institute of Social Sciences, Allahabad, 1982.

Baruah, T.K.M., 1977, *The Singphos and their Religion*, Directorate of Research, Shillong.

Bhandari, Arvind, 1970, "Polyandry : Base of Ladakhi Buddhists", *Indian Express*, April 26, New Delhi.

Bhattacharjee, T.K., 1975, *The Tangams*. Research Department, Government of Arunachal Pradesh, Shillong.

Bheghley, L., 1978, *Social Stratification in America*. Good Tear Publishing Company, California.

Bhowmick, P.K., 1980, *Shifting Cultivation : A Plea for New Strategies in Shifting Cultivation in North-East India*. NEICS, Shillong.

Bordoloi, B.N., 1980, "An Ethnographic Note on the Hmars of the North Cachar Hill District of Assam". *Bulletin of the Tribal Research Institute*, Vol. 1, No. 1, Gauhati.

—,—, 1984, *The Dimasa Kacharis of Assam*. Tribal Research Institute, Gauhati.

Bordoloi, B.N., Thakur, Saikia and Das, 1985, "Traditional Tribal

Institutions. *Bulletin of the Tribal Research Institute*, Vol. 1, No. 3, Gauhati.

Borgohain, H., 1961, "Socio-Religious Prohibition Among the Adis". *Resarun Journal of Research Department*, No. 1+2, Government of Arunachal Pradesh, Shillong.

Borthakur, D.N., 1976, "Improving Productivity with Special Reference to the North Hill Region", Paper Presented at Indian Science Congress.

Bose, Saradindu., 1967, *Carrying Capacity Under Shifting Cultivation*, Calcutta.

Briffault, R., 1927, *The Mothers*.

Bromley, Yu. V., 1976, *Soviet Ethnography - Main Trends*, USSR, Academy of Sciences, Moscow.

Buckley, Walter, 1968, "Social Stratification and the Functional Theory of Social Stratification". *American Sociological Review*, Vol. 23, August.

Burling, Robins., 1963, *Rengsanggri : Family and Kinship in a Garo Village*. University of Pennsylvania, Philadelphia.

Census of India, 1901, Census Report of Bengal.

—,—, 1911, Punjab.

—,—, 1931, Vol. I, Part I, Also Vol. XVII.

—,—, 1892, Punjab.

Chakravarti, Rama., 1986, *People of India*. B.R. Publishing Corporation, Delhi.

Chattarjee, B.B. and T.C. Jha, 1965, "Changing Family in Polyandrous Community". *The Eastern Anthropologist*, Vol. XVII, No. 2.

Chattopadhyay, K.P., 1957, "On Polyandry". *Journal of the Asiatic Society of Bengal*, Vol. XXII, No. 2.

Chaturvedi, D.N., 1968, "The Bhils of Rajasthan through Ages". *Tribe*, Vol. 5, No. 3, Udaipur.

Conklin, H.C., 1961, "The Study of Shifting Cultivation". *Current Anthropology*, February.

Council for Social Science Research, 1980, *Shifting Cultivation in North East India*, Shillong.

Cunningham Alexander, 1854, *Ladakh : Physical, Historical and Statistical*. Sagar Publications, New Delhi. Also 1970 edition.

Dahrendorf, Ralf, 1959, *Class and Class Conflict in Industrial Society*, Routledge and Kegan Paul, London.

Das Gupta, D.K., 1982, "A Brief Note on Sherdukpen Language", *Resarun Journal of Research Department*, Directorate of Research, Shillong.

Das Gupta, P.K., 1983, *Life and Culture of Matrilineal Tribes of*

Meghalaya, Inter-India Publication, Delhi.

Das, A.K. and M.K. Raha, 1967, *The Rabhas of West Bengal*, Government of West Bengal, Calcutta.

Dasgupta, P.K. and N.K. Das, 1984, "Socio-Cultural Aspects of Cultivation and Soil Conservation in North-East India" in *Socio-Economic Aspects in Soil Conservation Activities with Special Reference to North-East Region*. Government of Meghalaya, Shillong.

Datta, P.S., 1988, "Shifting Cultivation in Hills of North-East: A Case for Reassessment", Paper presented in Seminar organised by IASSI.

Dave, P.C., 1960, *The Garasia, Bharatiya Adimyati Sewak Sangh*, Delhi.

Davis, K. and W.E. Moore, 1945, "Some Principles of Stratification". *American Sociological Review*, No. 7.

Davis Kingsley, 1960, *Human Society*. The Macmillan, New York.

Deb Roy, H., 1981, *A Tribe in Transition : The Jaintia in Meghalaya*, Cosmo Publication, New Delhi.

Deori, R.K., 1981, "Marriage System of the Mijis of West Kameng District" Resarun, Government of Arunachal Pradesh, Shillong.

Deori, R.K., 1978, "A Brief Note on the Inter-relationship of the Sulung and the Bangnis of Kameng District, Arunachal Pradesh". In *Research in Arunachal,* Directorate of Research, Government of Arunachal Pradesh, Shillong.

—,—, 1982, The Sulung. Research Department, Government of Arunachal Pradesh, Shillong.

Dev, Bimal J. and D.K. Lahiri, 1983, *Lushai Customs and Ceremonies*. Mittal Publications, Delhi.

Dhar, Bibhas, 1982, "Chhos Kor : The Festival of the Monpa and the Sherdukpen". *Journal of Indian Anthropological Society*, No. 17: 265-68.

Directorate of Information, 1984, *Mizoram, News Magazine*, No. 1, Mizoram.

Directorate of Information and Public Relations, 1982, North-Eastern Council : A Decade of Service, North Eastern Council, Shillong.

Dilthey, Witgenstein, 1978, Referred to by Quinton Skinnee Social Meaning and Social Explanation, ed., P. Gardiner. *The Philosophy of History*, Oxford University Press.

Doshi, J.K., 1976, *Social Structure and Cultural Change in a Bhil Village*, New Heights, Delhi.

Dube, S.M., 1978, "North-East India : A Sociological Perspective", In *North-East India : A Sociological Study*, ed., S.M. Dube, Concept Publishing Company, Delhi.

Dutta, Parul, 1973, *The Noctes. The Directorate of Research of Arunachal Pradesh,* Shillong. Also 1978 edition.

—,—, 1984, "*Cultural and Historical Background* of the Noctes of Arunachal Pradesh", in *Tribes of North-East India*, ed., S. Karotempral, Vendrame Missiological Institute, Shillong.

Dutta, B.B., 1980, "Shifting Cultivation : A Few Comments from the Angle of Productivity", in *Shifting Cultivation in North-East India*, NEICS, Shillong.

Dutta, P.C., 1982, "Agricultural System of the Wanchos", *Resarun*, Vol. VIII, No. 2, Shillong.

Dutta, P. S., Sinha and L. Devi, 1978, "Festival of North-East India", in *Souvenir Anthropological Students Convention*, Gauhati University, Gauhati.

Duarah, D.K., 1981, "Food Habits of the Tribes of Arunachal Pradesh", *Resarun* No. 1+2, Government of Arunachal Pradesh, Shillong.

Durant, Will, 1954, *The Story of Civilization*, Part I.

Ellen, R., 1982, *Environment, Subsistence and System*, Cambridge University Press, Cambridge.

Elwin, Verrier, 1959, *A Philosophy for NEFA*, Shillong.

—,—, 1959, *The Art of the North-East Frontier of India*, Shillong.

Epstein, A.L., 1978, *Ethnos and Identity*, Tavistock Publications.

FAO, 1980, Report on Population Data Regarding Forest Communities Practising Shifting Cultivation.

Featherstone, B.K., 1926, *An Unexplored Pass.* Hatchinson & Co., London.

Fernandes, Walter, 1988, "Shifting Cultivation, Deforestation and Technical Changes". Paper presented in Seminar organised by IASSI.

Fernandes, Walter and Geet Menon, 1987, "Tribal Women and Forest Economy", in *Deforestation, Exploitation and Status Change.* Tribes of India Series, Indian Social Institute, New Delhi.

Fischer, H.T., 1952, *Polyandry. International Archives for Ethnography*, Vol. XLVI, Leiden.

Fosbery, F.R. 1963, *Man's place in the Island Eco-system*, Bishop Museum Press, Honolulu.

Frunck, A.H., 1907, *A History of Western Tibet*, Patridge.

Gassah, L.S., 1980, "Village Administration in Jaintia Hills : A Comparative Study of Two Villages". *The Journal of NEICSR*, Vol. IV, No. 1.

Geertz, Clifford, 1963, "Religious Beliefs and Economic Behaviour in a Central Javanese Town : Some Preliminary Consideration", *Economic Development and Culture Change* - 2.

Ghosh, B.B., 1979, Nagaland District Gazetteers : Mokokchong, Government of Nagaland, Kohima.

—,—, 1979, *Nagaland District Gazetteers*: Zumheboto, Government of Nagaland, Kohima.

—,—, 1981, *History of Nagaland*, S. Chand and Company Limited, Delhi.

Glazer, Nathan and D.P. Moynihan, 1975, *Ethnicity*, Harvard University Press.

Gluckman, Max., 1958, "Analysis of a Social Situation in Modern Zululand". The Rhodes Livingstone Papers No. 28.

Goswami, M.C., 1972, "The Role of Samadhi in a Changing Lalung Society". *Bulletin of the Department of Anthropology*, Vol. 1.

Goswami, M.C., and Kamkhenthang, 1974, "Nicotine Habbit of Paite". *Bulletin of the Department of Anthropology*, Gauhati University, Gauhati.

Goswami, B.B., 1970, "Relationship Between Family Size and Agriculture in a Hill Region of Assam". *Tribe*, Vol. VII, No. 3.

Gough, K., 1952, A Comparison of Incest Prohibitions and the Rules of Exogamy in Three Matrilineal Groups of Malabar Coast, *International Archives of Ethnography*, Vol. XLVI, No. 1, Leiden.

—,—, 1952, Changing Kinship Usages in the Setting of Political and Economic Change among the Nayars of Malabar, *Journal of the Royal Anthropological Institute*, Vol. LXXXII.

Haimendorf, C. Von F., 1946, *The Naked Nagas*, Thacker Spink and Co., Calcutta.

—,—, 1962, *The Apatanis and Their Neighbour*, Routledge and Kegan Paul, London.

—,—, 1973, "Social-Cultural Change among the Konyak Nagas", *Highlander*, Vol. 1, Kohima.

—,—, 1982, *Highlanders of Arunachal Pradesh*. Vikas Publishing House, Delhi.

—,—, 1985, *Tribes of India : The Struggle for Survival*. Oxford University Press, Bombay.

Harris, Marvin, 1969, "The Cultural Ecology of India's Secred Cattle", *Current Anthropology*, No. 7.

Honigmann, John J., 1973, *Handbook of Social and Cultural Anthropology*, Rand McNally and Company, Chicago.

—,—, 1976, *The Development of Anthropological Ideas*. The Dorsey Press, Illinois.

Horam, H., 1977, *Social and Cultural Life of Nagas (The Tangkhul Naga)*, B.R. Publishing Corporation, Delhi.

Hungyo, Pearson, 1985. "Land Tenure System in the Hills of Manipur",

An unpublished Paper.

Hutton, J.H., 1969, *The Angami Nagas*. Oxford University Press, (First edition, 1921).

—,—, 1981, *The Sema Nagas*. Oxford University Press (First published in 1921).

Indian Council of Agricultural Research, 1983, *Shifting Cultivation in North-East India*, Research Complex, Shillong.

Iyer, L.K., 1932, "Nayar Polyandry" *Man*, Vol. 32, No. 320.

—,—, 1937, *Travancore Castes and Tribes*, Trivandrum.

Kabui, Gangmumei, 1985, *Anal : A Transborder Tribe of Manipur*, Mittal Publications, Delhi.

Kaith, D.C., 1958, *Shifting Cultivation Practices in India*, ICAR Review Series No. 24, New Delhi.

Kumar, K., 1979, *The Pailibos*, Government of Arunachal Pradesh, Shillong.

—,—, 1979, *The Boris*, Government of Arunachal Pradesh, Shillong.

Laitunga, C., 1981, Know Your Own Land, Firma KLM Private Ltd., Calcutta.

—,—, 1982, *Know Your Own Land*, Firma KLM Private Ltd., Calcutta.

Linton, R., 1936, *The Study of Man*. Apple Century Crafts, New York.

Locock, E.B., 1969, *Introduction to Lewis Henry Morgan's Ancient Society*.

Lowie, Robert H., 1948, *Primitive Society*. Boni and Liveright, New York. Also 1920 edition.

Madan, Sagar M., 1937, *Mina Purana*, Jaipur.

Mahapatra, L.K., 1953, "Shifting Cultivation in Orissa". Report of the Second Conference for Tribes and Tribal Areas, Lohardaga.

—,—, 1988, "Ecology and Economy of Swidden Cultivation in India", Paper presented in Seminar organised by IASSI.

Majumdar, D.N., 1956, *The Garos*, Lawer's Book Stall, Gauhati.

—,—, 1978, Culture Change in two Garo Villages, *Anthropological Survey of India*, Calcutta.

—,—, 1980, "North-East India : A Profile", in *Eastern Himalayas : A Study on Anthropology and Tribalism*, Cosmos Publications, New Delhi.

—,—, 1984, "A Decaying Institution—What has happened to the Nokpante, A Study among the Garo", In *Tribes of North-East India*, ed. S. Karotemporal Vendrome Missiological Institute, Shillong.

Majumdar, D.N., 1940, "Some Aspects of the Cultural Life of the Khasas of Cis - Himalayan Region, *JRASB*, Vol. 6.

—,—, 1954, "Family and Marriage in a Polyandrous Society", *The*

Eastern Anthropologist, Vol. VIII.

Mann, R.S., 1966, "Social Problems in the Process of Tribal Integration", *Social Welfare*, vol. XII, No. 10, New Delhi.

Mann, R. S. 1968, "Static Garasias of South Rajasthan in an era of planned change", *Indian Sociological Bulletin*, Vol. V. No. 4.

—,—, 1977, "Intra and Inter-family Relations Among the Ladakhis of Ladakh". *Bulletin of the Anthropological Survey of India*, vol. XXI.

—,—, 1978, "Eco-System and Society in Ladakh", *Journal of Social Research*, Vol. XXI, No. 1.

—,—, 1978, "Ladakhi Polyandry - Reinterpreted", *Indian Anthropologist*, Vol. 8, No. 1, Delhi.

—,—, 1978, "Social Stratification and Interaction in Ladakh Village", *Bulletin of Anthropological Survey of India*, Vol. XXI, No. 3-4.

—,—, 1978, "Bhils and Culture Contact: Case of Social Grouping", in *Rajasthan Bhils*, ed., N.N. Vyas, R.S. Mann and N.D. Chowdhary, T.R.I. Udaipur.

—,—, 1979, "Anthropo-Geography: An Important Methodological Issue", *Man in India*, Vol. 59, No. 3, Ranchi.

—,—, 1981, *Nature, Man, Spirit Complex in Tribal India*, Concept Publishing Company, New Delhi.

—,—, 1982, "Economic System among the Western Indian Tribes", in *Economics of the Tribes and their Transformation*, ed., K.S. Singh, Concept Publishing Company, Delhi.

—,—, 1983, "Structure and Role Dynamics among the Bhils of Rajasthan" in *Tribal Movements in India*, ed., K.S. Singh, Manohar Publications, New Delhi.

—,—, 1984, *Anthropological and Sociological Theory*, Rawat Publications, Jaipur.

—,—, 1985, "Role of Monastery in Ladakhi Life and Culture", *Indian Anthropologist*, Vol. 15, No. 1.

—,—, 1986, The Ladakhi: A Study in Ethnography and Change, *Anthropological Survey of India*, Calcutta.

—,—, 1987, "Social-Cultural and Economic Dimensions of Shifting Cultivation in North-East India, *Journal of Social and Economic Studies*, 4, 2.

—,—, 1988, "Religion and Society among the Ladakhi Highlanders of Northern India", *South Asian Anthropologist*, Vol. 9, No. 1.

—,—, 1990, "Culture and Ecology in Ladakh", *Man in India*, Vol. 70, No. 3.

Mann, R.S., and K. Mann, 1989, *Tribal Cultures and Change*, Mittal Publications, New Delhi.

Mann, K., 1987, *Tribal Women in a Changing Society*, Mittal Publications, Delhi.

Ministry of Agriculture, 1981, *Sixth Five Year Plan*, 201.

Mandelbaum, David G., 1938, "Polyandry in Kota Society", *American Anthropologist*, Vol. 40, No. 4.

Marak, Julius, 1985, *The Garo Customary Laws and Practices*, Vendrame Missiological Institute, Shillong.

McLenan, J.F., 1986, *Studies in Ancient History.*

Mills, J.P., 1926, *The Ao Nagas*, Macmillan Co., London. Also 1973 edition.

Moorcraft, William and George Trebeck, 1873, *Travels in the Himalayas Provinces of Hindustan and Punjab in Ladakh and Kashmir*, John Murray, London.

Nag, D.S., 1958, *Tribal Economy—an Economic Study of the Baiga*, Bharatiya Adimjati Sewak Sangh, New Delhi.

Nakane, Chie, 1967, *Garo and Khasi : A Comparative Study in Matrilineal Systems*, Mouton and Company, Paris.

—,—, 1975, "Women in a Cross-Cultural Perspective". *Social Change*, Vol. 5, No. 122.

Nair, P.T., 1985, *Tribes of Arunachal Pradesh*, Spectrum Publications, Gauhati.

National Commission on Agriculture, 1976, *Forestry*, Vol. IX, Government of India, New Delhi.

Nongbri, Tiplut, 1984, "The Problems of Matriliny : A Short Review of the Khasi Kinship Structure", *Journal of North-East India Council for Social Science Research*, Vol. 8, No. 1.

Opler, Marvin K., 1943, "Women Social Status and the Forms of Marriage", *The American Journal of Sociology*, Vol. XVIX.

Pandey, B.B., 1974, The Hill Miris, Government of Arunachal Pradesh, Shillong.

Panikkar, "Some Aspects of Nayar Life, *JRAI*, Vol. XLVIII.

Parmar, Y.S., 1975, *Polyandry in the Himalayas*, Vikas Publishing House, Delhi.

Parry, N.E., 1976, *The Lakhers*, Firma K.L.M. Private Limited, T.R.I. Aizawal, Mizoram. First Published in 1932.

Parsons, Talcott, 1964, *An Analytical Approach to the Theory of Social Stratification*. Essays in Sociological Theory. The Free Press, Glencoe.

Pathy, Jaganath, 1988, "Shifting Cultivators : Bearing the Brunt of Development", Paper presented in Seminar Organised by IASSI.

Piddington, Ralph, 1950, *An Introduction to Social Anthropology*, Vol. I.

Prasad, R.N., 1981, "The Political Institution of the Lakher Chieftainship in Mizoram", *Journal of North-East India Council for Social Science Research*, Shillong.

Prince Peter, H.R.H., 1963, *The Study of Polyandry*, Mouton and Co., Hague.

Punjab State Gazetteer, Bashahr, 1910.

Ramkrishnan, P.S., 1983, "Socio-economic and Cultural Aspects of Jhum in North-East and Options for eco-development in tribal areas", in *Tribal Technique, Social Organisation and Development Distribution and Alternatives*, ed., N.P. Chaube.

Report of the United Nation's Survey Team on the Economic and Social Needs of the Opium-Producing Areas in Thailand, 1967.

Rivers, W.H.R., 1906, *The Todas*, Macmillan, London.

Rockhill, W.W., 1895, *The Land of the Lamas*, Longmans Green, London.

Roth, G., 1971, "Historical Relationships to Marxism" in *Scholarship and Partisanship : Essays on Max Weber*, ed., R. Bendix and G. Roth, University of California Press, Berkeley.

Roy Burman, B.K., 1984, "Crisis of Identity among Mizos", *Mainstream*, July, New Delhi.

—,—, 1988, "Shifting Cultivation : A Closer Look", Paper presented in Seminar Organised by IASSI.

Roy Burman, B.K. and Alemchiba Ao, 1966, *Waromung : Ao Naga Village*. Office of the Registrar General of India, Monograph Series, Census of India, 1961.

Roy Burman, B.K. and P.S. Sharma, 1970, "Tribal Agriculture in India", *Indian Journal of Agriculture Economics*, Vol. XXV, No. 3.

Roy, Sachin, 1966, *Aspects of Padam Minyong Culture*, North East Frontier Agency, Shillong.

Royal Anthropological Institute, 1954, *Notes and Queries in Anthropology*.

Sachchidananda, 1985, "Swidden Cultivation among the Wanchos of Arunachal Pradesh", *Swidden Cultivation in Asia*, Vol. 2, UNESCO.

Sahlins, Marshall D., 1969, "Culture and Environment : The Study of Cultural Ecology", in *Theory in Anthropology*, ed. Manners and Kaplan, Routledge and Kagan Paul, London.

—,—, 1969, "Evolution : Specific and General" in *Theory in Anthropology*, ed. Manners and Kaplan, Routledge and Kegan Paul, London.

Saikia, P.D., 1978, "The Sociological Problems Associated with Economic Development", in *North-East India : Sociological Study*, ed., S.M. Dube, Concept Publishing Company, Delhi.

—,—, 1980, "Kinship System of the Nisis of Arunachal Pradesh", in *Eastern Himalayas : A Study on Anthropology and Tribalism*, ed., T.C. Sharma and D.N. Majumdar, Cosmo, Delhi.

Saikia, P.D. and D. Borah, 1984, "Socio-Economic Aspects of Soil Conservation activities in the Hill Areas of North-East India", in *Socio-Economic Aspects in Soil Conservation Activities with special reference to North-Eastern Region*, Government of Meghalaya, Shillong.

Saigal, Omesh, 1978, *Tripura : Its History and Culture*, Concept Publishing Company, Delhi.

Samant, R.K., 1984, "The Reangs of Tripura—Their Socio-Cultural and Agro-Economic Changes", in *Tribes of North-East India*, ed., S. Karotemprol, Vendrome, Missiological Institute, Shillong.

Sangma, Milton, 1984, "History and Culture of the Garos", in *Garo Hill Land and the People*, ed., L.S. Gassah, Omsons Publication, Gauhati.

Sapolia, Kamla, 1984, "Women of Mizoram". *Mizoram News Magazine*, No. 1, Directorate of Information, Mizoram.

Saraswati, R., 1968, *Mina Itihas*, Jheethalal Nandlal, Jaipur.

Sarkar, Niranjan, 1973, "The So-called Polyandry among the Gallongs", *Man in India*, Vol. 53, No. 2.

Saxena, R.N., 1953, "Marriage and Divorce in Jaunsar Bawar", *Vanyajati*, October.

Schneider, D.M. and K. Gough, 1961, *Matrilineal Kinship*, University of California Press, Berkley and Los Angeles.

Sema, Hokishe, 1986, *Emergence of Nagaland*, Vikas Publishing House Pvt. Ltd. Delhi.

Sen Soumen, 1985, *A Tribe in Transition : The Jaintias of Meghalaya*, Cosmos Publication, Delhi.

Sharma, T.C., 1980, "The pre-Historic Background of a Shifting Cultivation in Shifting Cultivation in North-East India", ICAR, Shillong.

Sharma, T.C. and D.N. Majumdar, 1980, *Eastern Himalayas : A Study on Anthropology and Tribalism*, Cosmos Publications, New Delhi.

Simla State Gazetteer, 1910.

Singh, Thakur, 1912, *Code of Tribal Custom of the Ladakh Tehsil*, Pioneer Press, Allahabad.

Spencer, Herbert, 1904, *Principles of Sociology*, Vol. 1, Part III, Williams and Nargate.

Spurgeon, David, 1982, "Making the most of Forests", *Spnn*, Vol. XXIII, No. 4.

Srivastava, 1975, *Adivasi Jaunsar Bawar Ke*, Sarita.

Srivastava, L.R.N., 1973., *Among the Wanchos*. Research Department, Arunachal Administration, Shillong.

Steward, Julian H., 1955, *Theory of Culture Change*, University of Illinois Press, Urbana.

—,—, 1968, "Cultural Ecology", in *International Encyclopaedia of Social Sciences*.

Syam Choudhury, N.K. and M.M. Das, 1973, The Lalung Society, *Anthropological Survey of India*, Calcutta.

Tamotse, Shibutani and M.K. Kian, 1965, *Ethnic Stratification*, Macmillan Company, New York.

Tanley; 1946, *Introduction to Plant Ecology*, George Allen and Unwin, London.

Tax Sol, 1951, Acculturation in Americas, *Proceedings and Selected Papers of XXIX International Congress of Americanists*, Illinois.

The Law Research Institute, 1979, *The Customary Laws and Practices of the Wancho*. The Law Research Institute, Gauhati.

—,—, 1979, The Customary Laws and Practices of the Ao of Nagaland. Typed Report.

—,—, 1979, The Customary Laws and Practices of the Tangkhul of Manipur. Typed Report.

INDEX